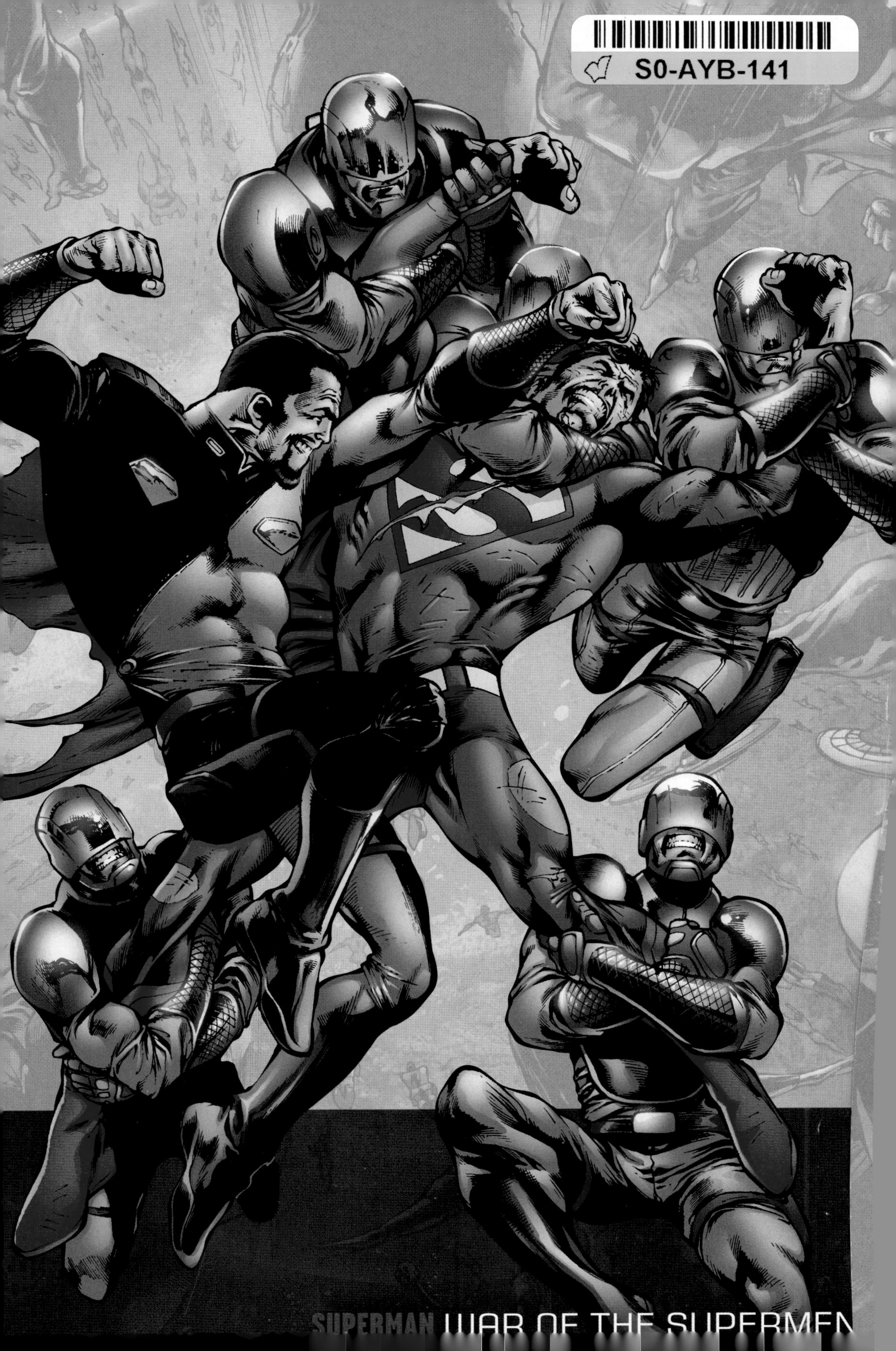

SUPERMAN WAR OF THE SUPERMEN

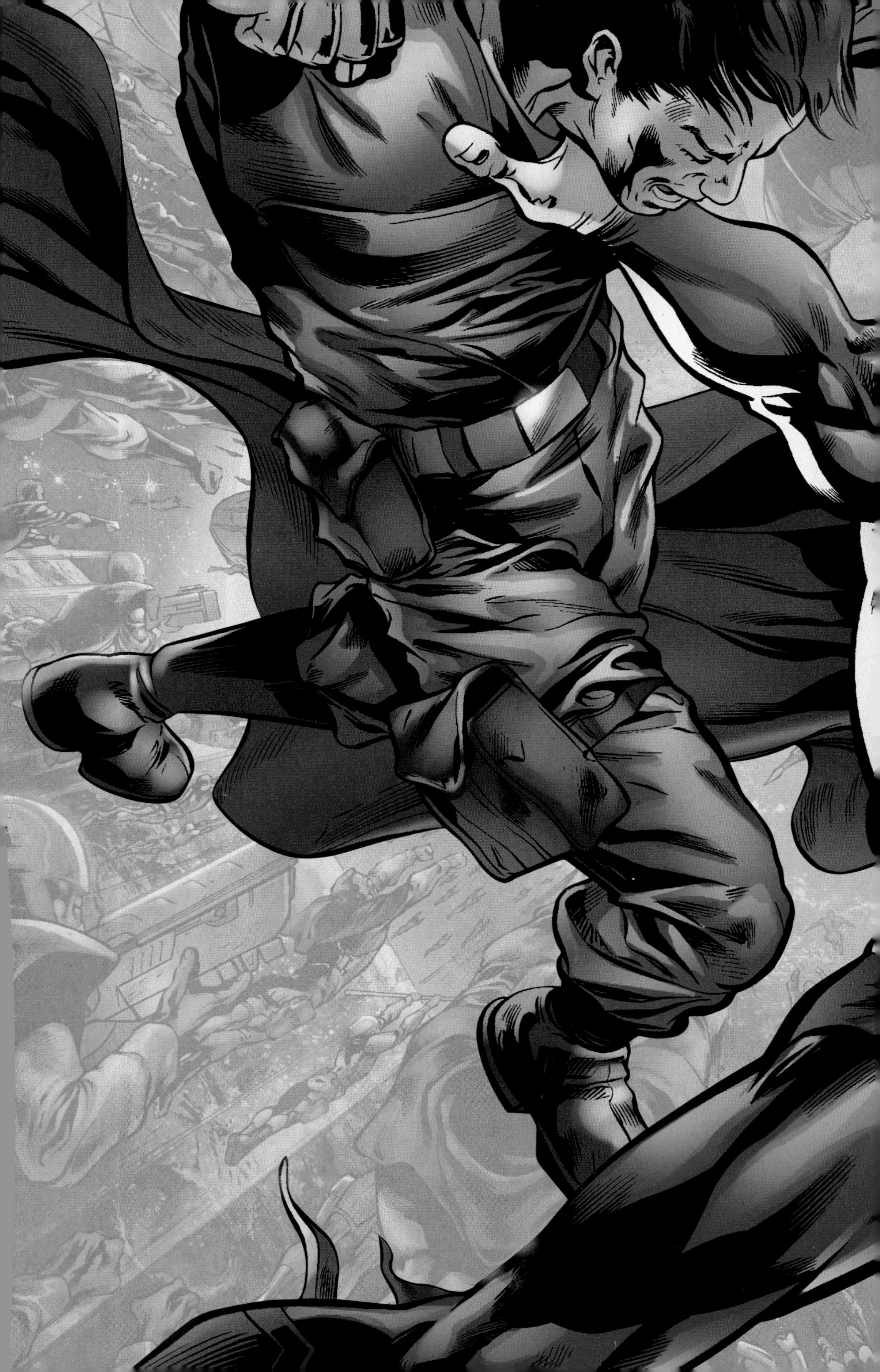

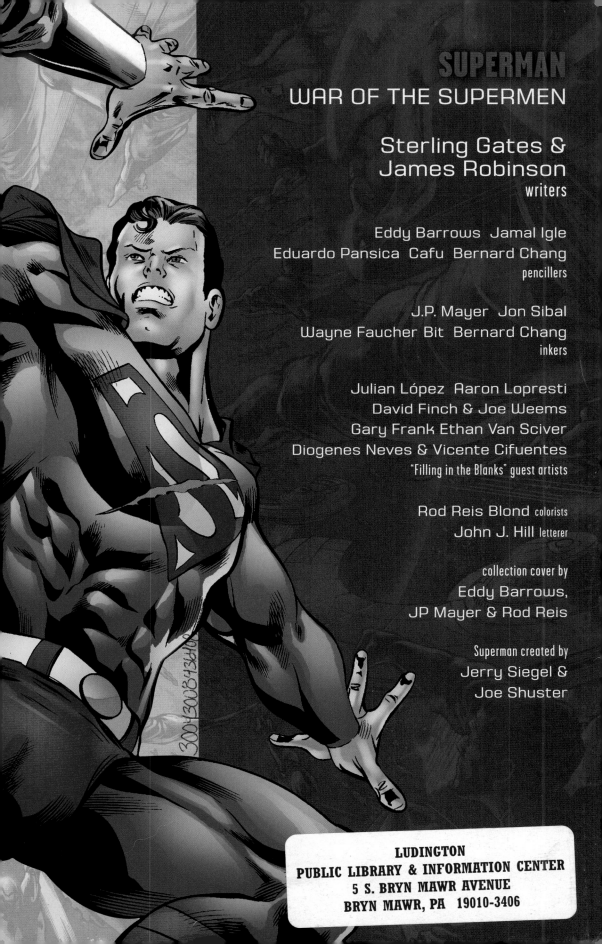

SUPERMAN
WAR OF THE SUPERMEN

**Sterling Gates &
James Robinson**
writers

Eddy Barrows Jamal Igle
Eduardo Pansica Cafu Bernard Chang
pencillers

J.P. Mayer Jon Sibal
Wayne Faucher Bit Bernard Chang
inkers

Julian López Aaron Lopresti
David Finch & Joe Weems
Gary Frank Ethan Van Sciver
Diogenes Neves & Vicente Cifuentes
"Filling in the Blanks" guest artists

Rod Reis Blond colorists
John J. Hill letterer

collection cover by
Eddy Barrows,
JP Mayer & Rod Reis

Superman created by
Jerry Siegel &
Joe Shuster

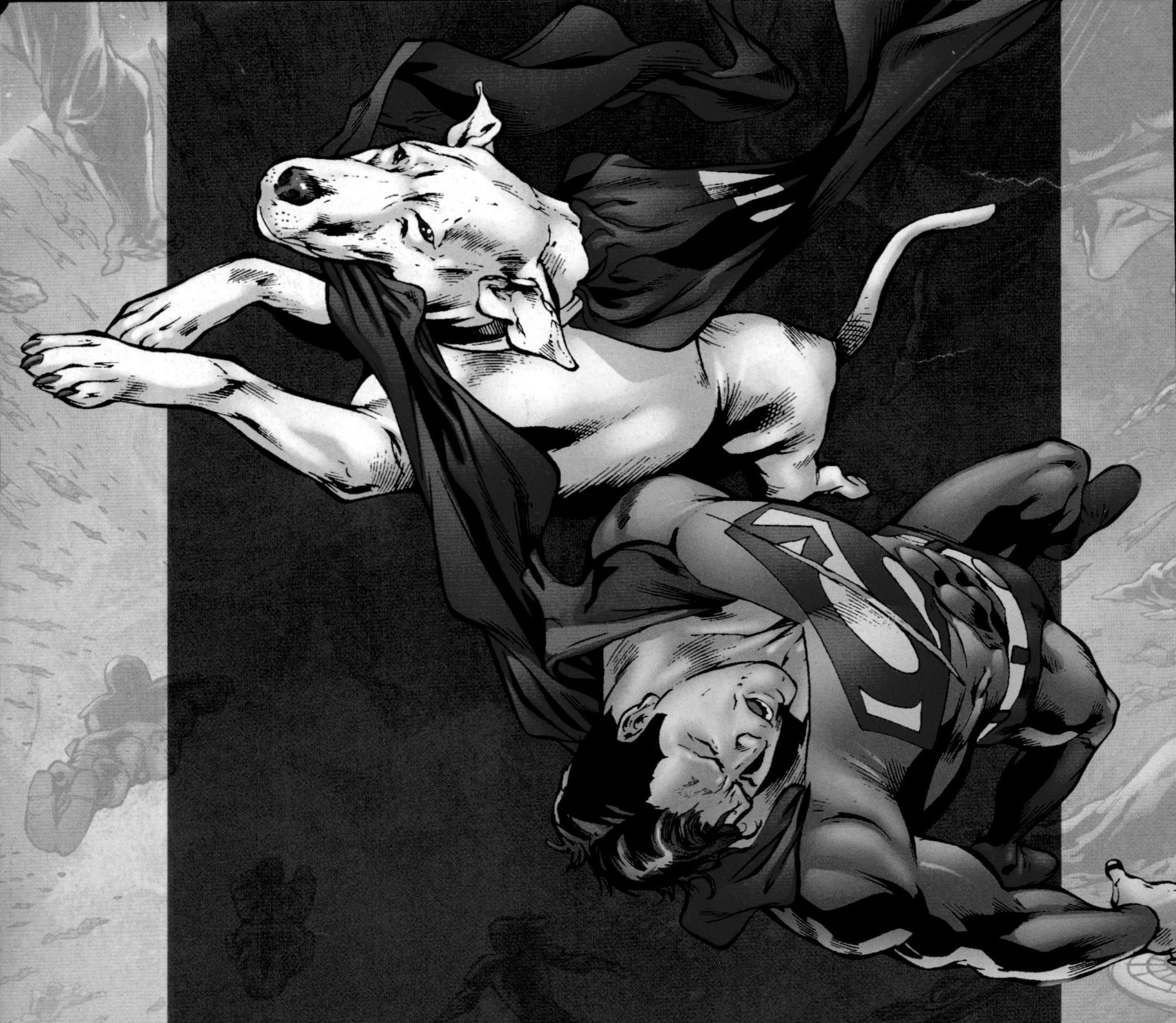

MATT IDELSON Editor – Original Series WILL MOSS Associate Editor – Original Series
IAN SATTLER Director – Editorial, Special Projects and Archival Editions SEAN MACKIEWICZ Editor ROBBIN BROSTERMAN Design Director – Books

EDDIE BERGANZA Executive Editor
BOB HARRAS VP – Editor-in-Chief

DIANE NELSON President DAN DIDIO and JIM LEE Co-Publishers GEOFF JOHNS Chief Creative Officer JOHN ROOD Executive VP – Sales, Marketing and Business Development AMY GENKINS Senior VP – Business and Legal Affairs NAIRI GARDINER Senior VP – Finance JEFF BOISON VP – Publishing Operations MARK CHIARELLO VP – Art Direction and Design JOHN CUNNINGHAM VP – Marketing TERRI CUNNINGHAM VP – Talent Relations and Services ALISON GILL Senior VP – Manufacturing and Operations DAVID HYDE VP – Publicity HANK KANALZ Senior VP – Digital JAY KOGAN VP – Business and Legal Affairs, Publishing JACK MAHAN VP – Business Affairs, Talent NICK NAPOLITANO VP – Manufacturing Administration SUE POHJA VP – Book Sales COURTNEY SIMMONS Senior VP – Publicity BOB WAYNE Senior VP – Sales

SUPERMAN: WAR OF THE SUPERMEN

DC Comics, 1700 Broadway, New York, NY 10019
A Warner Bros. Entertainment Company
Printed by RR Donnelley, Salem, VA, USA. 12/16/11. First Printing.
ISBN: 978-1-4012-3187-3

SUSTAINABLE FORESTRY INITIATIVE
Certified Chain of Custody
Promoting Sustainable Forest Management

Fiber used in this product line meets the sourcing requirements of the SFI program.
www.sfiprogram.org SGS-SFI/COC-US10/81072

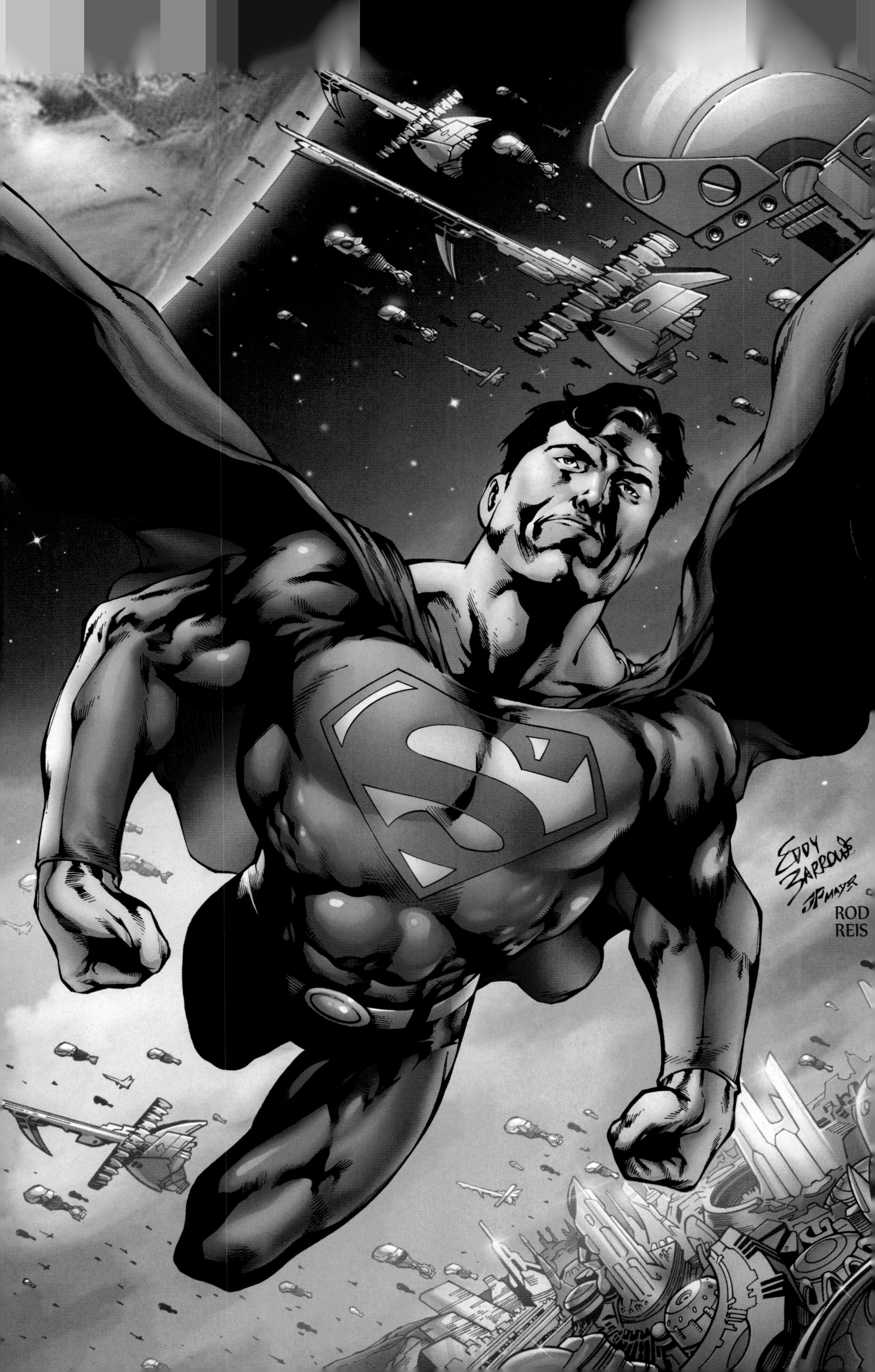
EDDY BARROWS
JP MAYER
ROD REIS

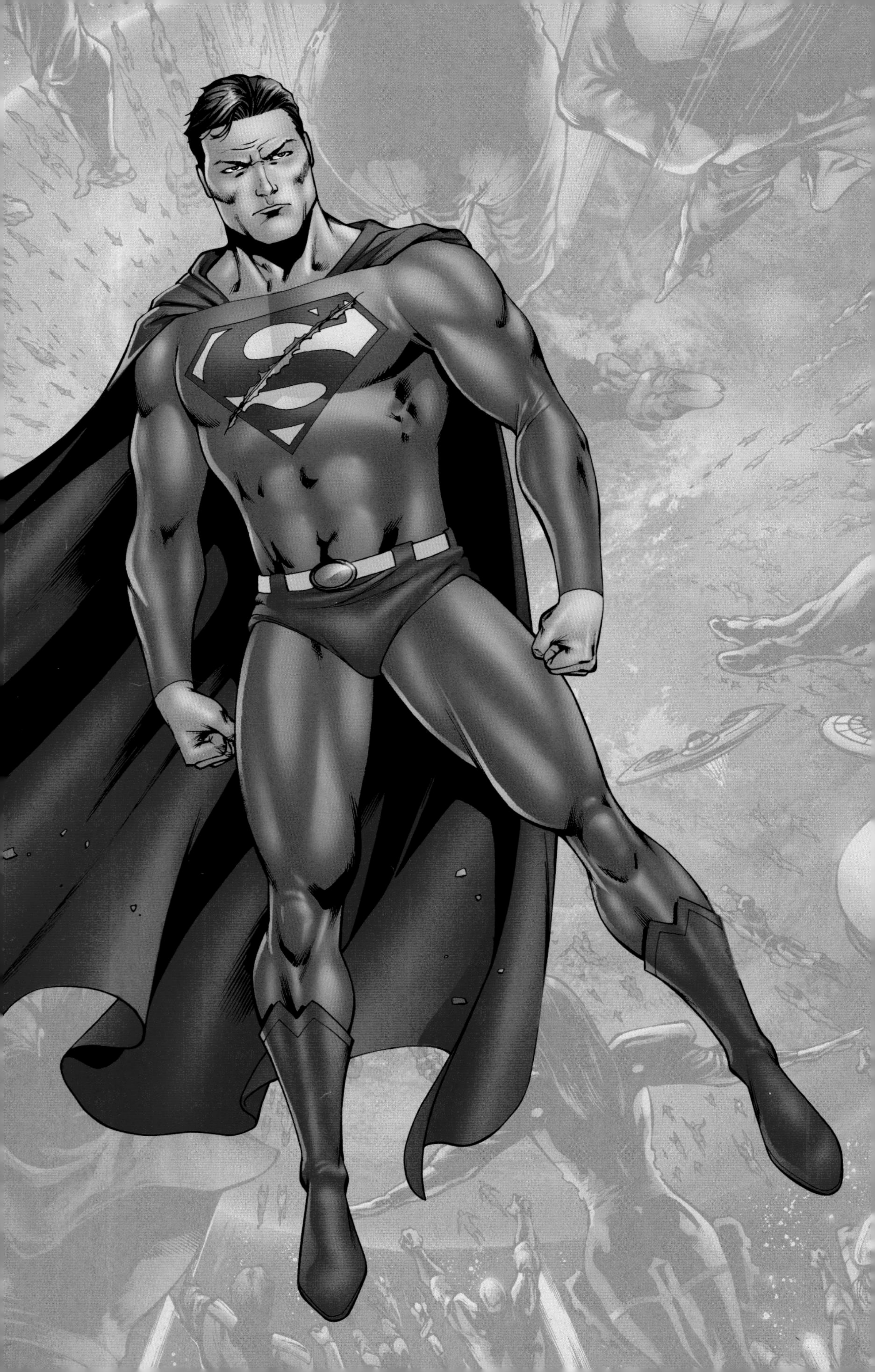

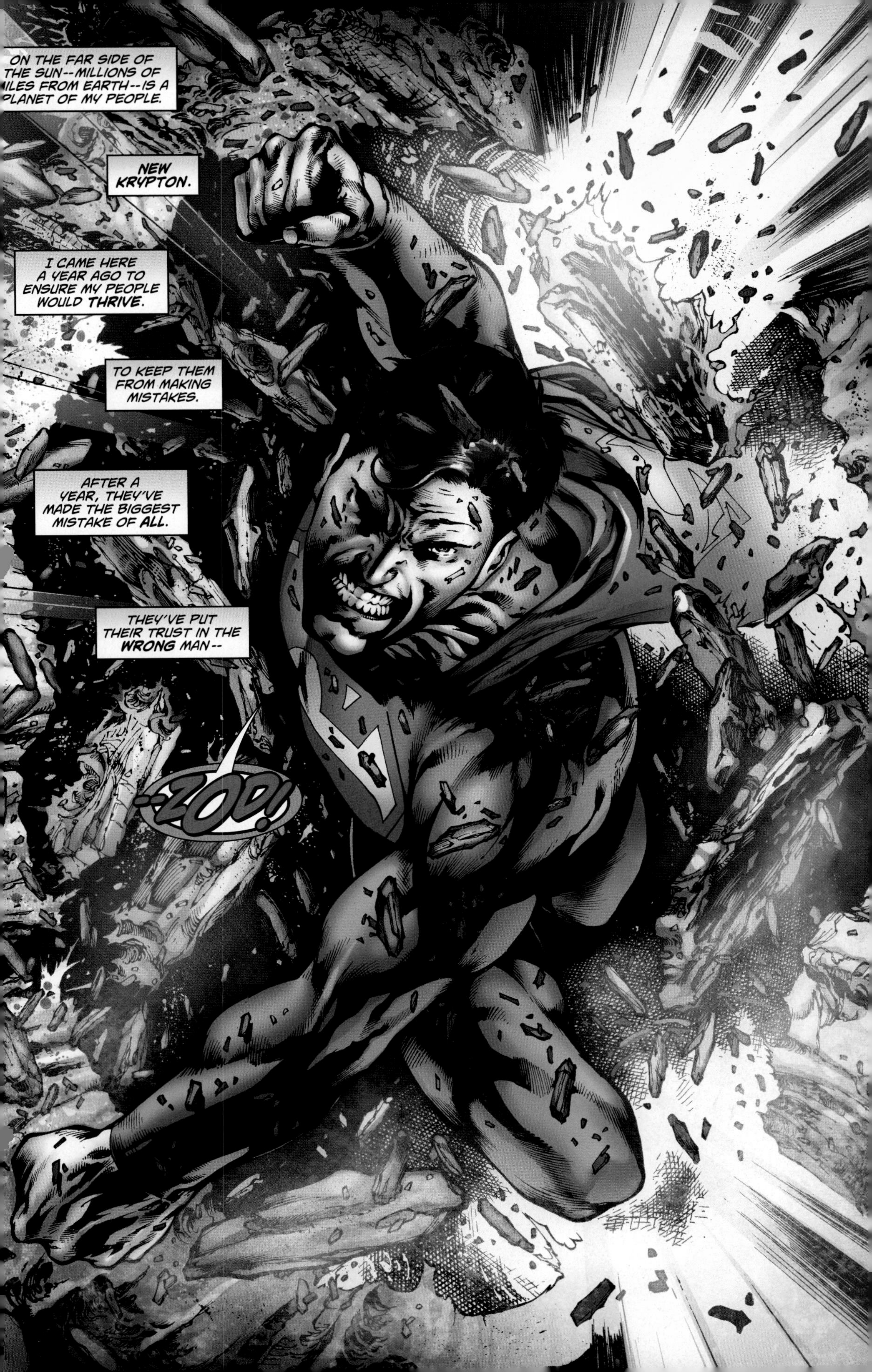

ON THE FAR SIDE OF THE SUN--MILLIONS OF MILES FROM EARTH--IS A PLANET OF MY PEOPLE.
NEW KRYPTON.
I CAME HERE A YEAR AGO TO ENSURE MY PEOPLE WOULD THRIVE.
TO KEEP THEM FROM MAKING MISTAKES.
AFTER A YEAR, THEY'VE MADE THE BIGGEST MISTAKE OF ALL.
THEY'VE PUT THEIR TRUST IN THE WRONG MAN--
--ZOD!

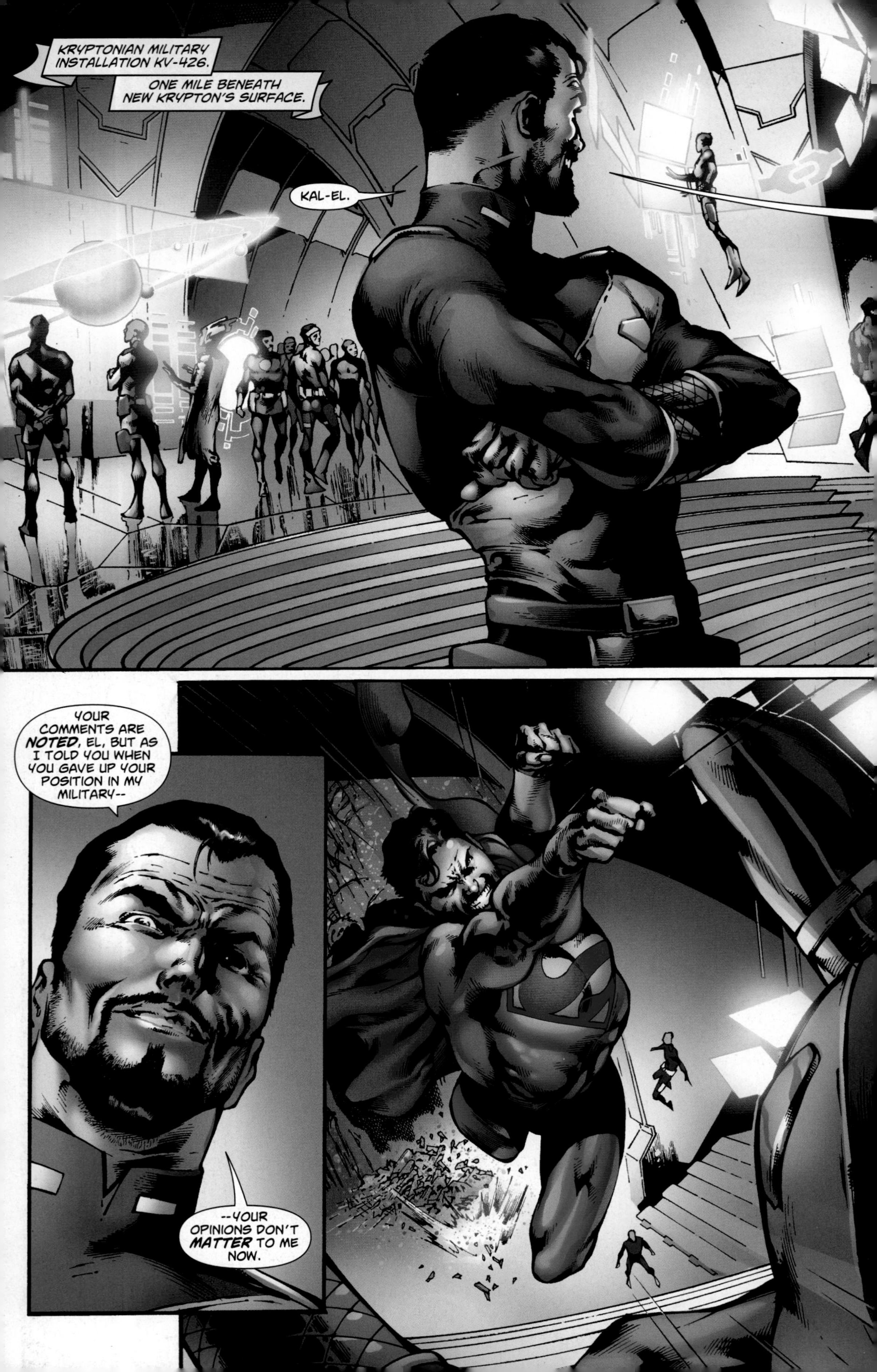
KRYPTONIAN MILITARY INSTALLATION KV-426.
ONE MILE BENEATH NEW KRYPTON'S SURFACE.
KAL-EL.
YOUR COMMENTS ARE NOTED, EL, BUT AS I TOLD YOU WHEN YOU GAVE UP YOUR POSITION IN MY MILITARY--
--YOUR OPINIONS DON'T MATTER TO ME NOW.

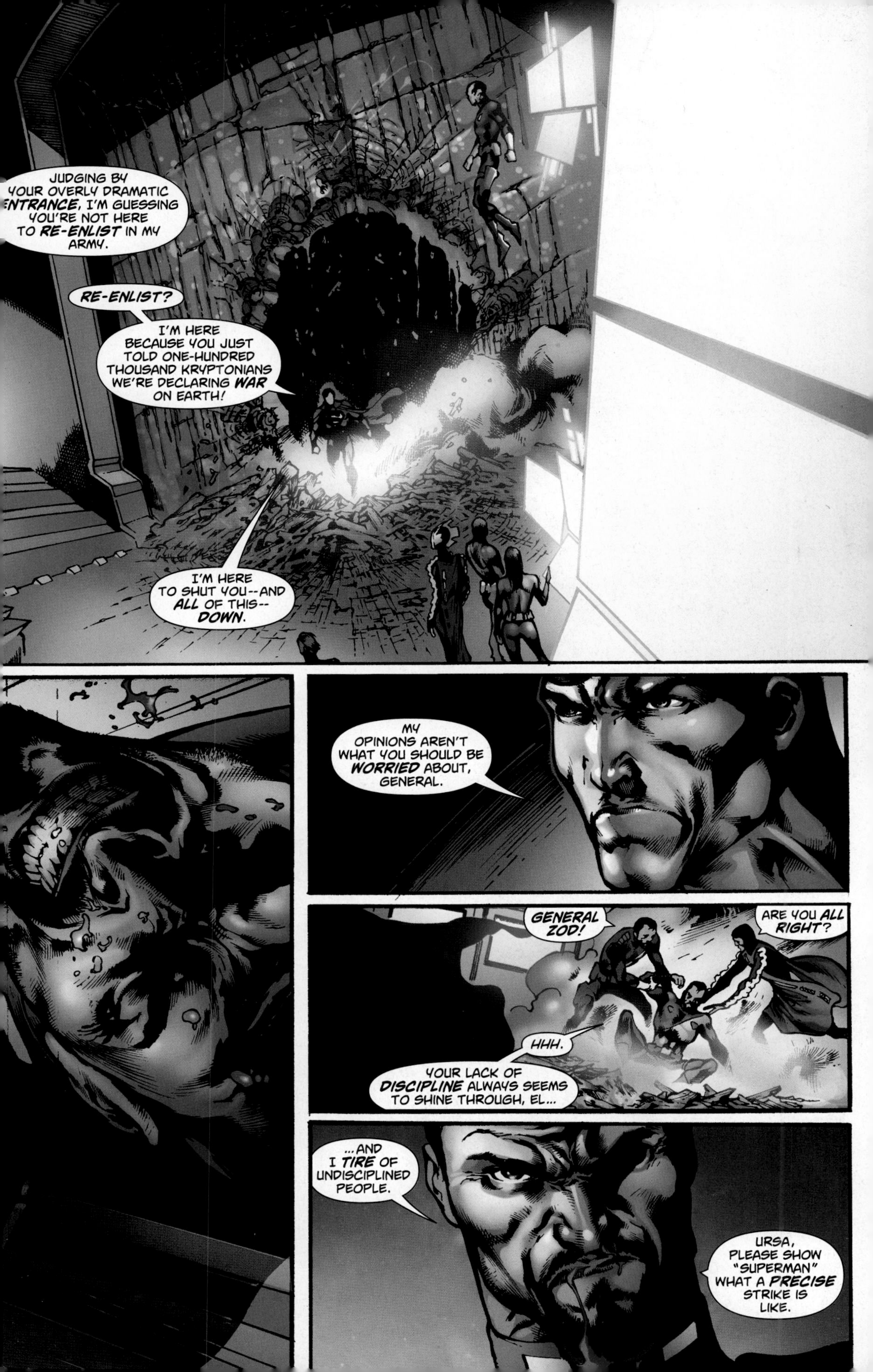
JUDGING BY YOUR OVERLY DRAMATIC ENTRANCE, I'M GUESSING YOU'RE NOT HERE TO RE-ENLIST IN MY ARMY.
RE-ENLIST?
I'M HERE BECAUSE YOU JUST TOLD ONE-HUNDRED THOUSAND KRYPTONIANS WE'RE DECLARING WAR ON EARTH!
I'M HERE TO SHUT YOU--AND ALL OF THIS-- DOWN.
MY OPINIONS AREN'T WHAT YOU SHOULD BE WORRIED ABOUT, GENERAL.
GENERAL ZOD!
ARE YOU ALL RIGHT?
HHH.
YOUR LACK OF DISCIPLINE ALWAYS SEEMS TO SHINE THROUGH, EL...
...AND I TIRE OF UNDISCIPLINED PEOPLE.
URSA, PLEASE SHOW "SUPERMAN" WHAT A PRECISE STRIKE IS LIKE.

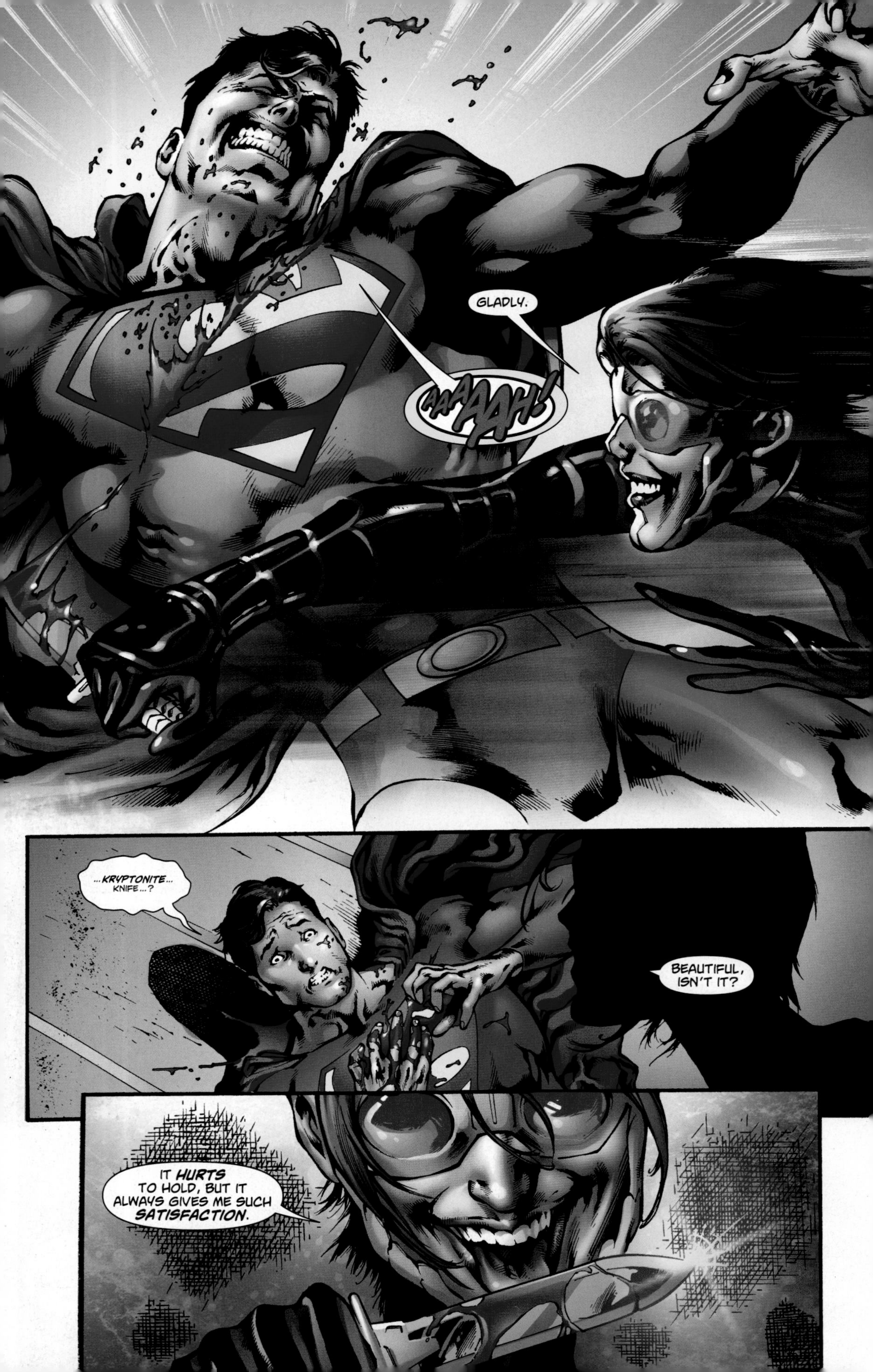
GLADLY.
AAAAAH!
...KRYPTONITE... KNIFE...?
BEAUTIFUL, ISN'T IT?
IT HURTS TO HOLD, BUT IT ALWAYS GIVES ME SUCH SATISFACTION.

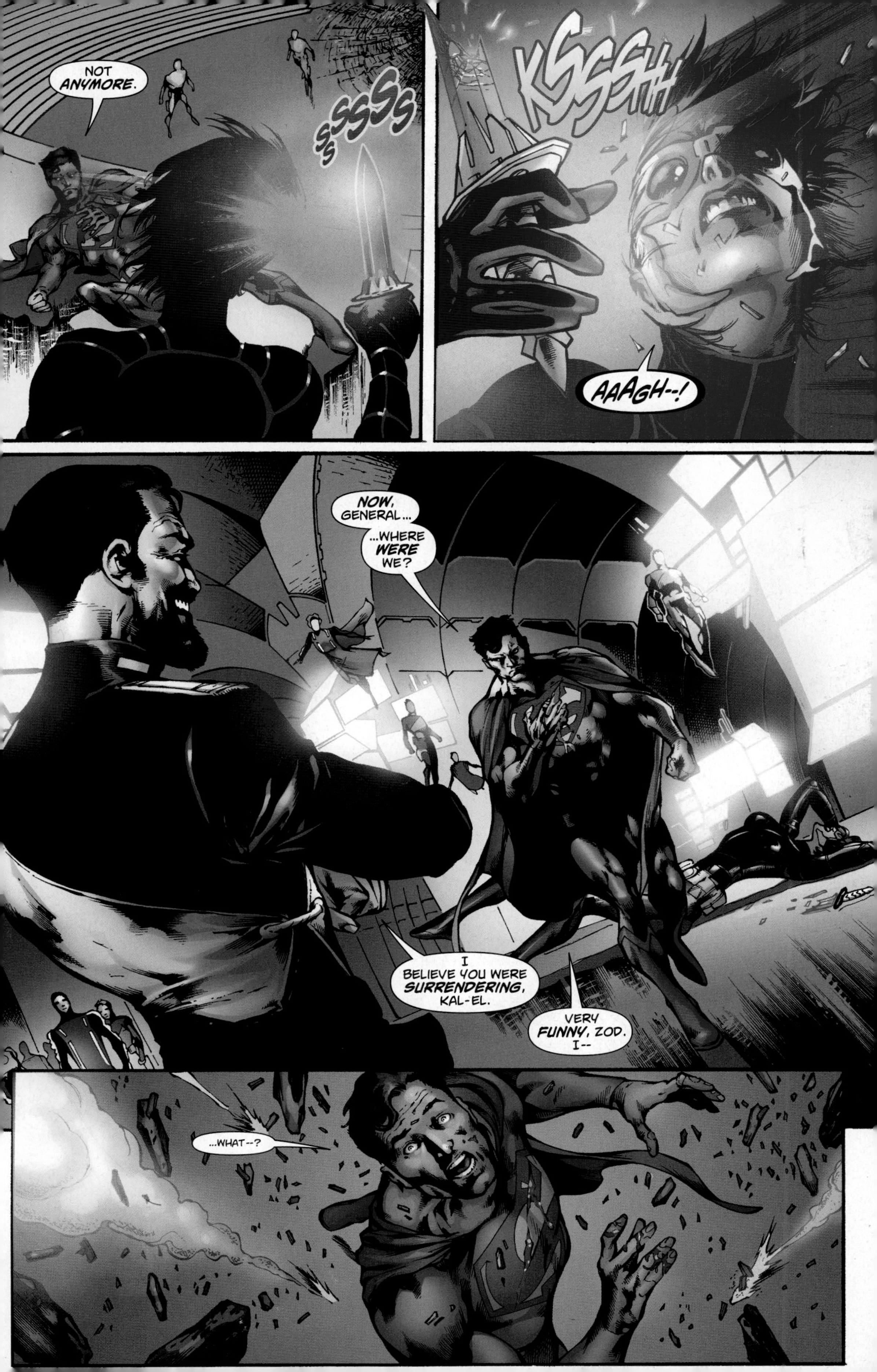
NOT ANYMORE.
SSSSSS
KSSSHH
AAAGH--!
NOW, GENERAL...
...WHERE WERE WE?
I BELIEVE YOU WERE SURRENDERING, KAL-EL.
VERY FUNNY, ZOD. I--
...WHAT--?

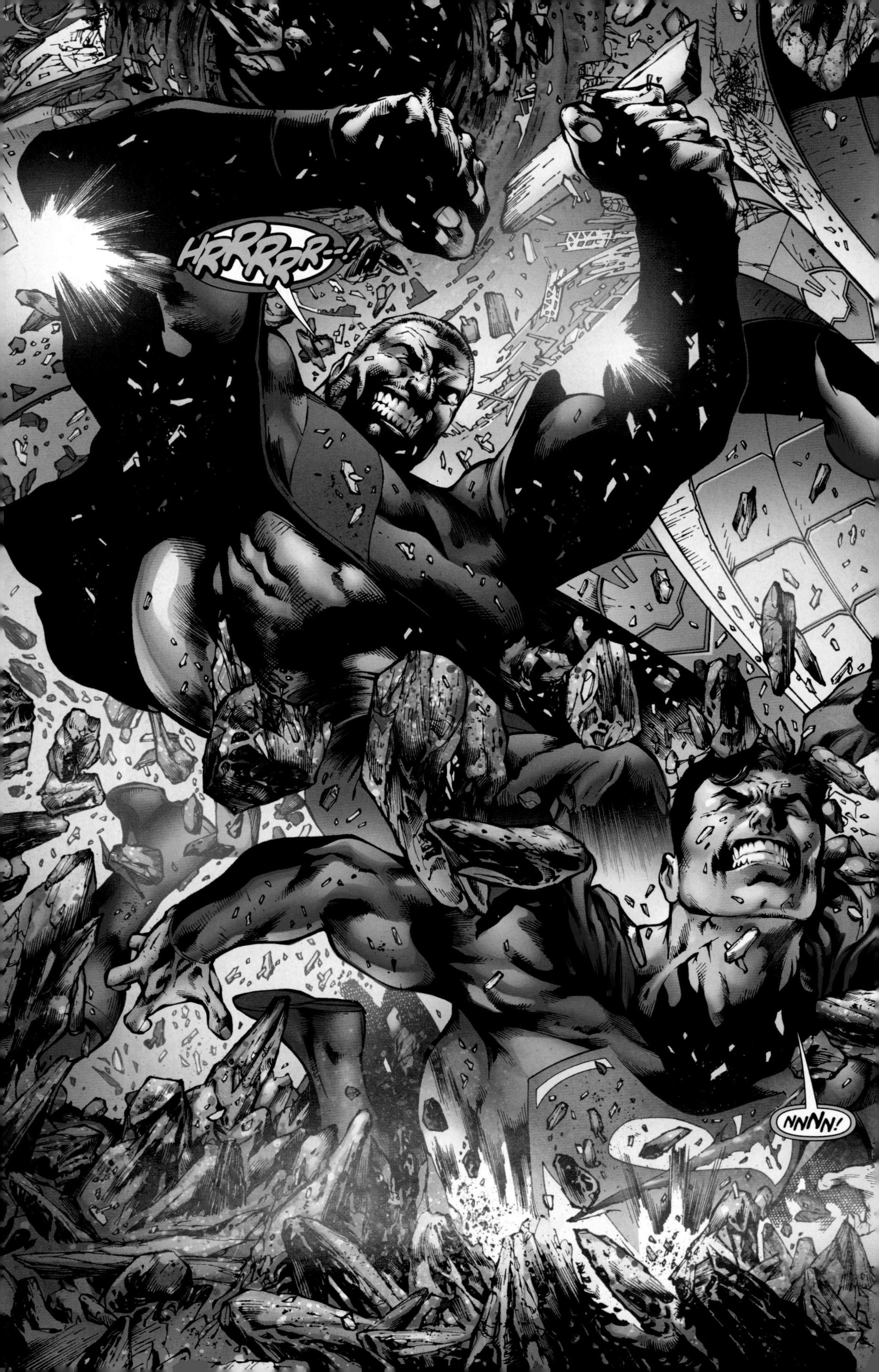
HRRRRR--!
NNNN!

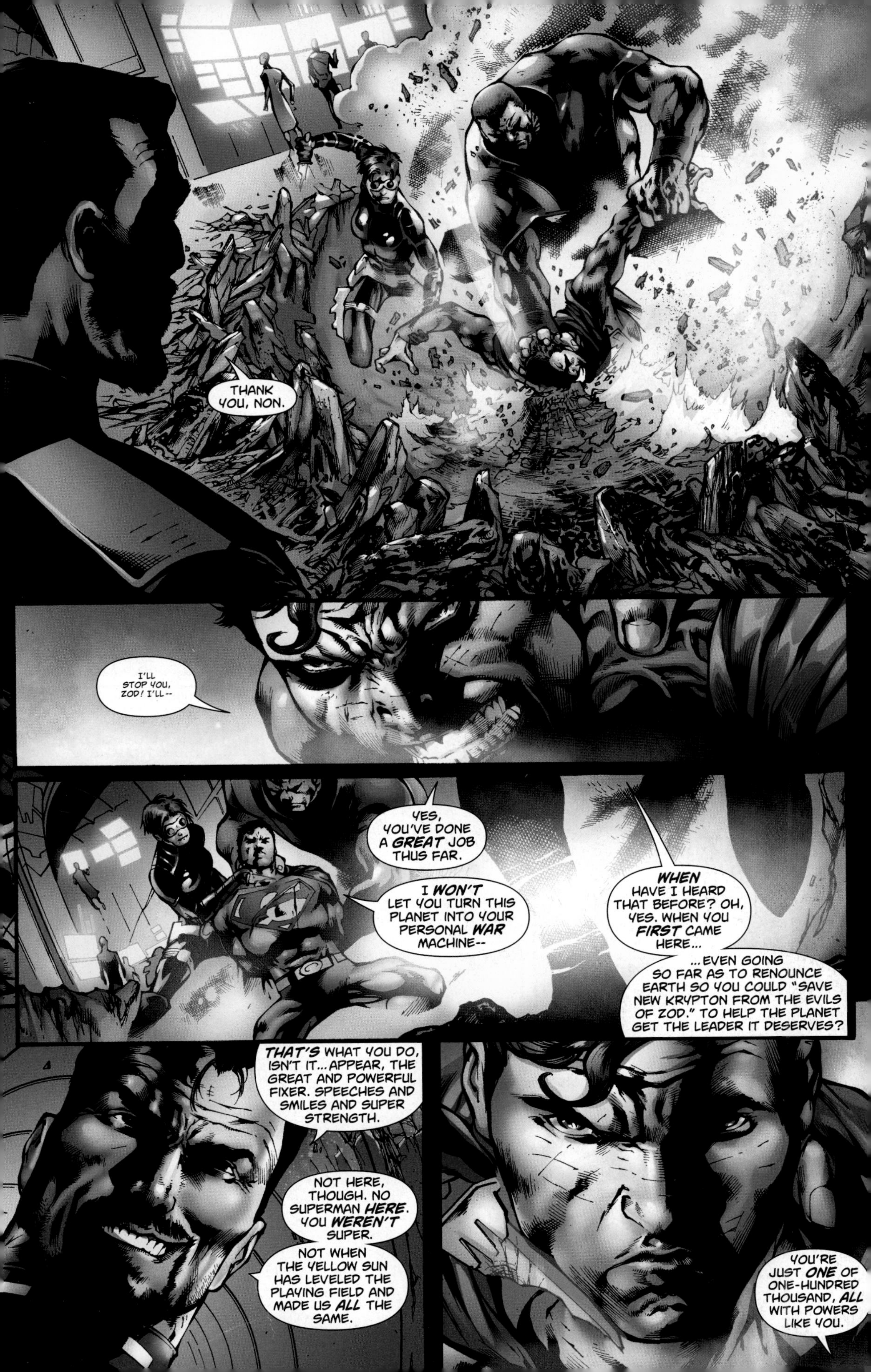
THANK YOU, NON.
I'LL STOP YOU, ZOD! I'LL--
YES, YOU'VE DONE A GREAT JOB THUS FAR.
I WON'T LET YOU TURN THIS PLANET INTO YOUR PERSONAL WAR MACHINE--
WHEN HAVE I HEARD THAT BEFORE? OH, YES. WHEN YOU FIRST CAME HERE...
...EVEN GOING SO FAR AS TO RENOUNCE EARTH SO YOU COULD "SAVE NEW KRYPTON FROM THE EVILS OF ZOD." TO HELP THE PLANET GET THE LEADER IT DESERVES?
THAT'S WHAT YOU DO, ISN'T IT... APPEAR, THE GREAT AND POWERFUL FIXER. SPEECHES AND SMILES AND SUPER STRENGTH.
NOT HERE, THOUGH. NO SUPERMAN HERE. YOU WEREN'T SUPER.
NOT WHEN THE YELLOW SUN HAS LEVELED THE PLAYING FIELD AND MADE US ALL THE SAME.
YOU'RE JUST ONE OF ONE-HUNDRED THOUSAND, ALL WITH POWERS LIKE YOU.

YOU CAME HERE TO PROTECT THE PEOPLE FROM *ME*? TO MONITOR *ME*?

MAYBE YOU SHOULD HAVE SPENT *MORE* TIME WATCHING THE PEOPLE, EL...*TRULY* PROTECTING THEM, LIKE I'VE DONE.

I KNOW IT MUST EAT AT YOU... THAT I DIDN'T WIN NEW KRYPTON'S LOVE THROUGH GUILE OR TRICKERY. I *EARNED* IT.

AND *ALL* THAT TIME YOU WERE WATCHING *ME*, RIGHT? I SEE THAT NOW...THAT'S THE REASON YOU KEPT ME CLOSE.

THAT'S WHY YOU MADE ME A COMMANDER IN THE ARMY.

NO, I HAD YOU JOIN THE MILITARY GUILD FOR A *MUCH* MORE SPECIFIC AND *IMPORTANT* REASON.

RED SHARD WAS YOUR DIRECT COMMAND, OF COURSE, BUT THE MASS TRAINING EXERCISES YOU OVERSAW... SHOWING THE SOLDIERS OF NEW KRYPTON HOW TO *BETTER* HANDLE THEIR NEW POWERS...

...IT WAS YOUR YEARS OF PRIOR EXPERIENCE THAT TURNED MY ARMY INTO THE CONSUMMATE FORCE IT NEEDED TO BECOME.

AND YOU'VE BEEN PLANNING TO ATTACK EARTH THIS *WHOLE* TIME, RIGHT?

THE ARMADA I UNCOVERED. CLASSIFIED AREAS I COULDN'T BREACH. THE WAY THE ARMY WAS TRAINED...INDEED, THE WAY *I* HELPED TRAIN THEM.

IT WAS *STUPID* OF ME TO HOPE YOU'D CHANGE FROM THE MAN YOU WERE, BUT--

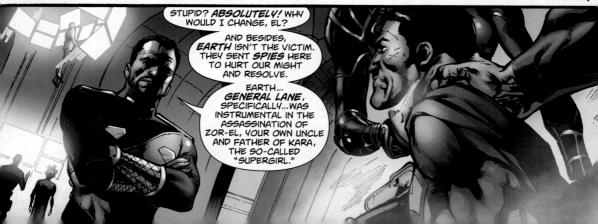

STUPID? *ABSOLUTELY!* WHY WOULD I CHANGE, EL?

AND BESIDES, *EARTH* ISN'T THE VICTIM. THEY SENT *SPIES* HERE TO HURT OUR MIGHT AND RESOLVE.

EARTH... *GENERAL LANE*, SPECIFICALLY...WAS INSTRUMENTAL IN THE ASSASSINATION OF ZOR-EL, YOUR OWN UNCLE AND FATHER OF KARA, THE SO-CALLED "SUPERGIRL."

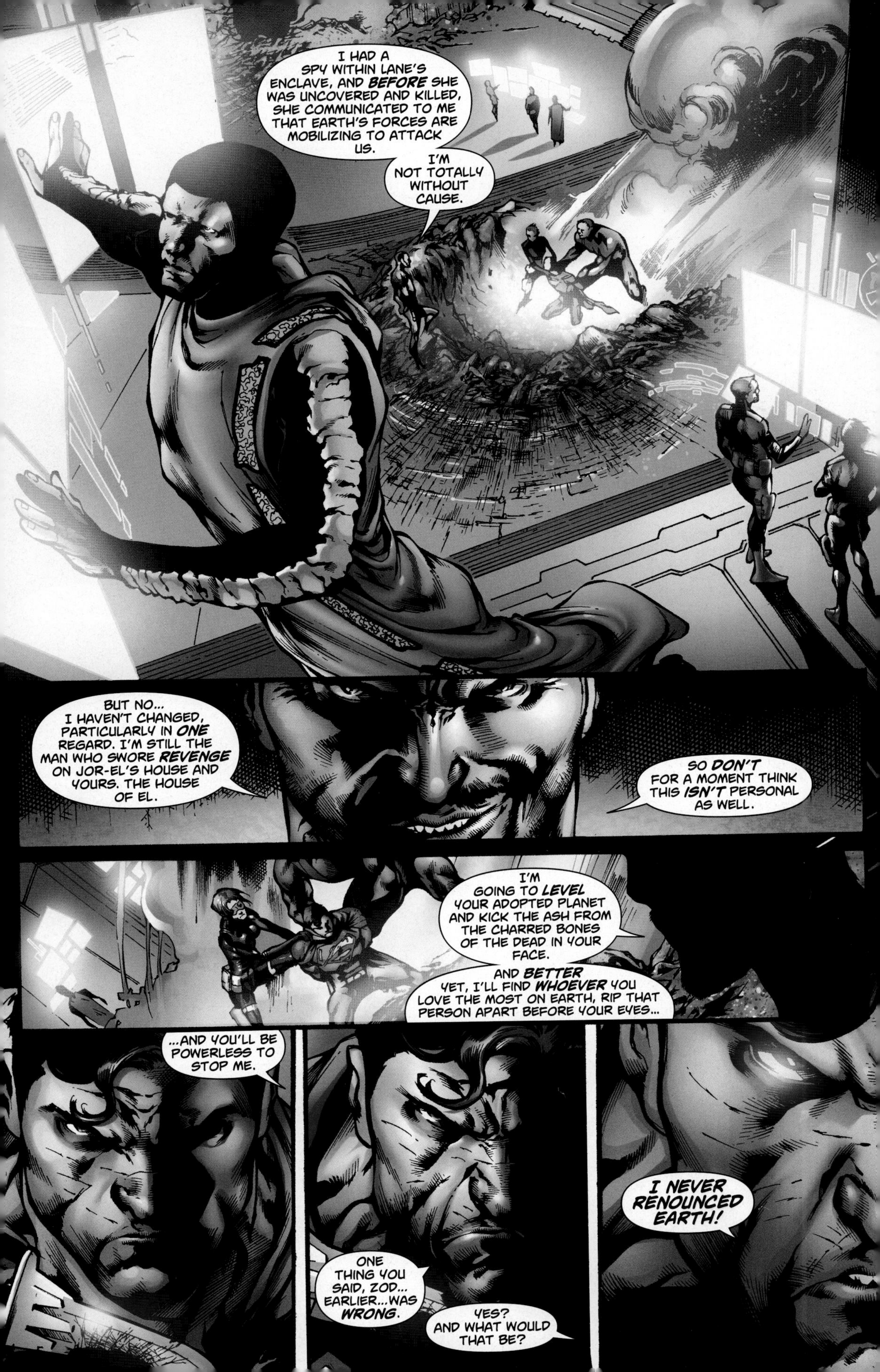

I HAD A SPY WITHIN LANE'S ENCLAVE, AND BEFORE SHE WAS UNCOVERED AND KILLED, SHE COMMUNICATED TO ME THAT EARTH'S FORCES ARE MOBILIZING TO ATTACK US.
I'M NOT TOTALLY WITHOUT CAUSE.
BUT NO... I HAVEN'T CHANGED, PARTICULARLY IN ONE REGARD. I'M STILL THE MAN WHO SWORE REVENGE ON JOR-EL'S HOUSE AND YOURS. THE HOUSE OF EL.
SO DON'T FOR A MOMENT THINK THIS ISN'T PERSONAL AS WELL.
I'M GOING TO LEVEL YOUR ADOPTED PLANET AND KICK THE ASH FROM THE CHARRED BONES OF THE DEAD IN YOUR FACE.
AND BETTER YET, I'LL FIND WHOEVER YOU LOVE THE MOST ON EARTH, RIP THAT PERSON APART BEFORE YOUR EYES...
...AND YOU'LL BE POWERLESS TO STOP ME.
ONE THING YOU SAID, ZOD... EARLIER...WAS WRONG.
YES? AND WHAT WOULD THAT BE?
I NEVER RENOUNCED EARTH!

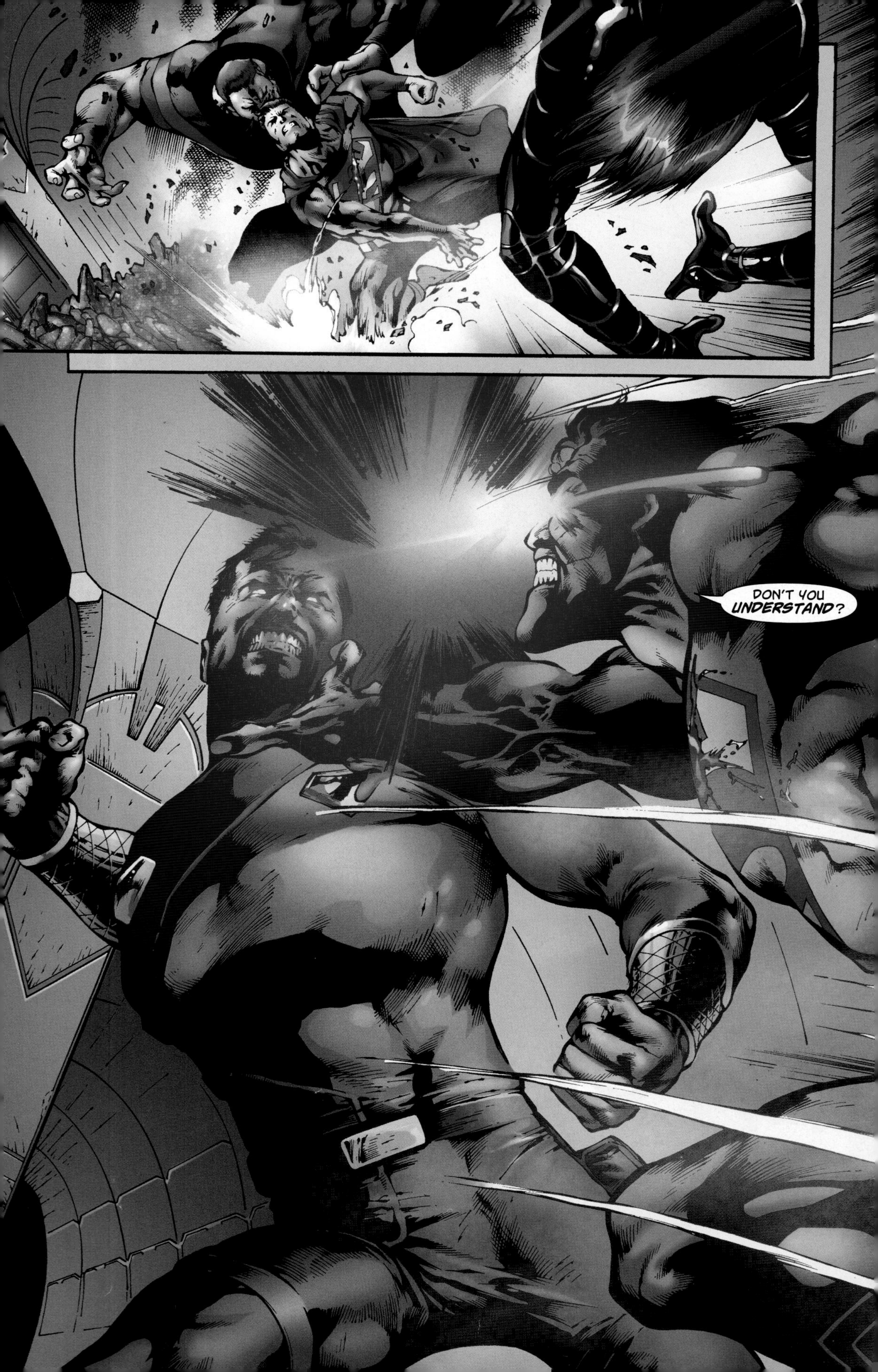
DON'T YOU UNDERSTAND?

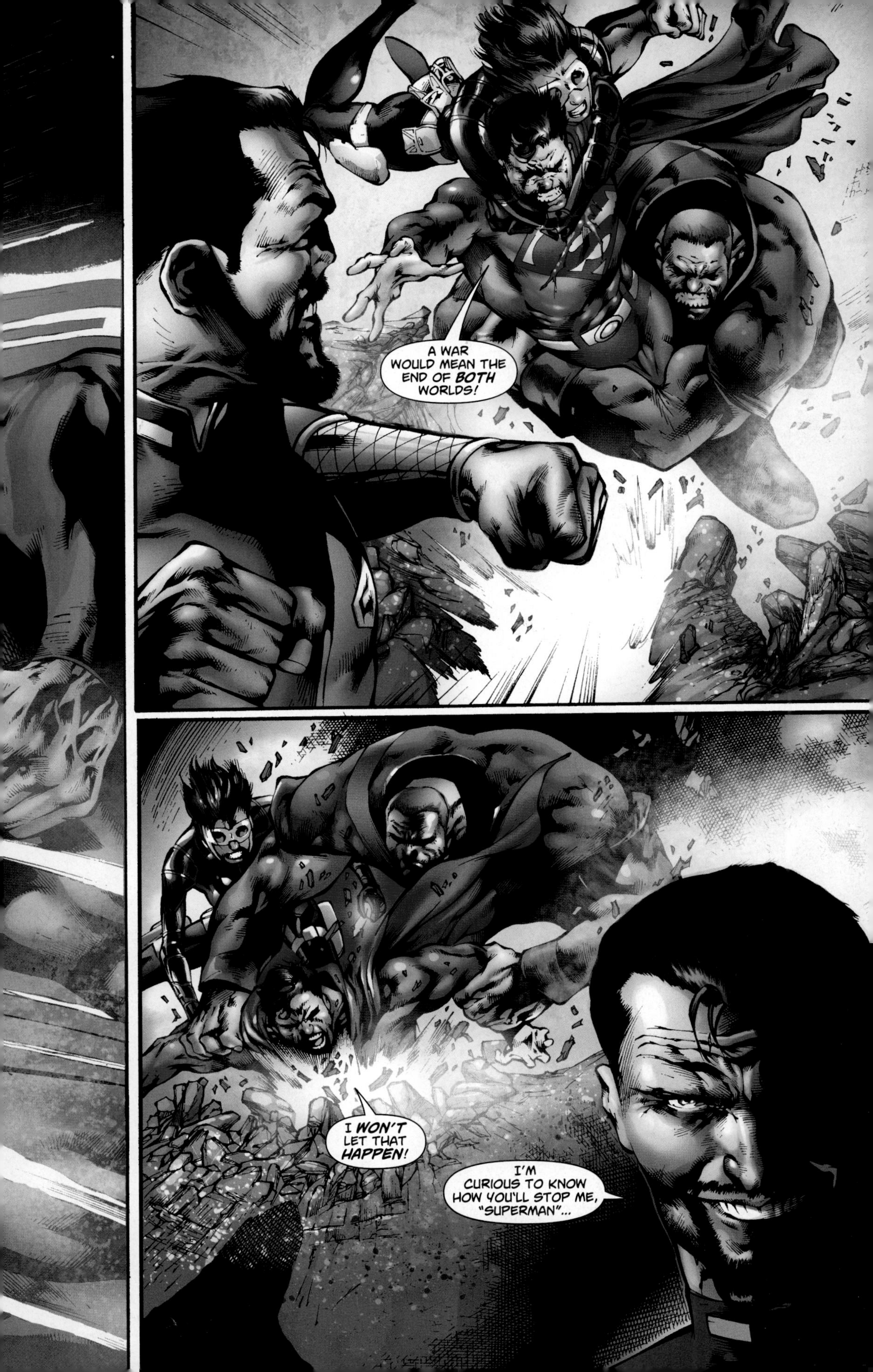
A WAR WOULD MEAN THE END OF *BOTH* WORLDS!
I *WON'T* LET THAT *HAPPEN*!
I'M CURIOUS TO KNOW HOW YOU'LL STOP ME, "SUPERMAN"...

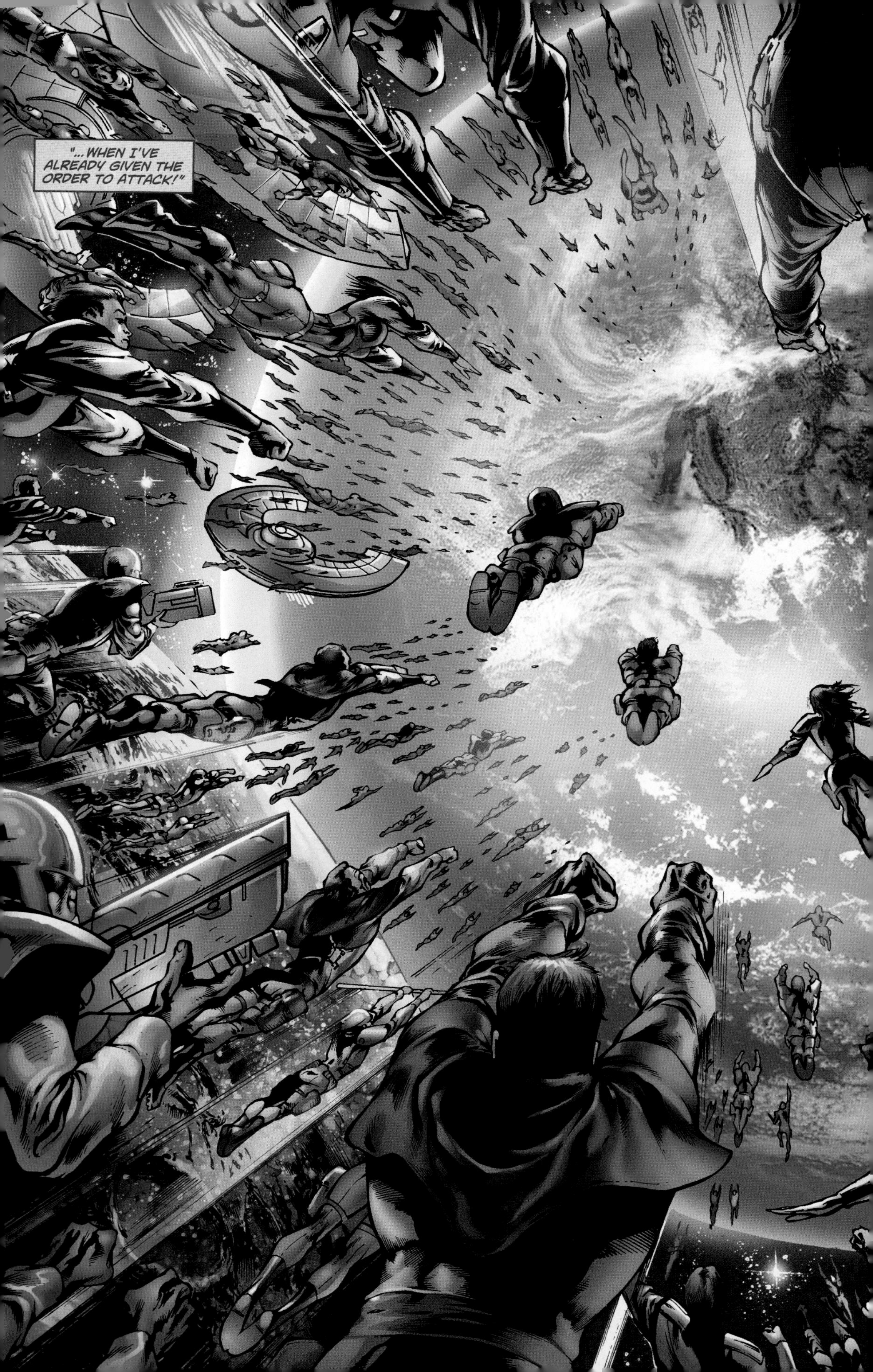
"...WHEN I'VE ALREADY GIVEN THE ORDER TO ATTACK!"

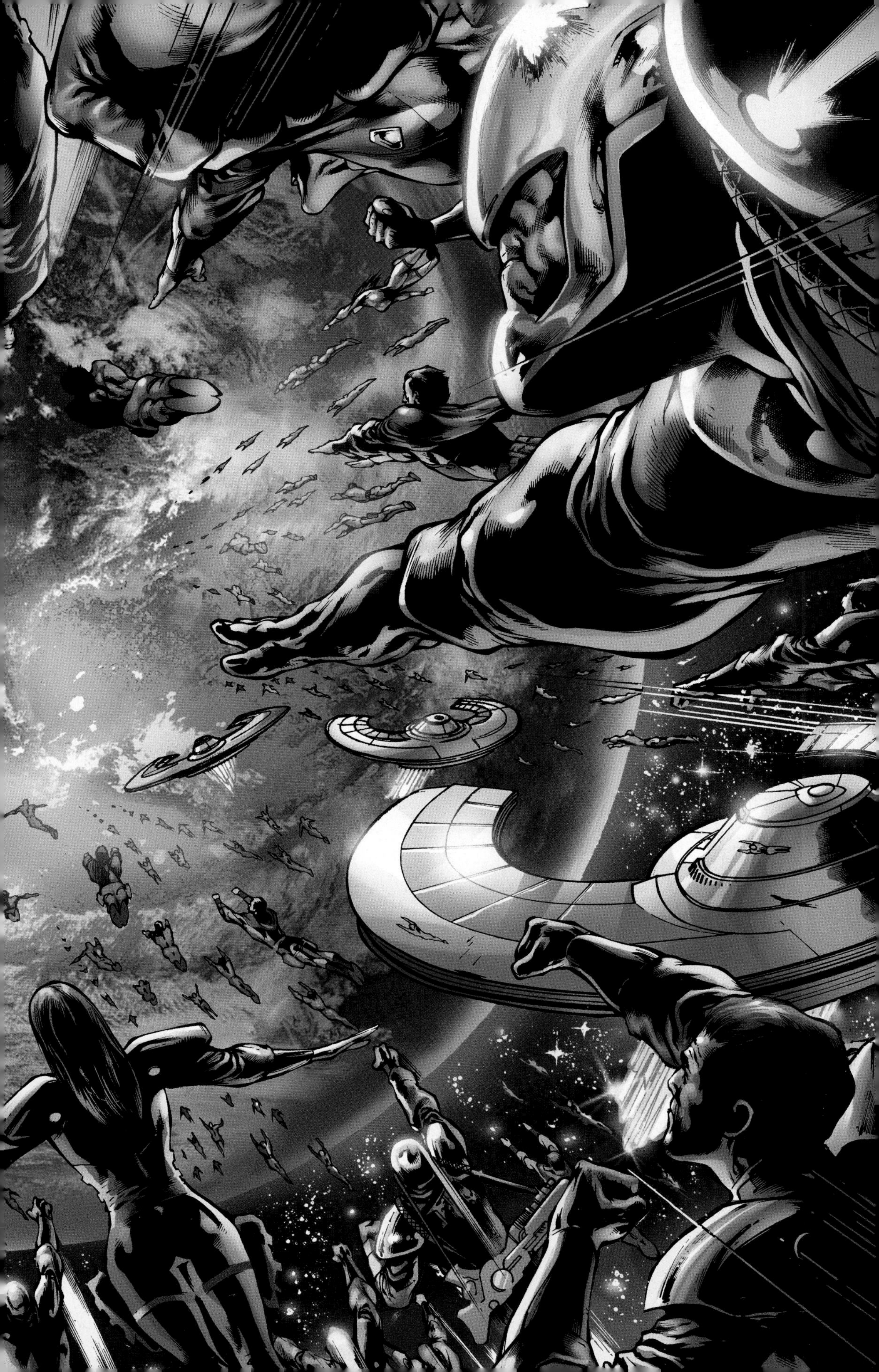

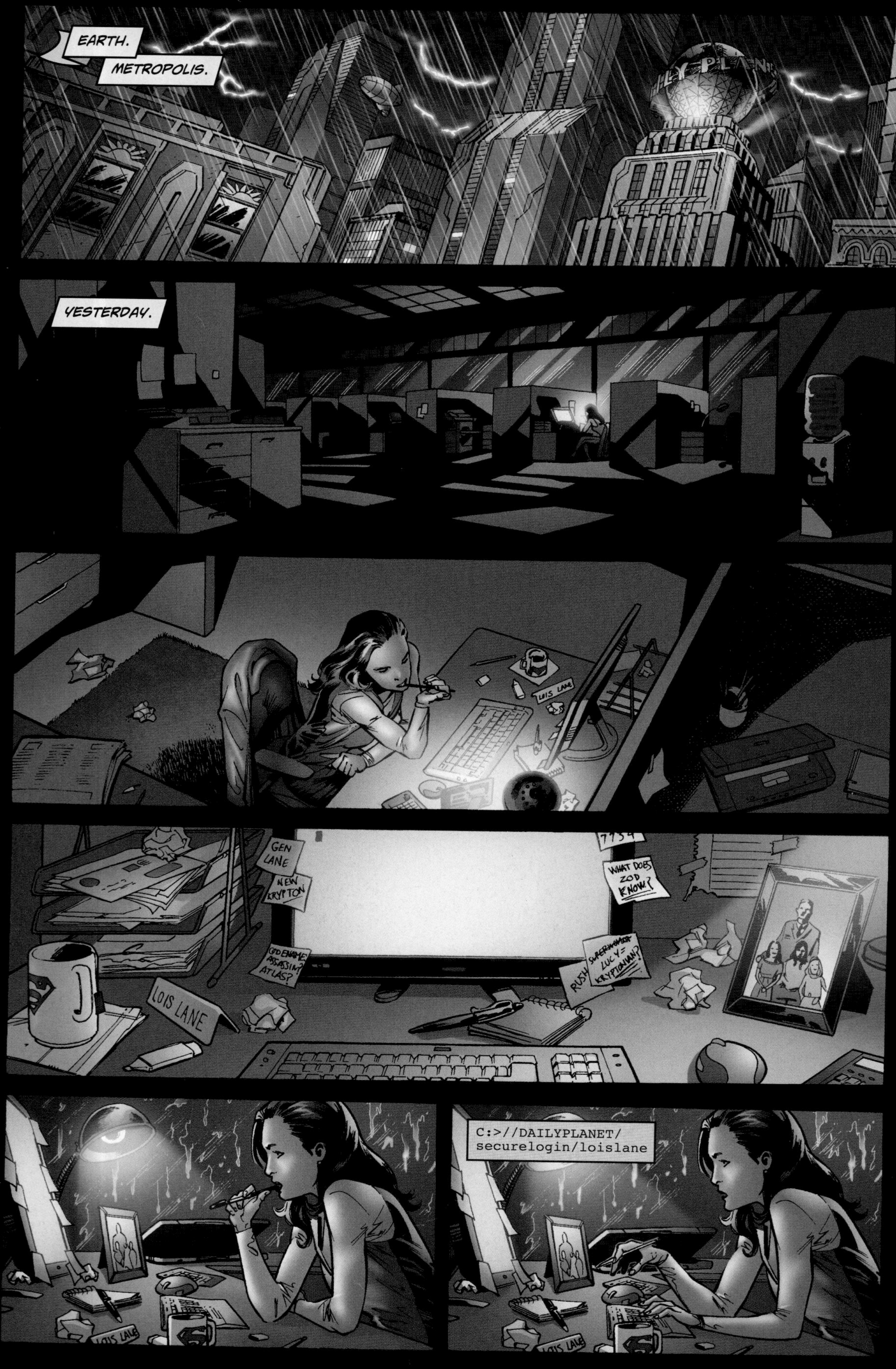
EARTH.
METROPOLIS.
YESTERDAY.
LOIS LANE
GEN LANE
NEW KRYPTON
WHAT DOES ZOD KNOW?
CODENAME ASSASSIN? ATLAS?
RUSH
LUCY= KRYPTONIAN?
LOIS LANE
C:>//DAILYPLANET/
securelogin/loislane

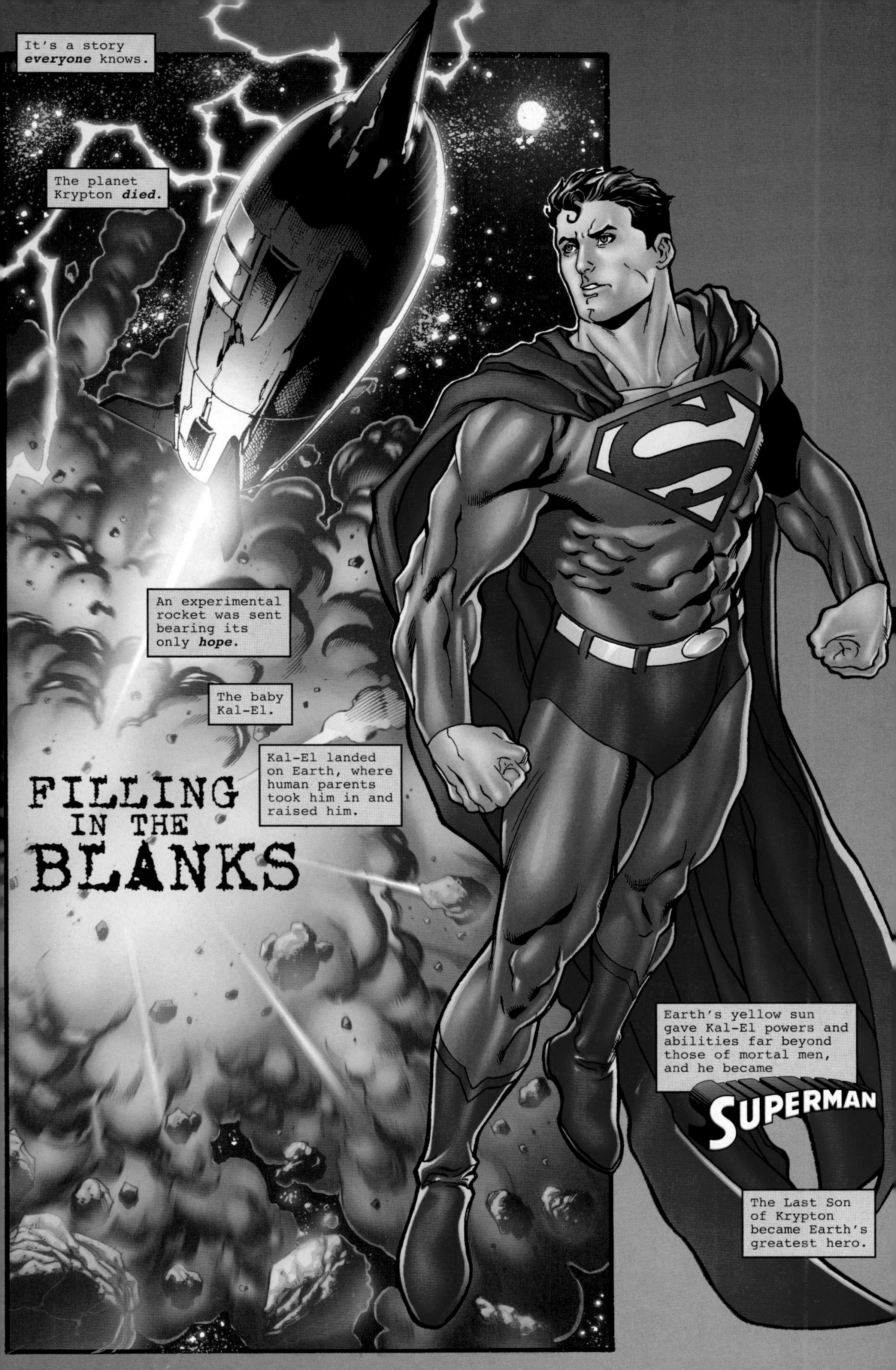
It's a story *everyone* knows.
The planet Krypton *died*.
An experimental rocket was sent bearing its only *hope*.
The baby Kal-El.
Kal-El landed on Earth, where human parents took him in and raised him.
FILLING IN THE BLANKS
Earth's yellow sun gave Kal-El powers and abilities far beyond those of mortal men, and he became
SUPERMAN
The Last Son of Krypton became Earth's greatest hero.

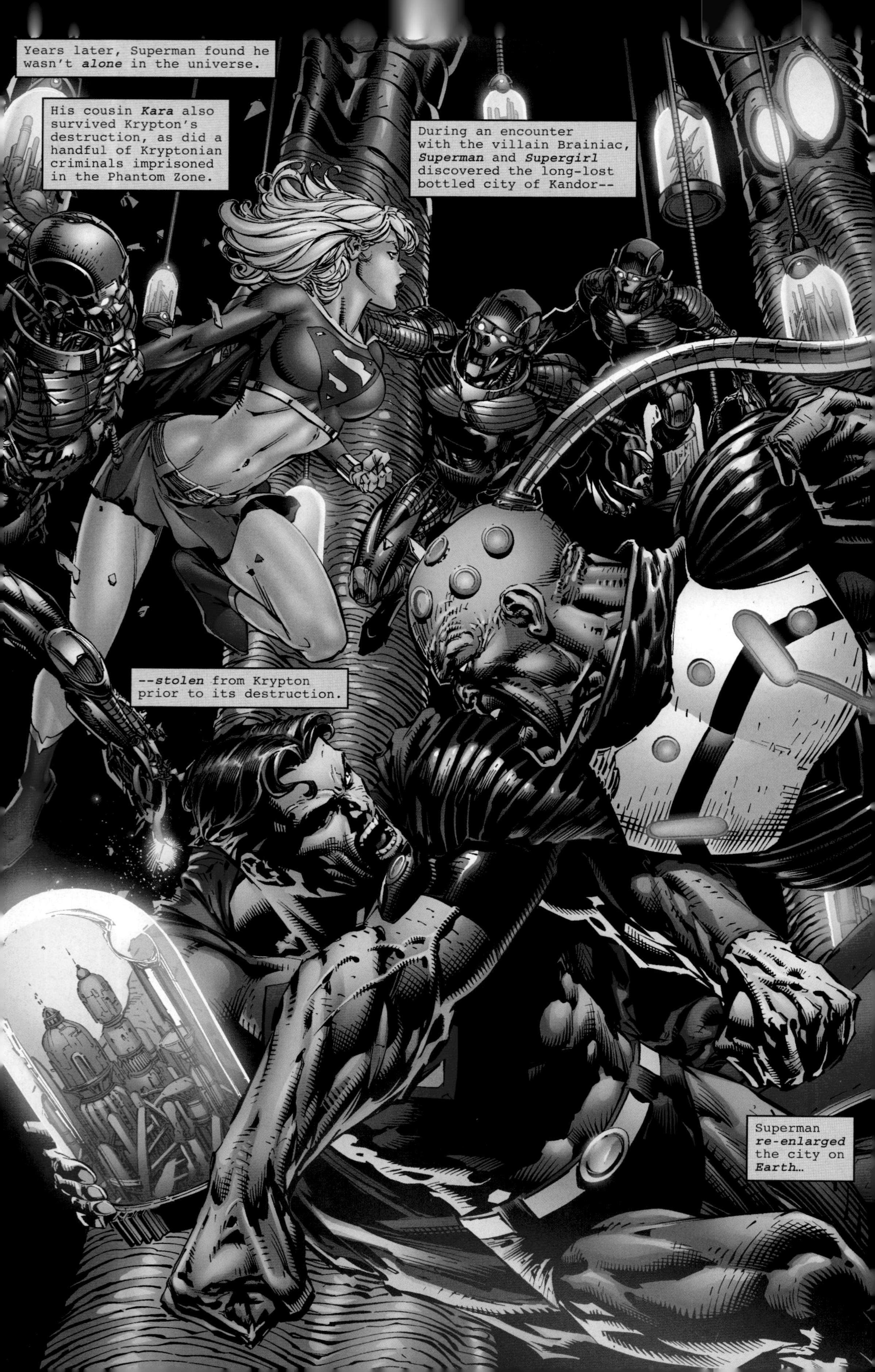
Years later, Superman found he wasn't *alone* in the universe.
His cousin *Kara* also survived Krypton's destruction, as did a handful of Kryptonian criminals imprisoned in the Phantom Zone.
During an encounter with the villain Brainiac, *Superman* and *Supergirl* discovered the long-lost bottled city of Kandor--
--*stolen* from Krypton prior to its destruction.
Superman *re-enlarged* the city on *Earth*...

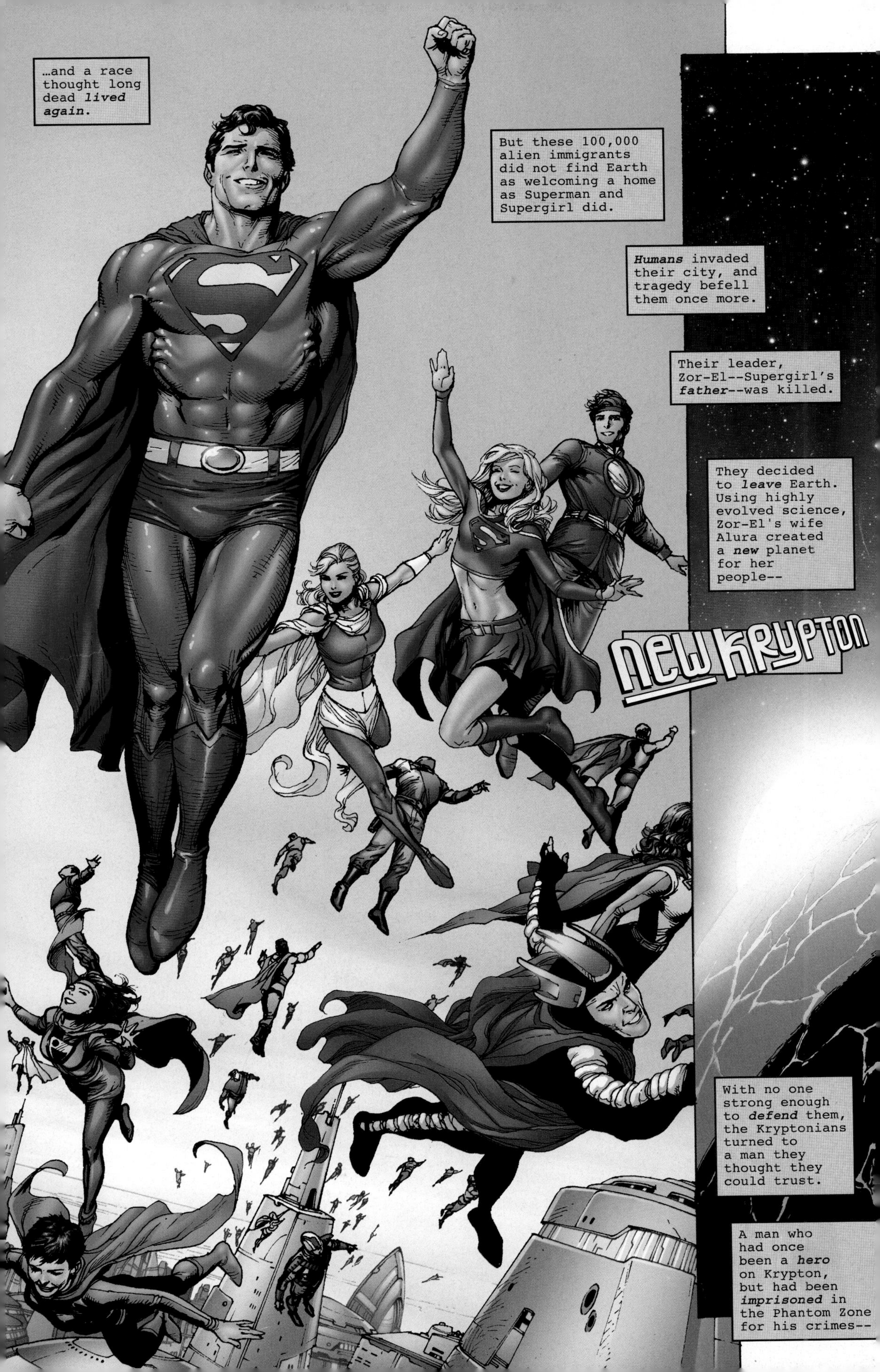
...and a race thought long dead *lived again*.
But these 100,000 alien immigrants did not find Earth as welcoming a home as Superman and Supergirl did.
Humans invaded their city, and tragedy befell them once more.
Their leader, Zor-El--Supergirl's *father*--was killed.
They decided to *leave* Earth. Using highly evolved science, Zor-El's wife Alura created a *new* planet for her people--
NEW KRYPTON
With no one strong enough to *defend* them, the Kryptonians turned to a man they thought they could trust.
A man who had once been a *hero* on Krypton, but had been *imprisoned* in the Phantom Zone for his crimes--

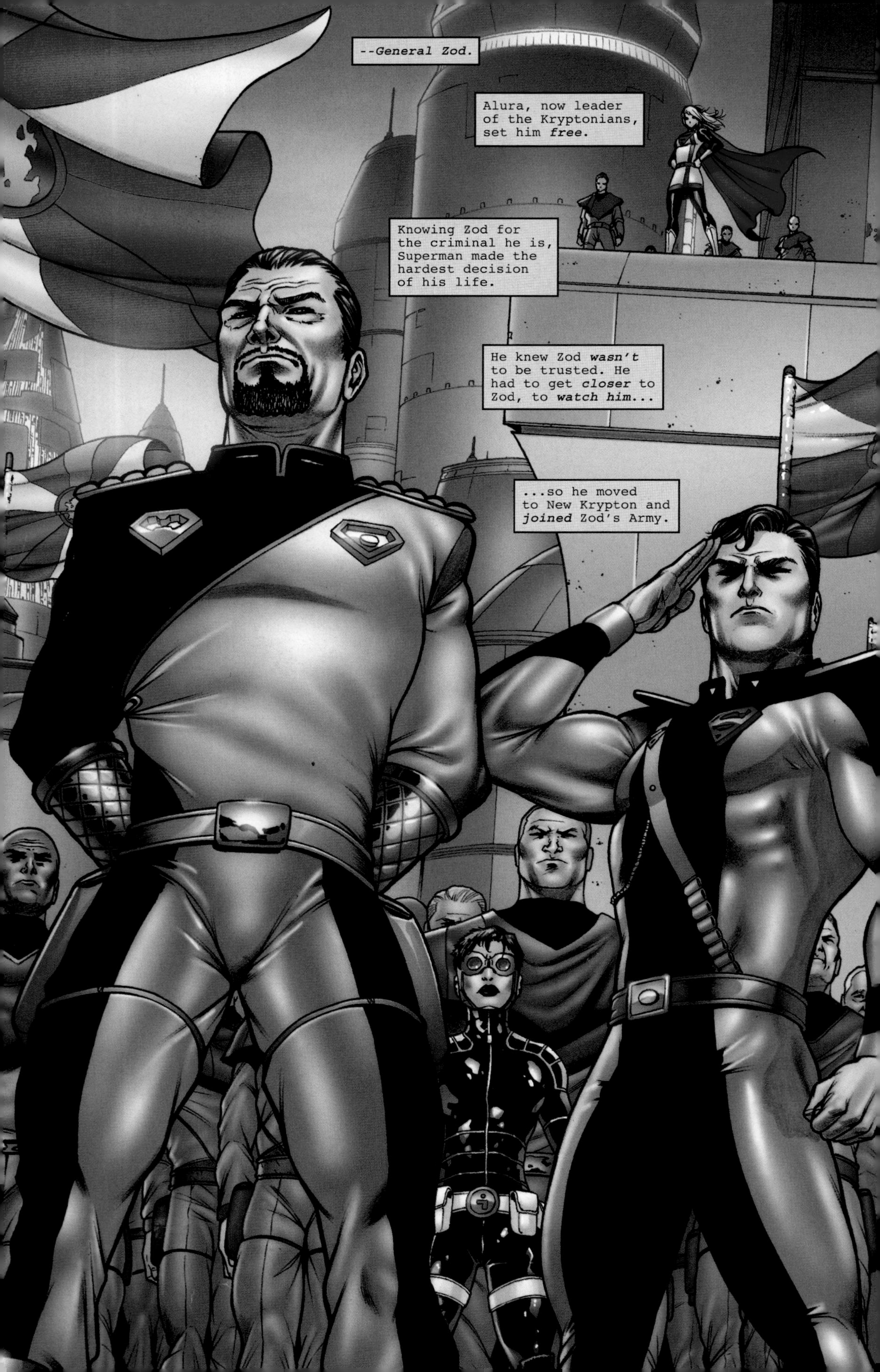
--*General Zod.*
Alura, now leader of the Kryptonians, set him *free.*
Knowing Zod for the criminal he is, Superman made the hardest decision of his life.
He knew Zod ***wasn't*** to be trusted. He had to get *closer* to Zod, to ***watch him...***
...so he moved to New Krypton and *joined* Zod's Army.

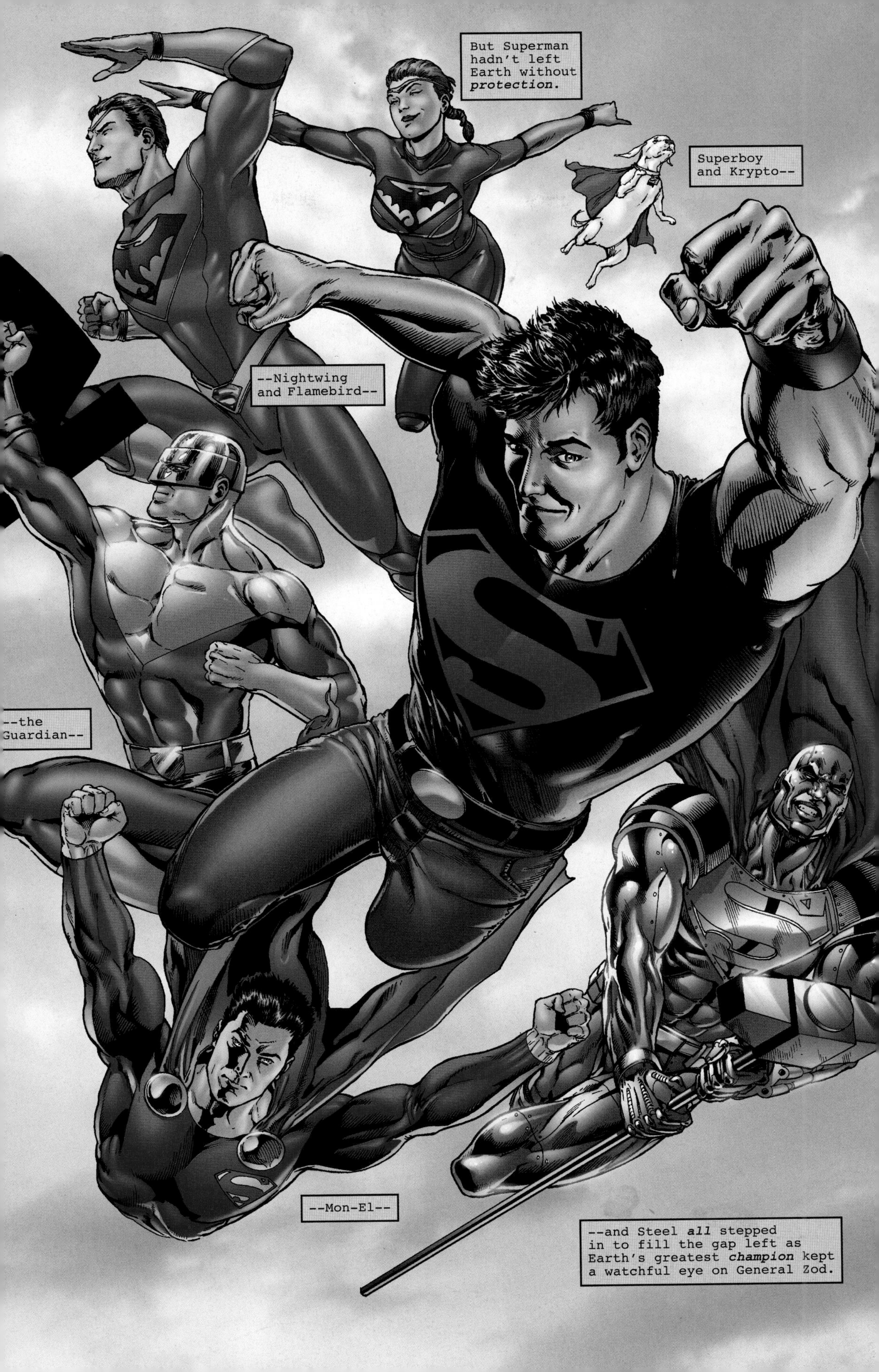
But Superman hadn't left Earth without *protection*.
Superboy and Krypto--
--Nightwing and Flamebird--
--the Guardian--
--Mon-El--
--and Steel *all* stepped in to fill the gap left as Earth's greatest *champion* kept a watchful eye on General Zod.

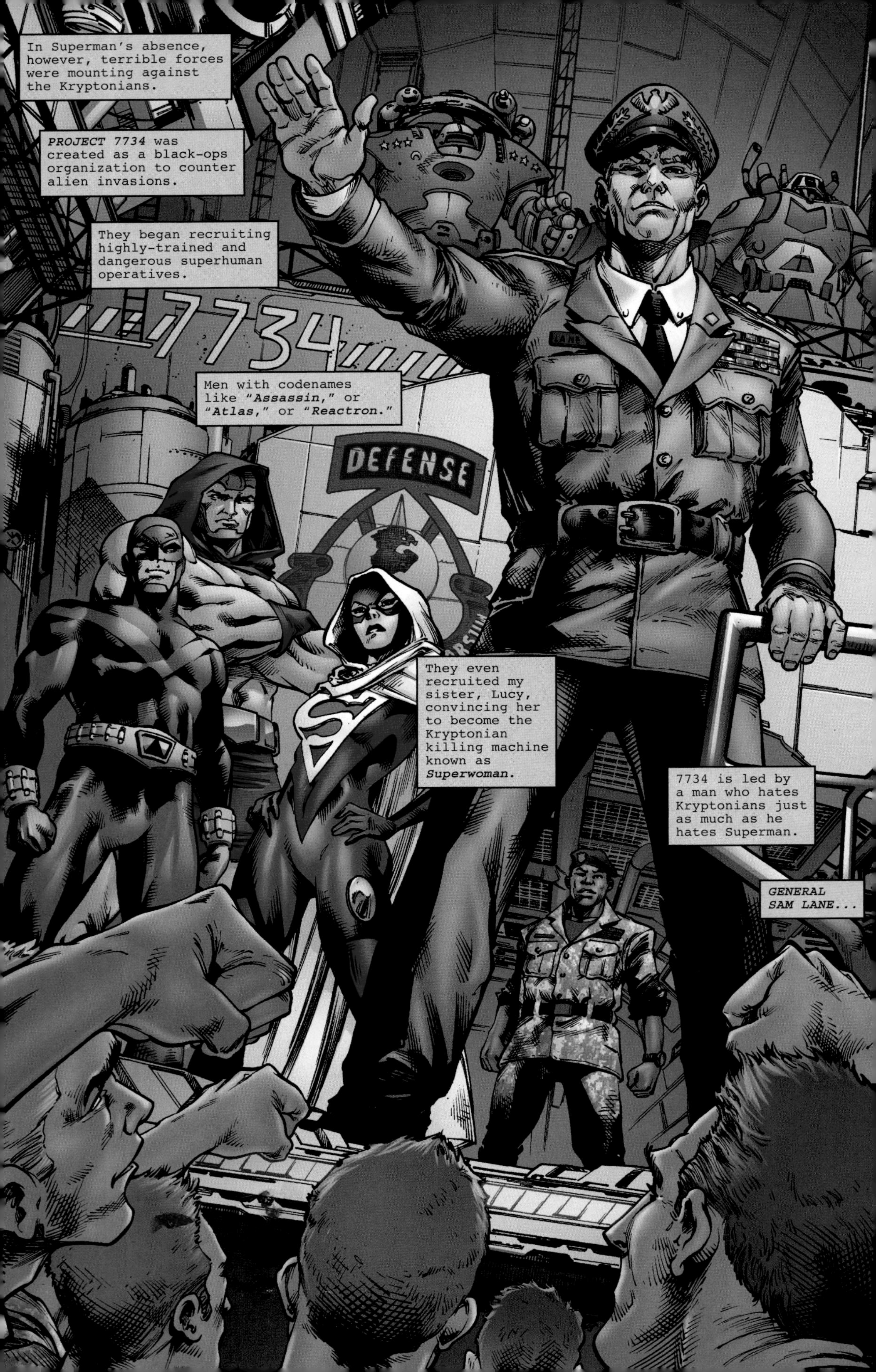
In Superman's absence, however, terrible forces were mounting against the Kryptonians.
PROJECT 7734 was created as a black-ops organization to counter alien invasions.
They began recruiting highly-trained and dangerous superhuman operatives.
7734
Men with codenames like "Assassin," or "Atlas," or "Reactron."
DEFENSE
They even recruited my sister, Lucy, convincing her to become the Kryptonian killing machine known as Superwoman.
7734 is led by a man who hates Kryptonians just as much as he hates Superman.
GENERAL SAM LANE...

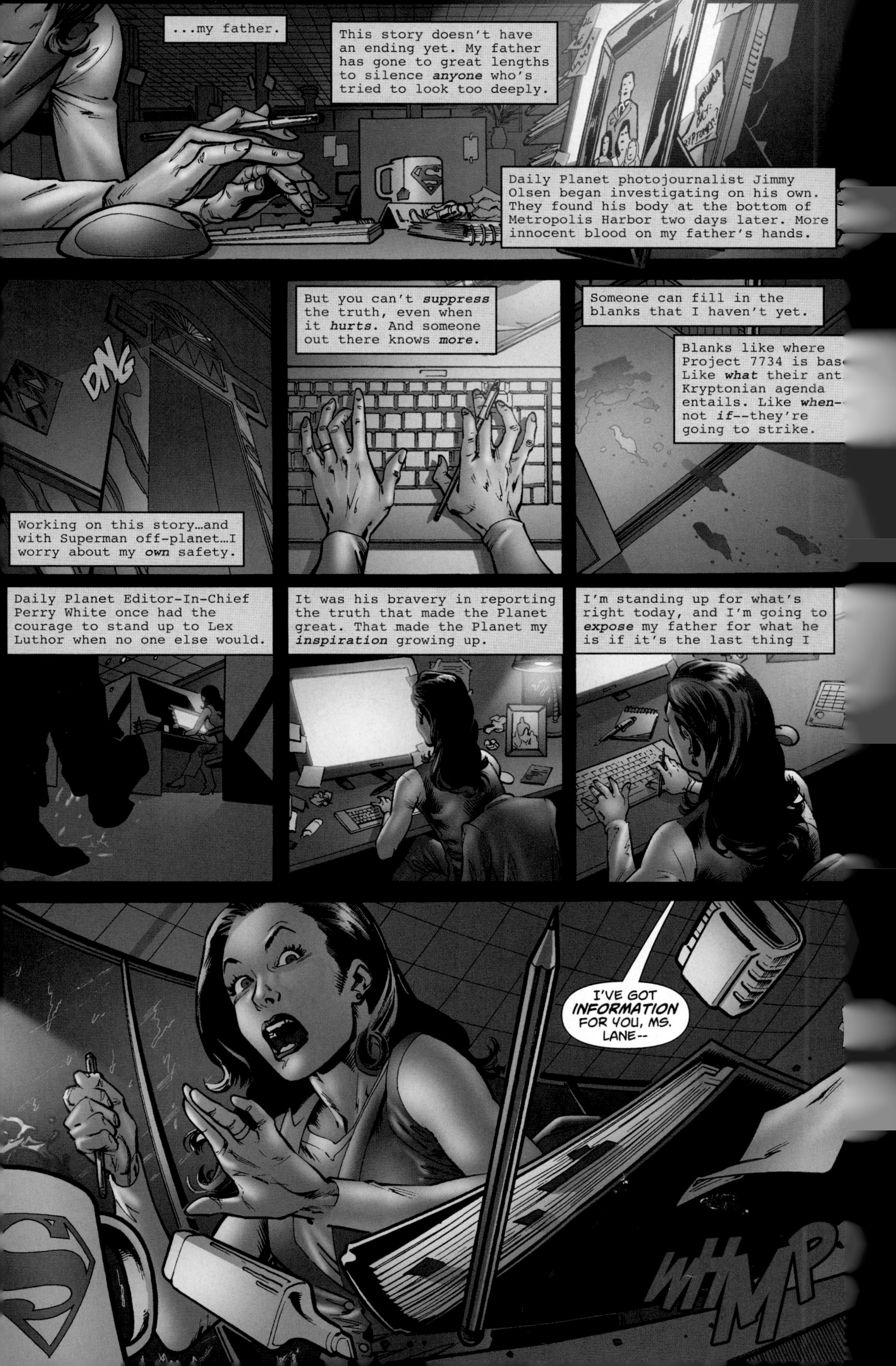
...my father.
This story doesn't have an ending yet. My father has gone to great lengths to silence *anyone* who's tried to look too deeply.
Daily Planet photojournalist Jimmy Olsen began investigating on his own. They found his body at the bottom of Metropolis Harbor two days later. More innocent blood on my father's hands.
DNG
Working on this story...and with Superman off-planet...I worry about my *own* safety.
But you can't *suppress* the truth, even when it *hurts*. And someone out there knows *more*.
Someone can fill in the blanks that I haven't yet.
Blanks like where Project 7734 is bas
Like *what* their ant
Kryptonian agenda
entails. Like *when*-
not *if*--they're going to strike.
Daily Planet Editor-In-Chief Perry White once had the courage to stand up to Lex Luthor when no one else would.
It was his bravery in reporting the truth that made the Planet great. That made the Planet my *inspiration* growing up.
I'm standing up for what's right today, and I'm going to *expose* my father for what he is if it's the last thing I
I'VE GOT *INFORMATION* FOR YOU, MS. LANE--
WHMP

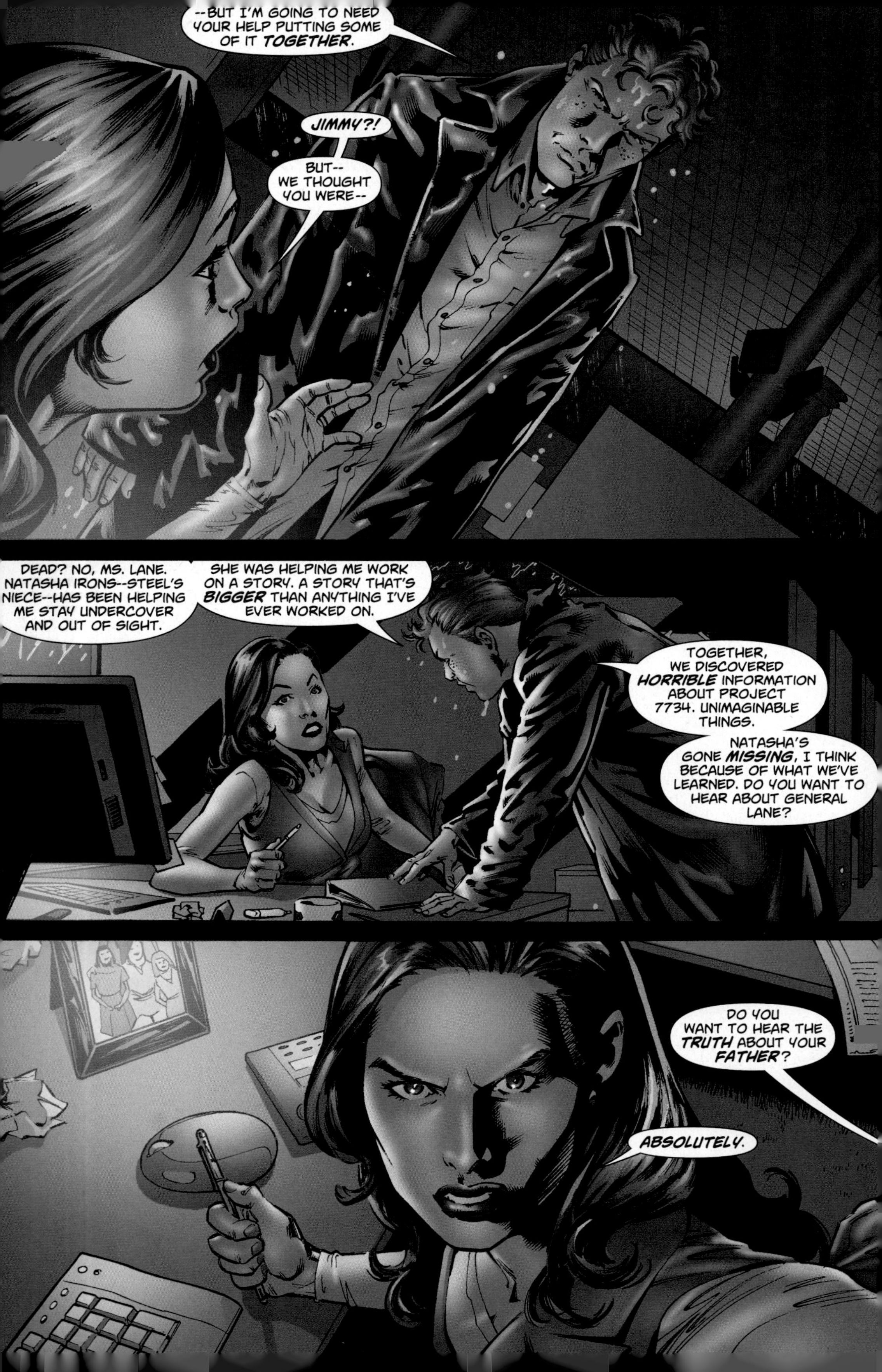
--BUT I'M GOING TO NEED YOUR HELP PUTTING SOME OF IT TOGETHER.
JIMMY?!
BUT-- WE THOUGHT YOU WERE--
DEAD? NO, MS. LANE. NATASHA IRONS--STEEL'S NIECE--HAS BEEN HELPING ME STAY UNDERCOVER AND OUT OF SIGHT.
SHE WAS HELPING ME WORK ON A STORY. A STORY THAT'S BIGGER THAN ANYTHING I'VE EVER WORKED ON.
TOGETHER, WE DISCOVERED HORRIBLE INFORMATION ABOUT PROJECT 7734. UNIMAGINABLE THINGS.
NATASHA'S GONE MISSING, I THINK BECAUSE OF WHAT WE'VE LEARNED. DO YOU WANT TO HEAR ABOUT GENERAL LANE?
DO YOU WANT TO HEAR THE TRUTH ABOUT YOUR FATHER?
ABSOLUTELY.

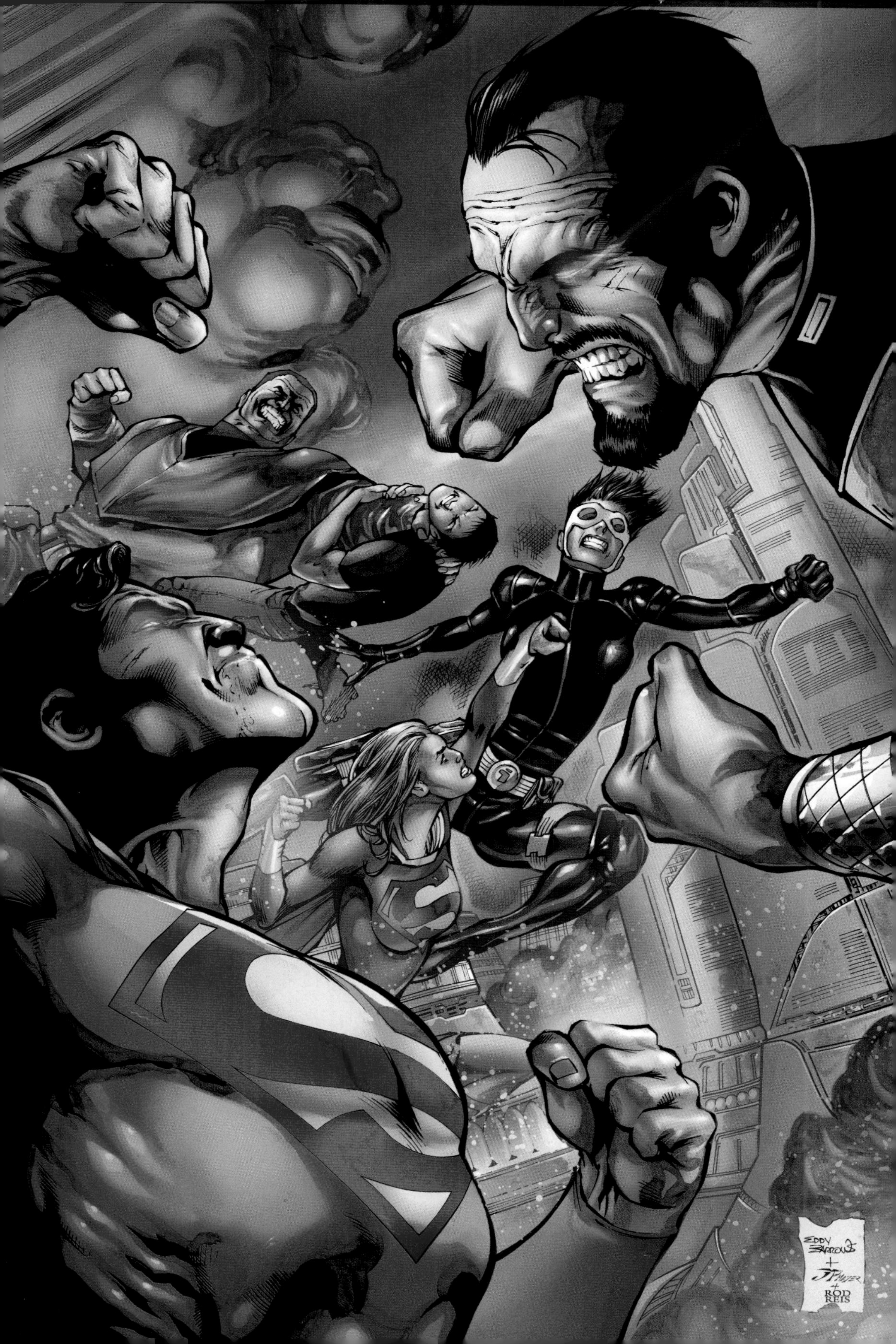
EDDY BARROWS
+
JP MAYER
+
ROD REIS

VARIANT by AARON LOPRESTI, MATT RYAN & BRAD ANDERSON

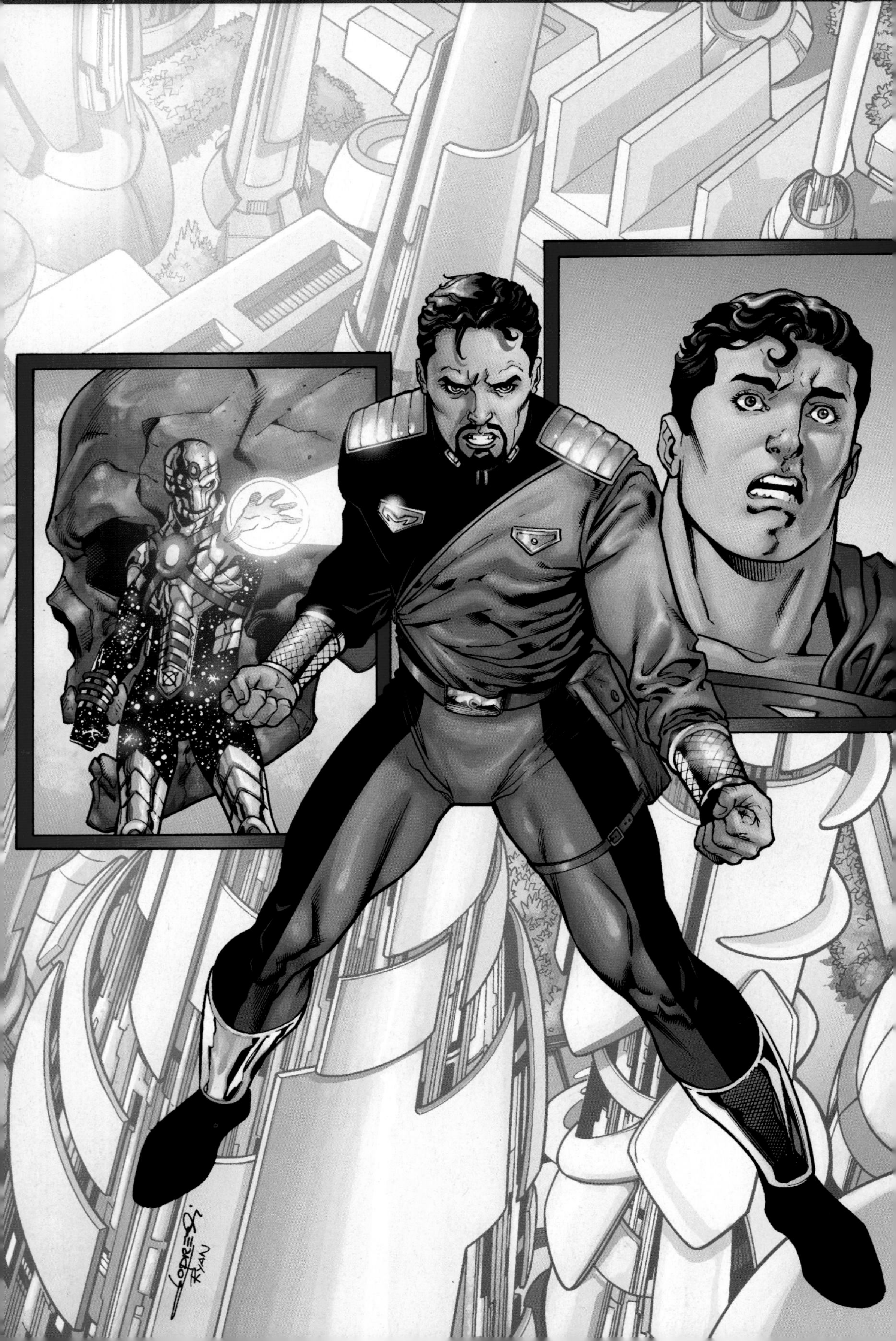

LOPRESTI
RYAN

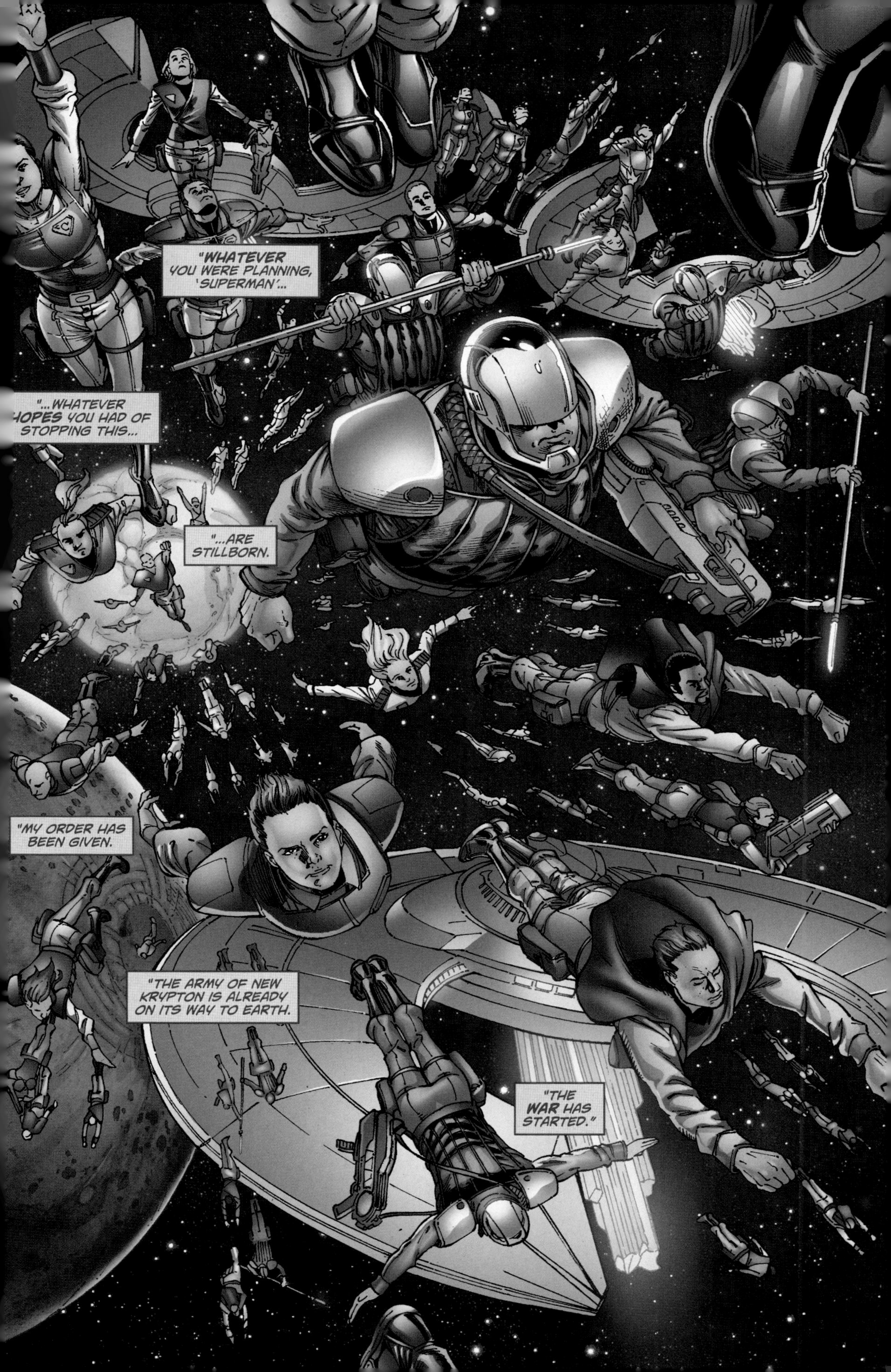
"WHATEVER YOU WERE PLANNING, 'SUPERMAN'...
"...WHATEVER HOPES YOU HAD OF STOPPING THIS...
"...ARE STILLBORN.
"MY ORDER HAS BEEN GIVEN.
"THE ARMY OF NEW KRYPTON IS ALREADY ON ITS WAY TO EARTH.
"THE WAR HAS STARTED."

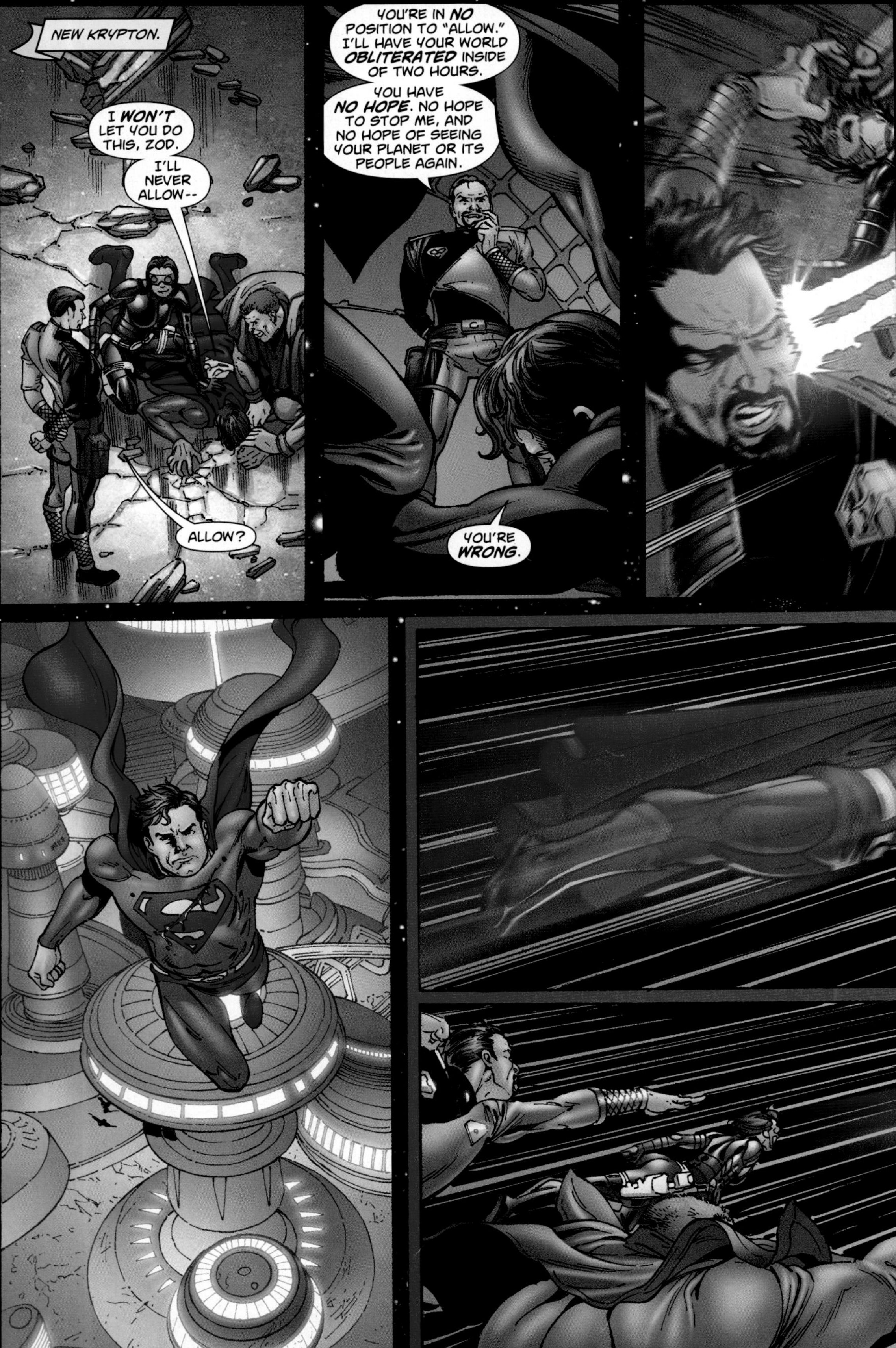
NEW KRYPTON.
I WON'T LET YOU DO THIS, ZOD.
I'LL NEVER ALLOW--
ALLOW?
YOU'RE IN NO POSITION TO "ALLOW." I'LL HAVE YOUR WORLD OBLITERATED INSIDE OF TWO HOURS.
YOU HAVE NO HOPE. NO HOPE TO STOP ME, AND NO HOPE OF SEEING YOUR PLANET OR ITS PEOPLE AGAIN.
YOU'RE WRONG.

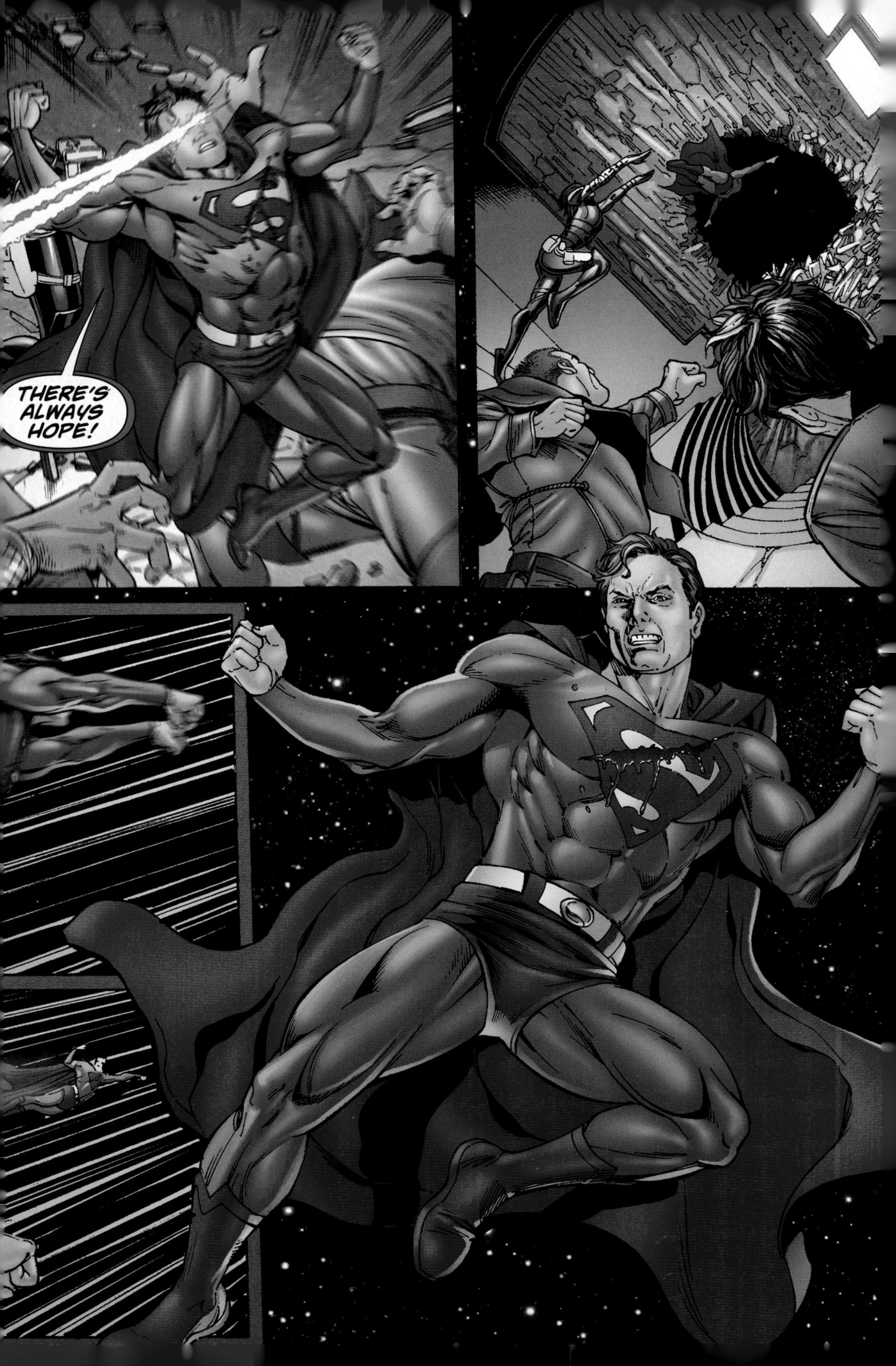
THERE'S ALWAYS HOPE!

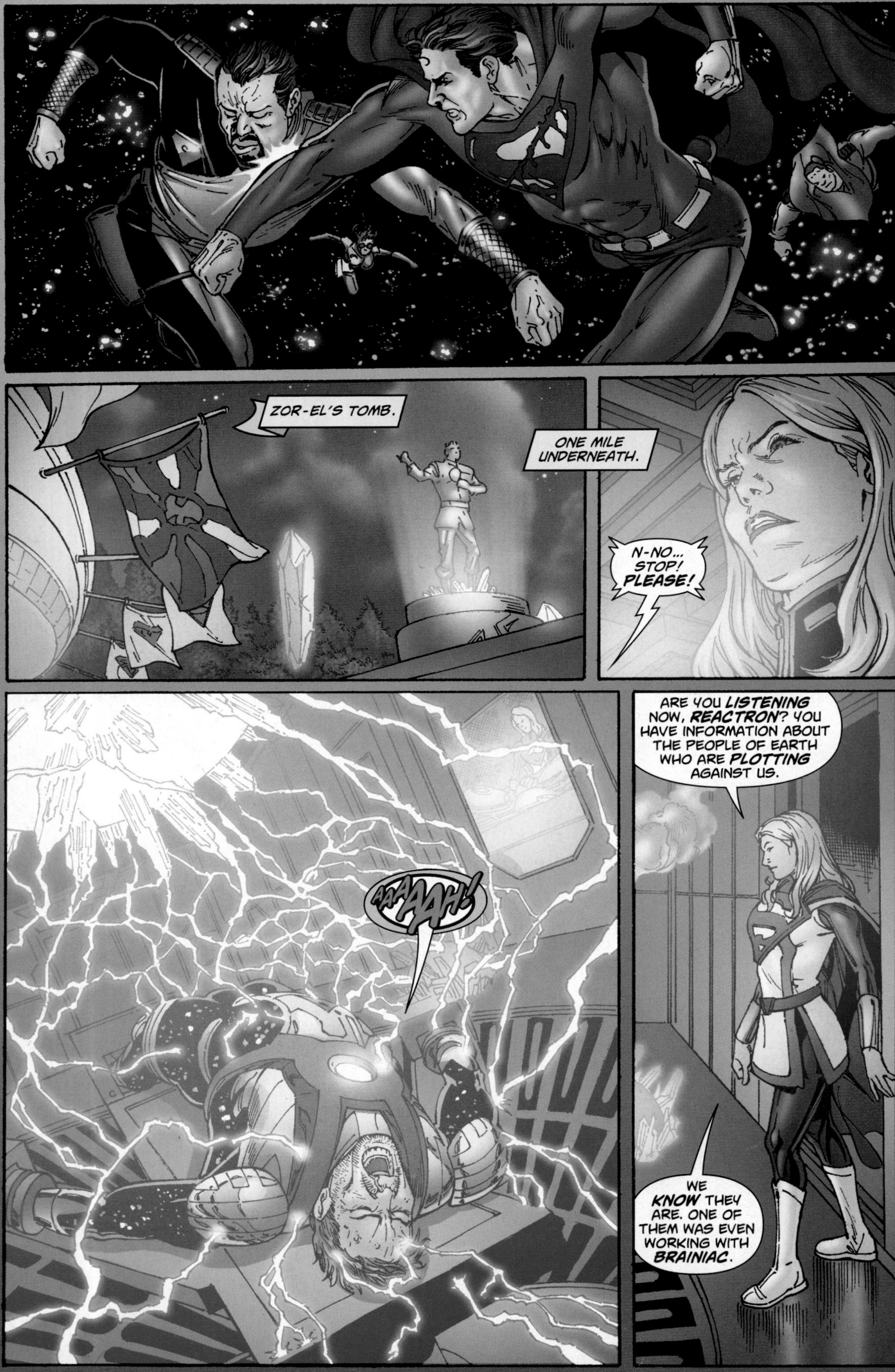
ZOR-EL'S TOMB.
ONE MILE UNDERNEATH.
N-NO... STOP! PLEASE!
AAAAAH!
ARE YOU LISTENING NOW, REACTRON? YOU HAVE INFORMATION ABOUT THE PEOPLE OF EARTH WHO ARE PLOTTING AGAINST US.
WE KNOW THEY ARE. ONE OF THEM WAS EVEN WORKING WITH BRAINIAC.

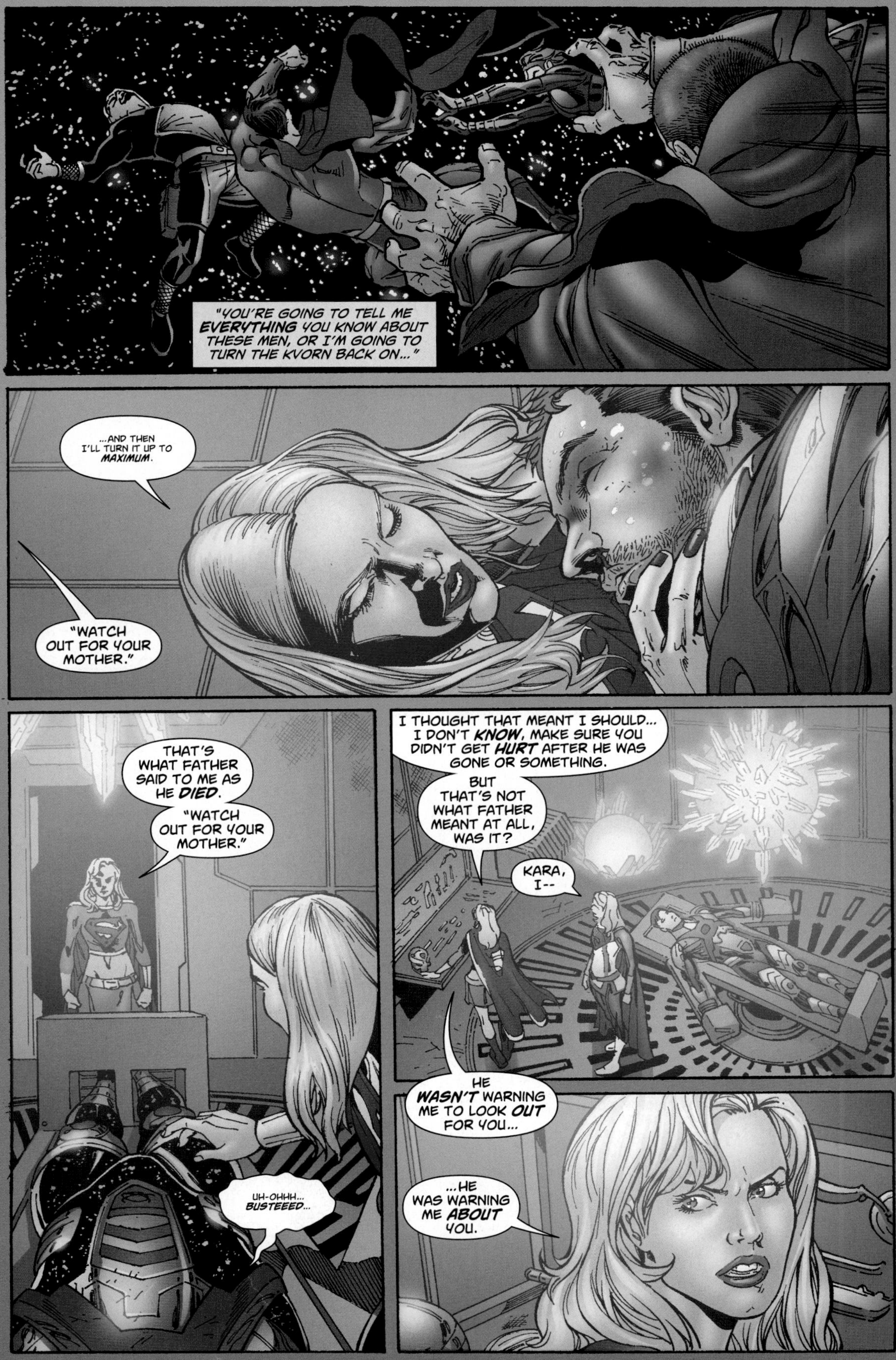
"YOU'RE GOING TO TELL ME EVERYTHING YOU KNOW ABOUT THESE MEN, OR I'M GOING TO TURN THE KVORN BACK ON..."
...AND THEN I'LL TURN IT UP TO MAXIMUM.
"WATCH OUT FOR YOUR MOTHER."
THAT'S WHAT FATHER SAID TO ME AS HE DIED.
"WATCH OUT FOR YOUR MOTHER."
UH-OHHH... BUSTEEED...
I THOUGHT THAT MEANT I SHOULD... I DON'T KNOW, MAKE SURE YOU DIDN'T GET HURT AFTER HE WAS GONE OR SOMETHING.
BUT THAT'S NOT WHAT FATHER MEANT AT ALL, WAS IT?
KARA, I--
HE WASN'T WARNING ME TO LOOK OUT FOR YOU...
...HE WAS WARNING ME ABOUT YOU.

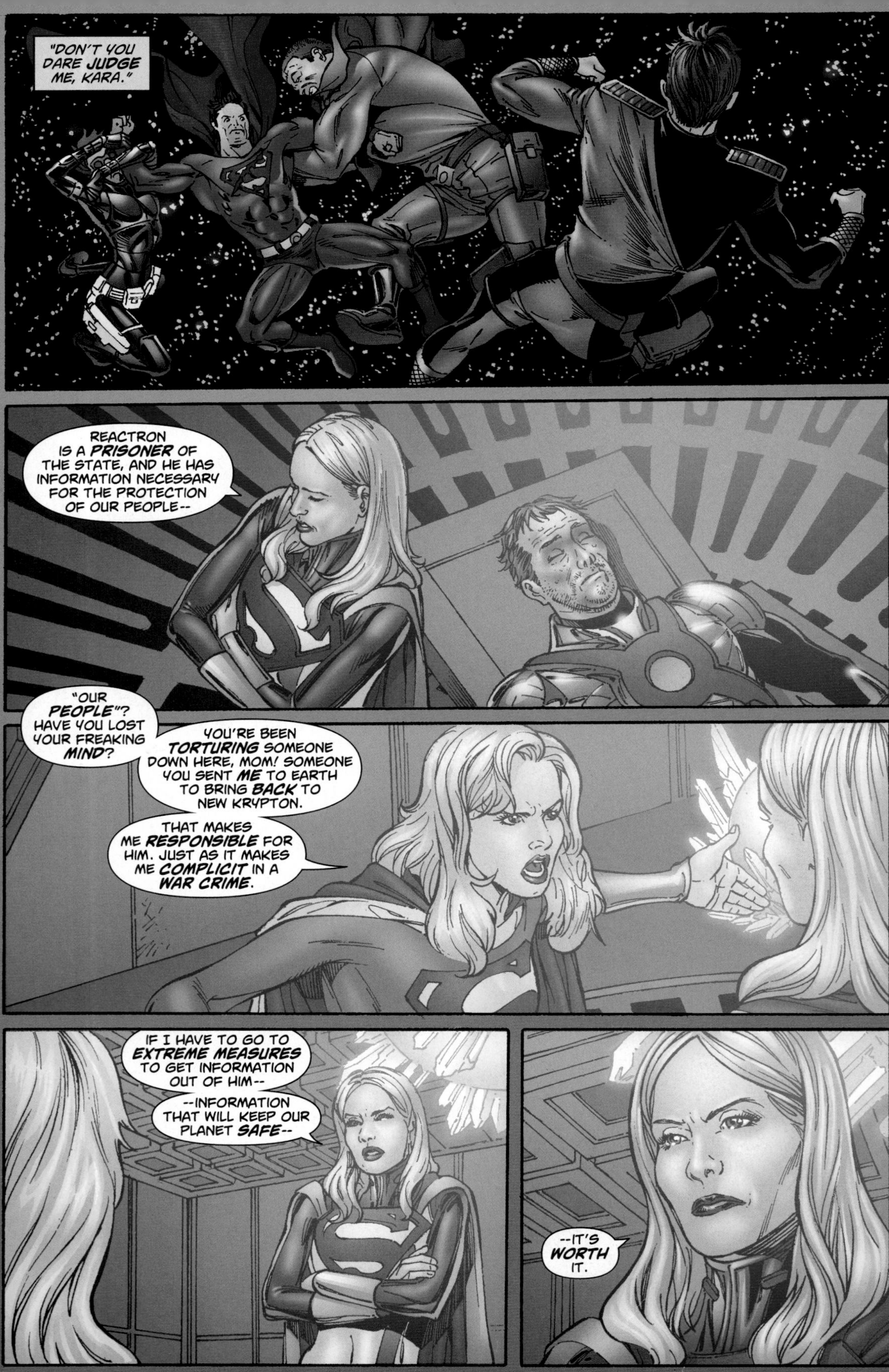
"DON'T YOU DARE JUDGE ME, KARA."
REACTRON IS A PRISONER OF THE STATE, AND HE HAS INFORMATION NECESSARY FOR THE PROTECTION OF OUR PEOPLE--
"OUR PEOPLE"? HAVE YOU LOST YOUR FREAKING MIND?
YOU'RE BEEN TORTURING SOMEONE DOWN HERE, MOM! SOMEONE YOU SENT ME TO EARTH TO BRING BACK TO NEW KRYPTON.
THAT MAKES ME RESPONSIBLE FOR HIM. JUST AS IT MAKES ME COMPLICIT IN A WAR CRIME.
IF I HAVE TO GO TO EXTREME MEASURES TO GET INFORMATION OUT OF HIM--
--INFORMATION THAT WILL KEEP OUR PLANET SAFE--
--IT'S WORTH IT.

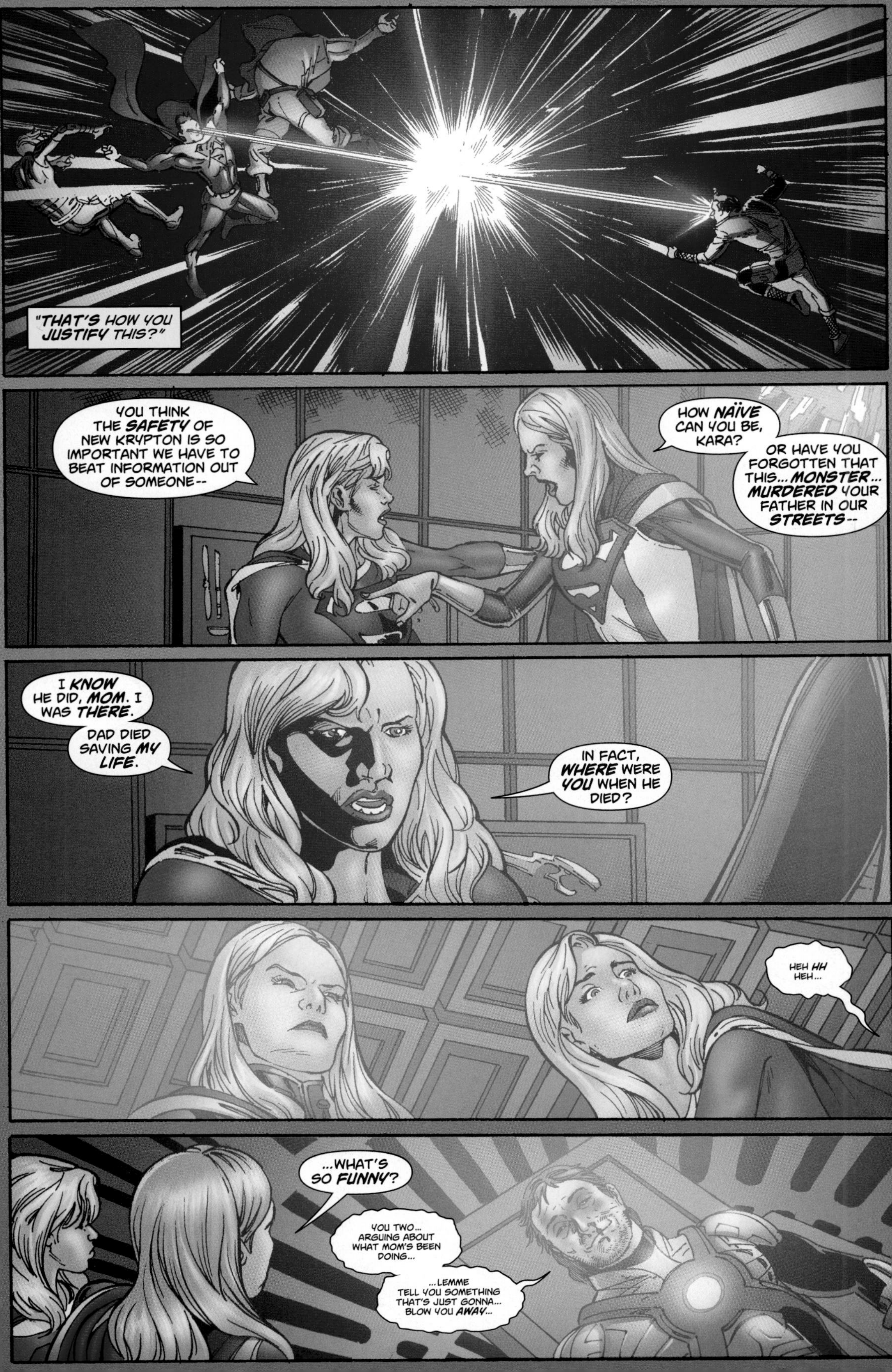
"THAT'S HOW YOU JUSTIFY THIS?"
YOU THINK THE SAFETY OF NEW KRYPTON IS SO IMPORTANT WE HAVE TO BEAT INFORMATION OUT OF SOMEONE--
HOW NAÏVE CAN YOU BE, KARA?
OR HAVE YOU FORGOTTEN THAT THIS... MONSTER... MURDERED YOUR FATHER IN OUR STREETS--
I KNOW HE DID, MOM. I WAS THERE.
DAD DIED SAVING MY LIFE.
IN FACT, WHERE WERE YOU WHEN HE DIED?
HEH HH HEH...
...WHAT'S SO FUNNY?
YOU TWO... ARGUING ABOUT WHAT MOM'S BEEN DOING...
...LEMME TELL YOU SOMETHING THAT'S JUST GONNA... BLOW YOU AWAY...

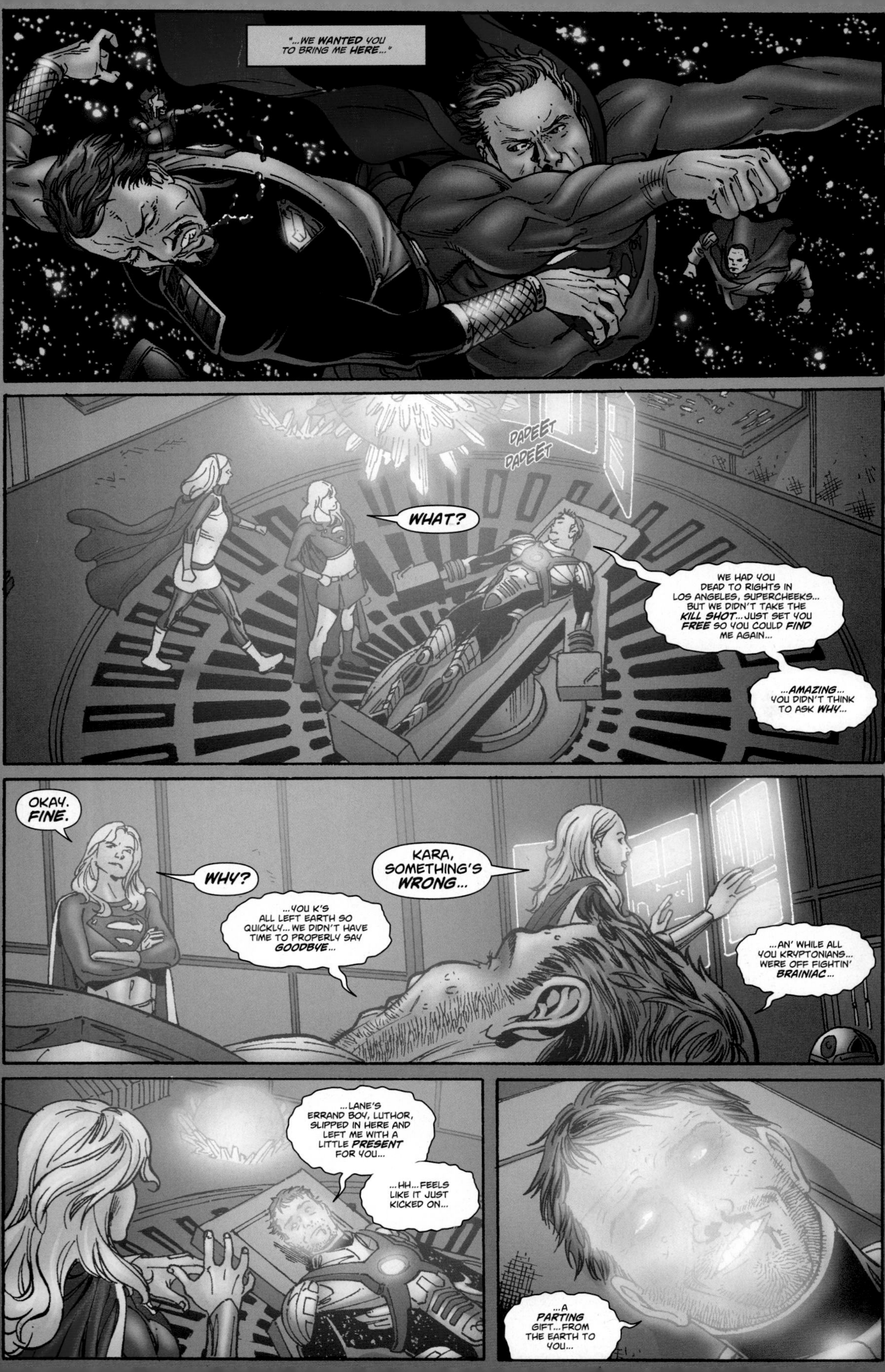
"...WE WANTED YOU TO BRING ME HERE..."
DADEET DADEET
WHAT?
WE HAD YOU DEAD TO RIGHTS IN LOS ANGELES, SUPERCHEEKS... BUT WE DIDN'T TAKE THE KILL SHOT...JUST SET YOU FREE SO YOU COULD FIND ME AGAIN...
...AMAZING... YOU DIDN'T THINK TO ASK WHY...
OKAY. FINE.
WHY?
KARA, SOMETHING'S WRONG...
...YOU K'S ALL LEFT EARTH SO QUICKLY...WE DIDN'T HAVE TIME TO PROPERLY SAY GOODBYE...
...AN' WHILE ALL YOU KRYPTONIANS... WERE OFF FIGHTIN' BRAINIAC...
...LANE'S ERRAND BOY, LUTHOR, SLIPPED IN HERE AND LEFT ME WITH A LITTLE PRESENT FOR YOU...
...HH...FEELS LIKE IT JUST KICKED ON...
...A PARTING GIFT...FROM THE EARTH TO YOU...

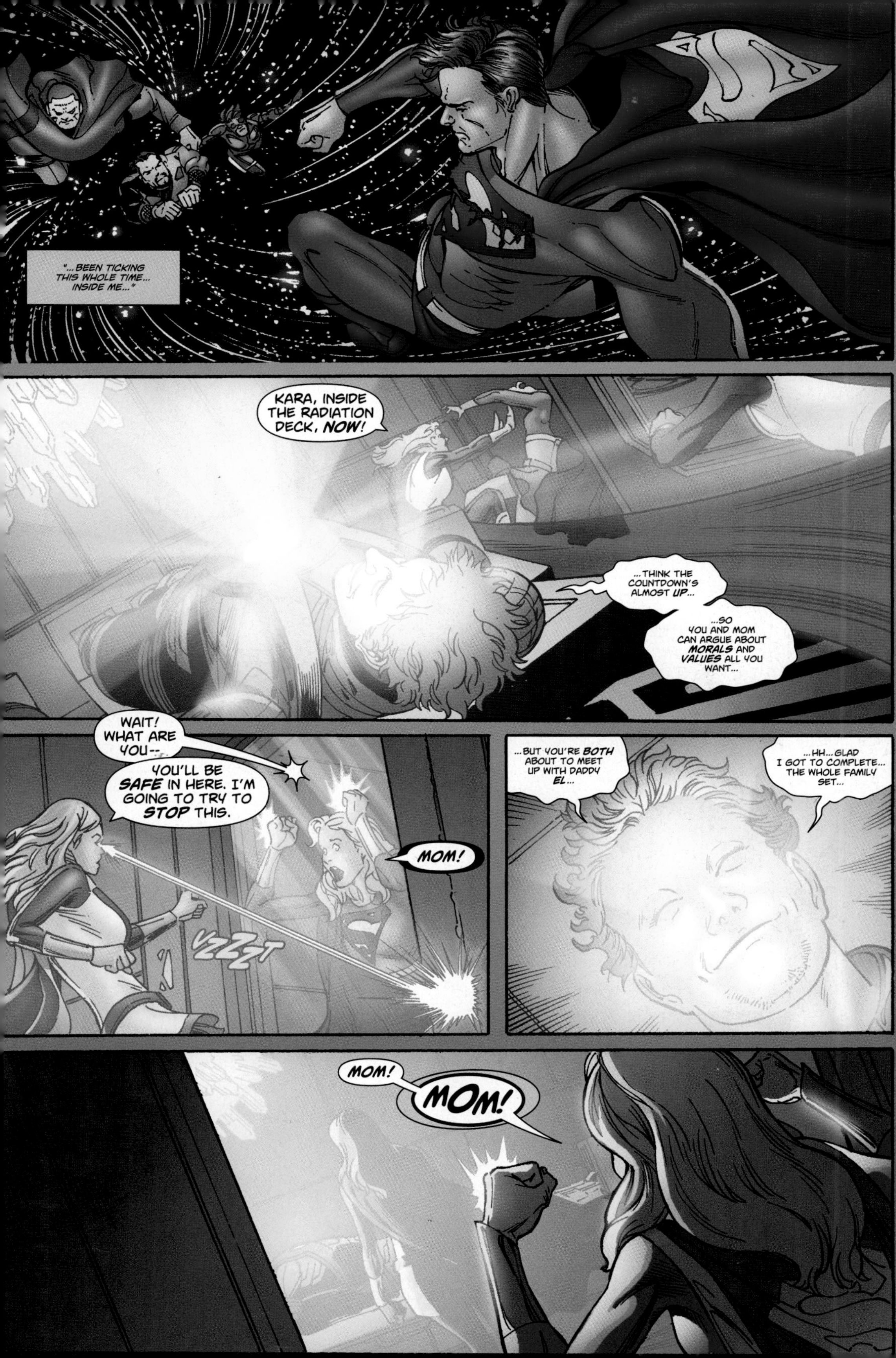
"...BEEN TICKING THIS WHOLE TIME... INSIDE ME..."
KARA, INSIDE THE RADIATION DECK, NOW!
...THINK THE COUNTDOWN'S ALMOST UP...
...SO YOU AND MOM CAN ARGUE ABOUT MORALS AND VALUES ALL YOU WANT...
WAIT! WHAT ARE YOU--
YOU'LL BE SAFE IN HERE. I'M GOING TO TRY TO STOP THIS.
MOM!
VZZZT
...BUT YOU'RE BOTH ABOUT TO MEET UP WITH DADDY EL...
...HH... GLAD I GOT TO COMPLETE... THE WHOLE FAMILY SET...
MOM!
MOM!

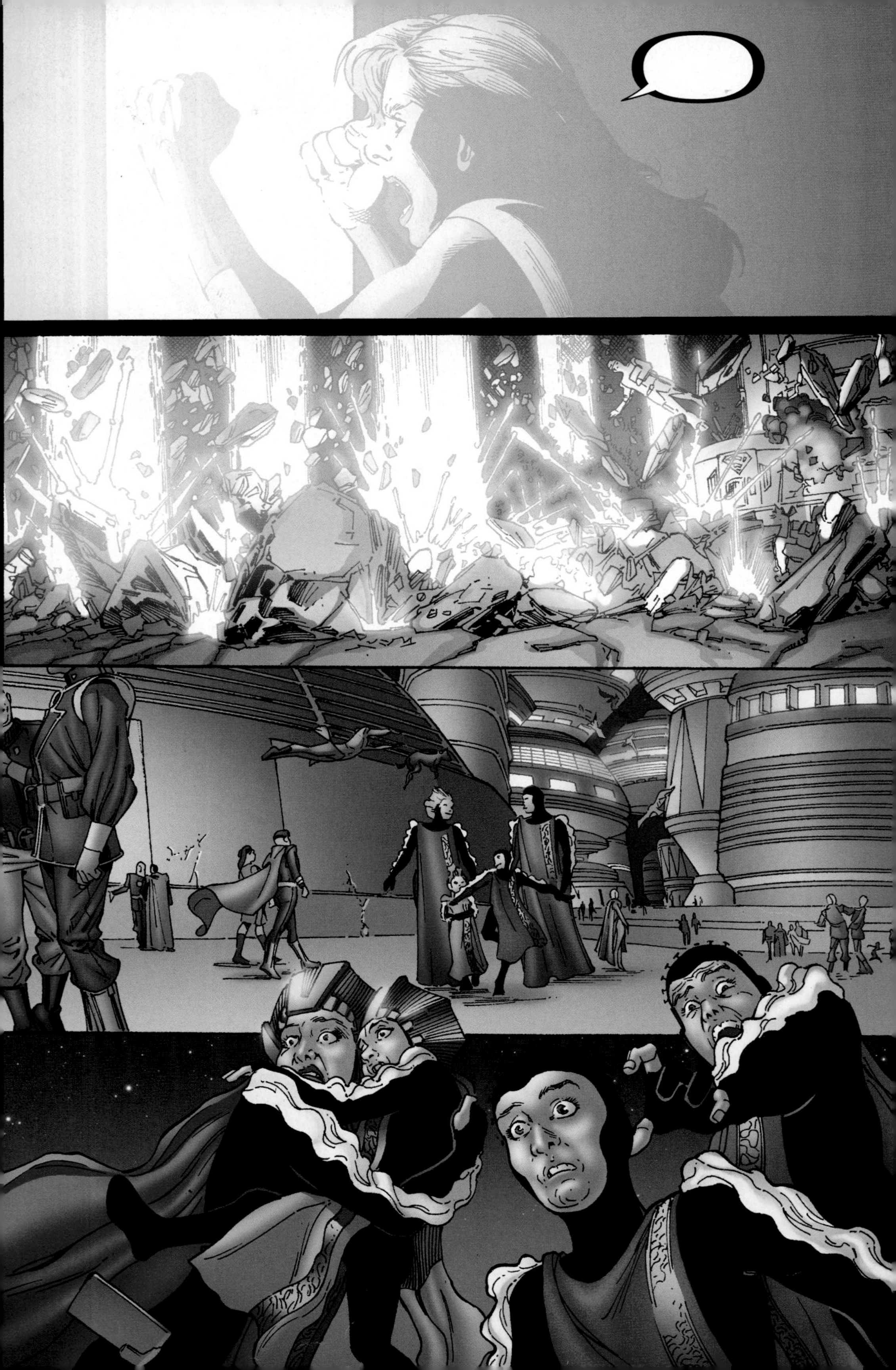

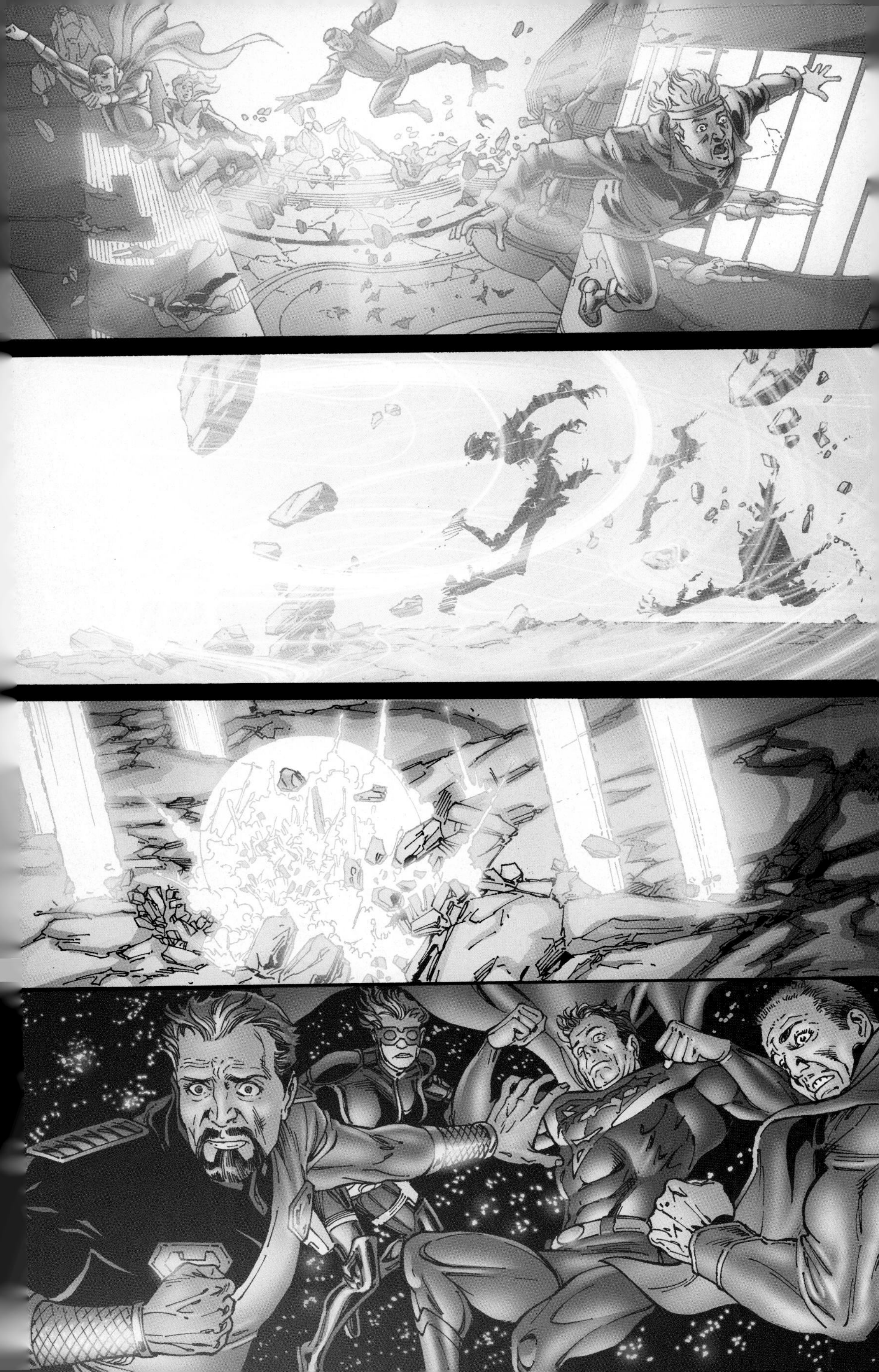

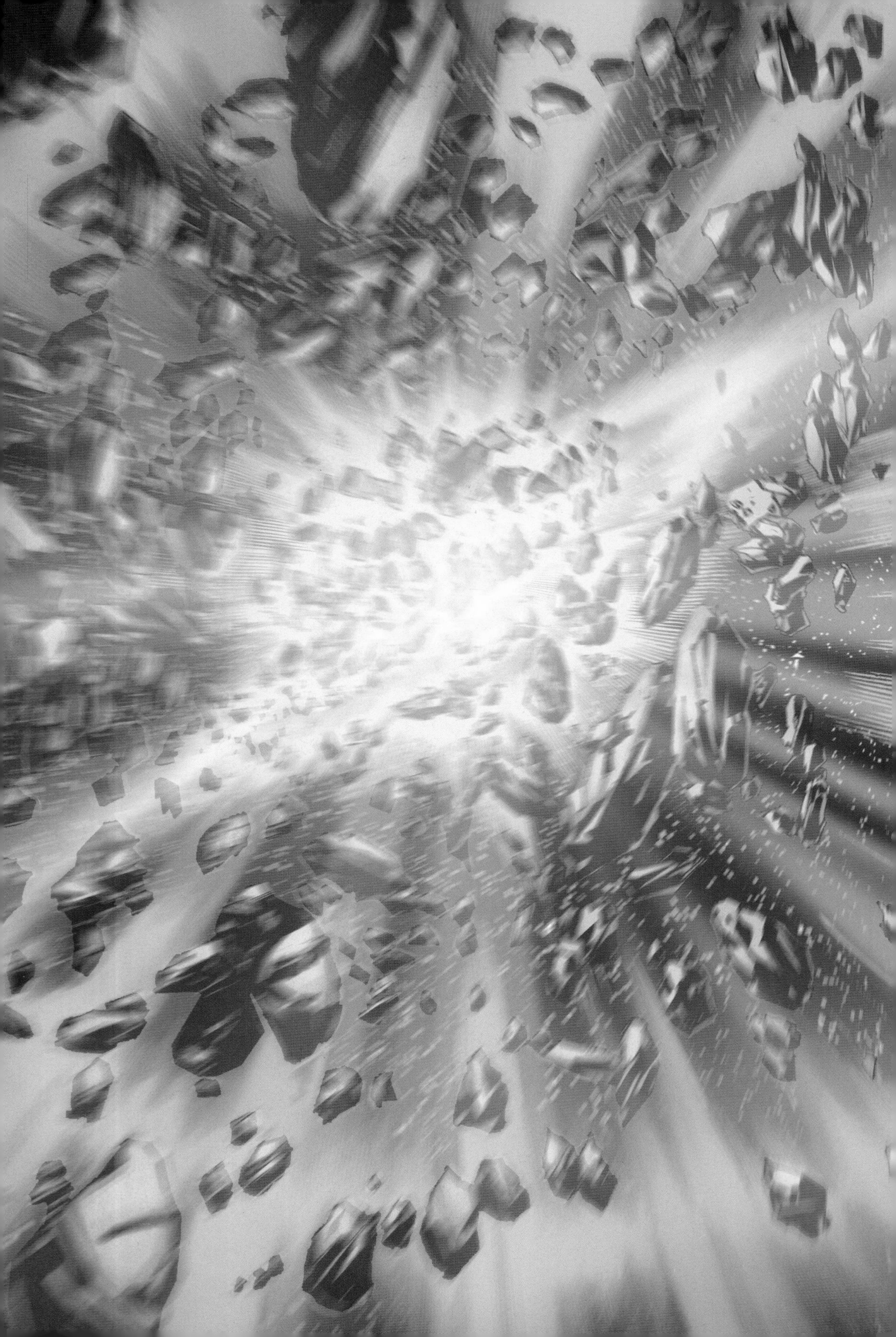

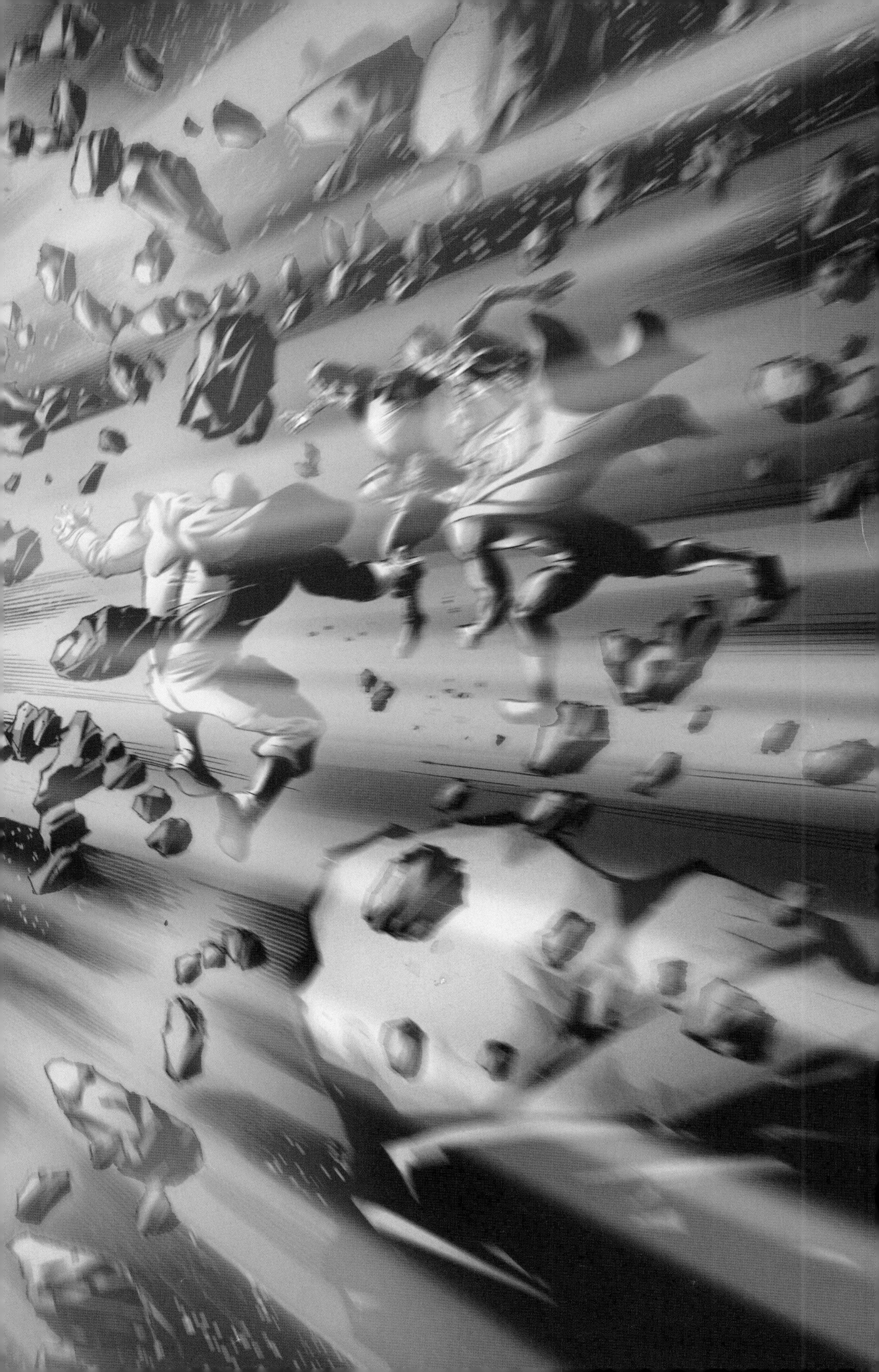

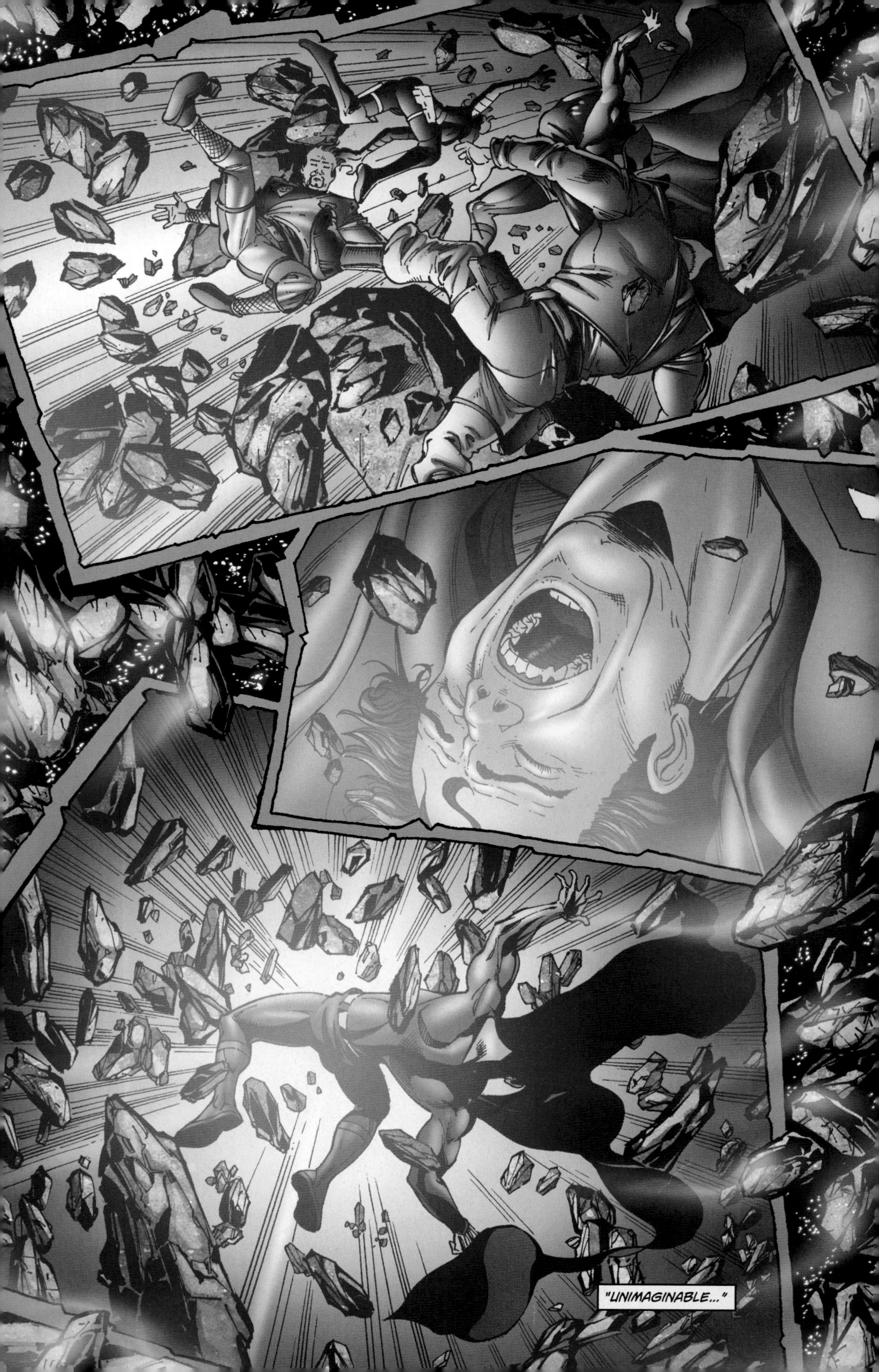
"UNIMAGINABLE..."

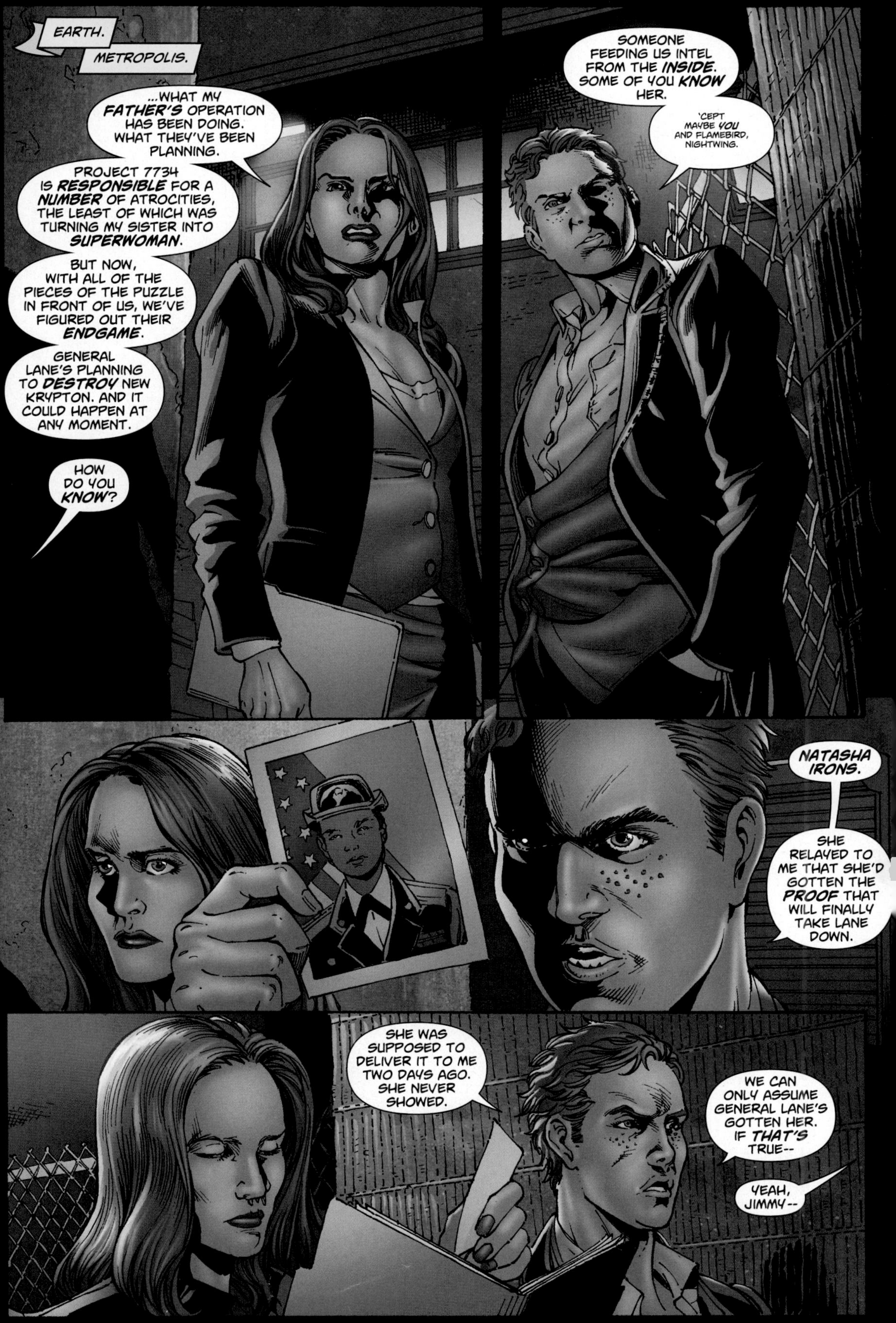
EARTH.
METROPOLIS.
...WHAT MY FATHER'S OPERATION HAS BEEN DOING. WHAT THEY'VE BEEN PLANNING.
PROJECT 7734 IS RESPONSIBLE FOR A NUMBER OF ATROCITIES, THE LEAST OF WHICH WAS TURNING MY SISTER INTO SUPERWOMAN.
BUT NOW, WITH ALL OF THE PIECES OF THE PUZZLE IN FRONT OF US, WE'VE FIGURED OUT THEIR ENDGAME.
GENERAL LANE'S PLANNING TO DESTROY NEW KRYPTON. AND IT COULD HAPPEN AT ANY MOMENT.
HOW DO YOU KNOW?
SOMEONE FEEDING US INTEL FROM THE INSIDE. SOME OF YOU KNOW HER.
'CEPT MAYBE YOU AND FLAMEBIRD, NIGHTWING.
NATASHA IRONS.
SHE RELAYED TO ME THAT SHE'D GOTTEN THE PROOF THAT WILL FINALLY TAKE LANE DOWN.
SHE WAS SUPPOSED TO DELIVER IT TO ME TWO DAYS AGO. SHE NEVER SHOWED.
WE CAN ONLY ASSUME GENERAL LANE'S GOTTEN HER. IF THAT'S TRUE--
YEAH, JIMMY--

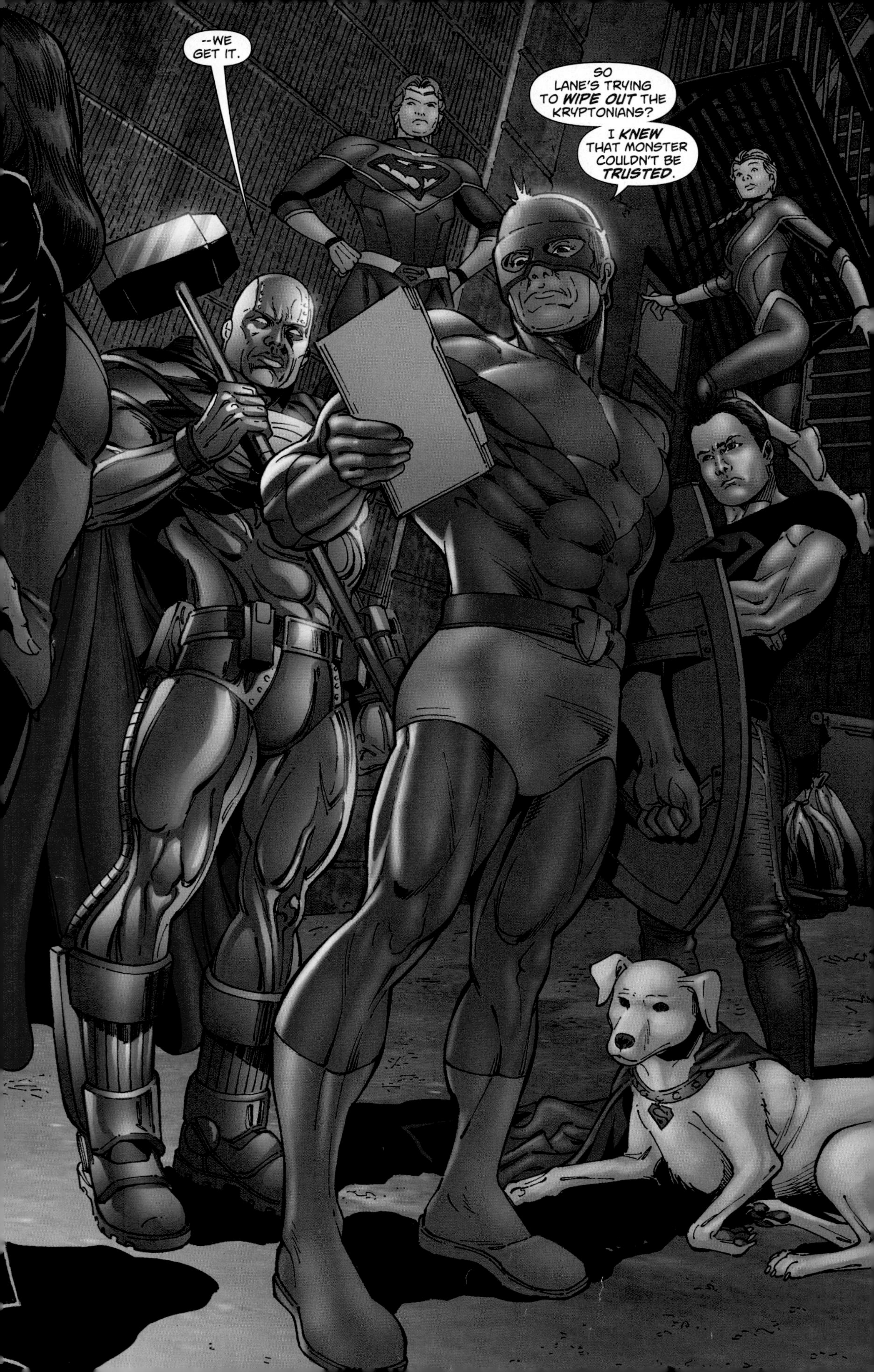
--WE GET IT.
SO LANE'S TRYING TO WIPE OUT THE KRYPTONIANS?
I KNEW THAT MONSTER COULDN'T BE TRUSTED.

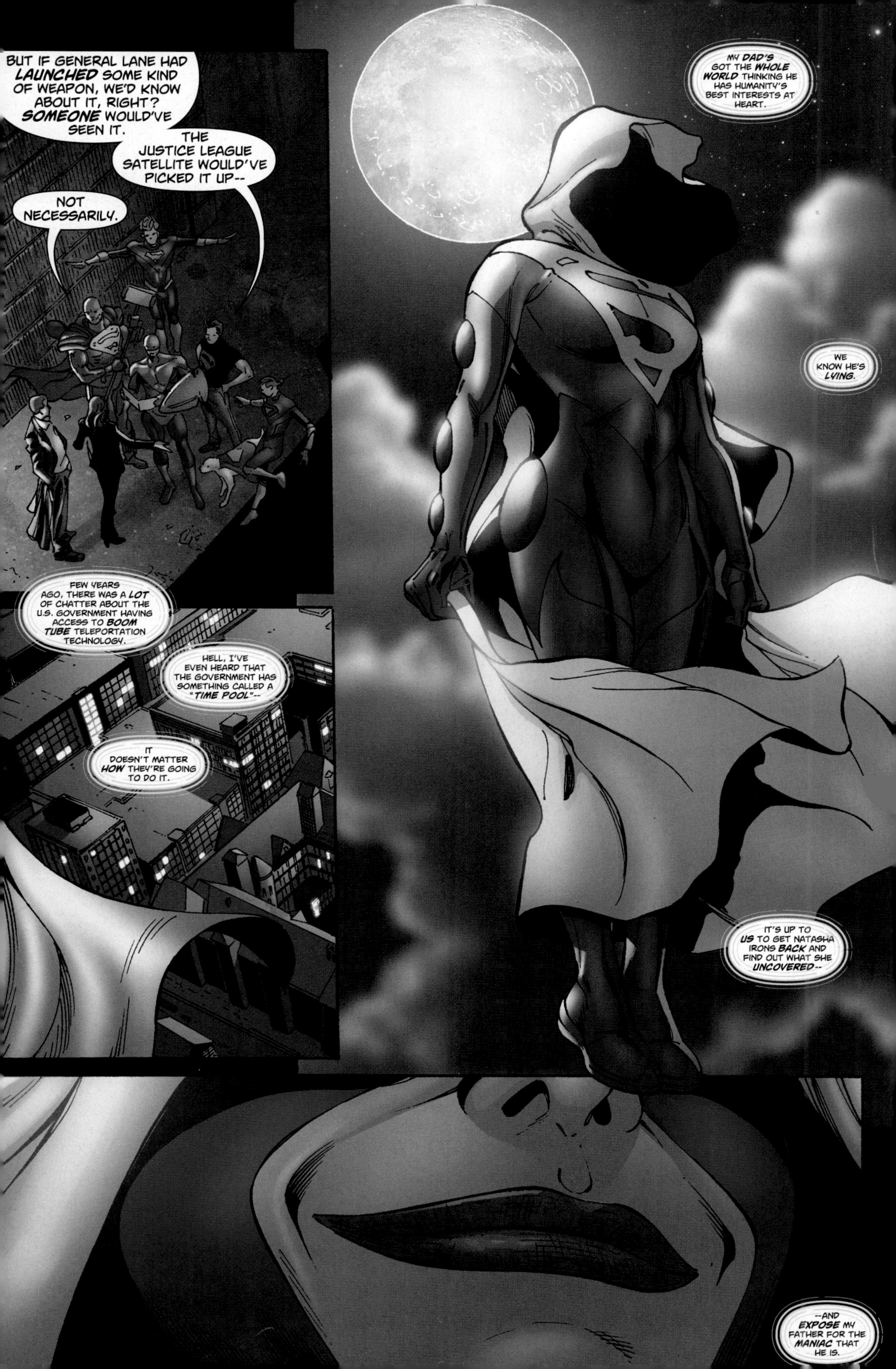
BUT IF GENERAL LANE HAD LAUNCHED SOME KIND OF WEAPON, WE'D KNOW ABOUT IT, RIGHT? SOMEONE WOULD'VE SEEN IT.
THE JUSTICE LEAGUE SATELLITE WOULD'VE PICKED IT UP--
NOT NECESSARILY.
MY DAD'S GOT THE WHOLE WORLD THINKING HE HAS HUMANITY'S BEST INTERESTS AT HEART.
WE KNOW HE'S LYING.
FEW YEARS AGO, THERE WAS A LOT OF CHATTER ABOUT THE U.S. GOVERNMENT HAVING ACCESS TO BOOM TUBE TELEPORTATION TECHNOLOGY.
HELL, I'VE EVEN HEARD THAT THE GOVERNMENT HAS SOMETHING CALLED A "TIME POOL"--
IT DOESN'T MATTER HOW THEY'RE GOING TO DO IT.
IT'S UP TO US TO GET NATASHA IRONS BACK AND FIND OUT WHAT SHE UNCOVERED--
--AND EXPOSE MY FATHER FOR THE MANIAC THAT HE IS.

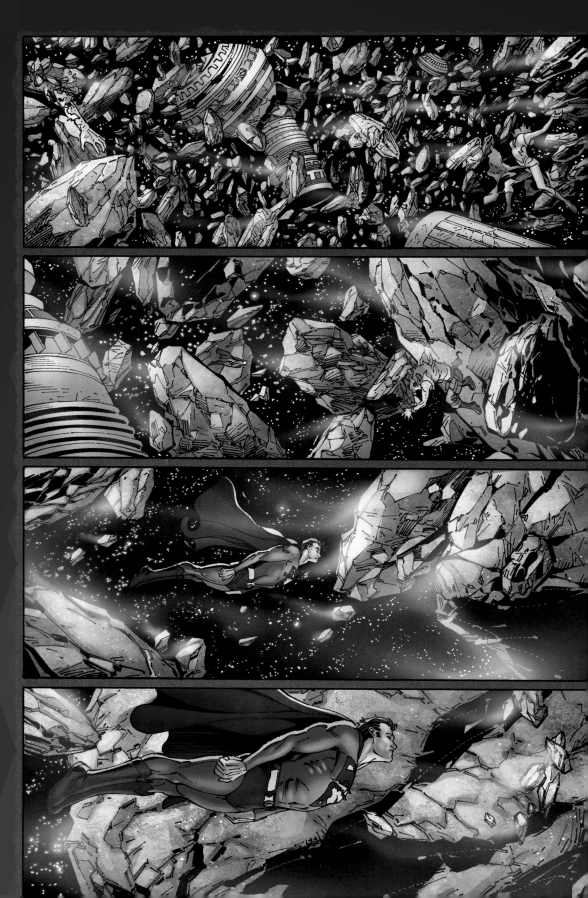

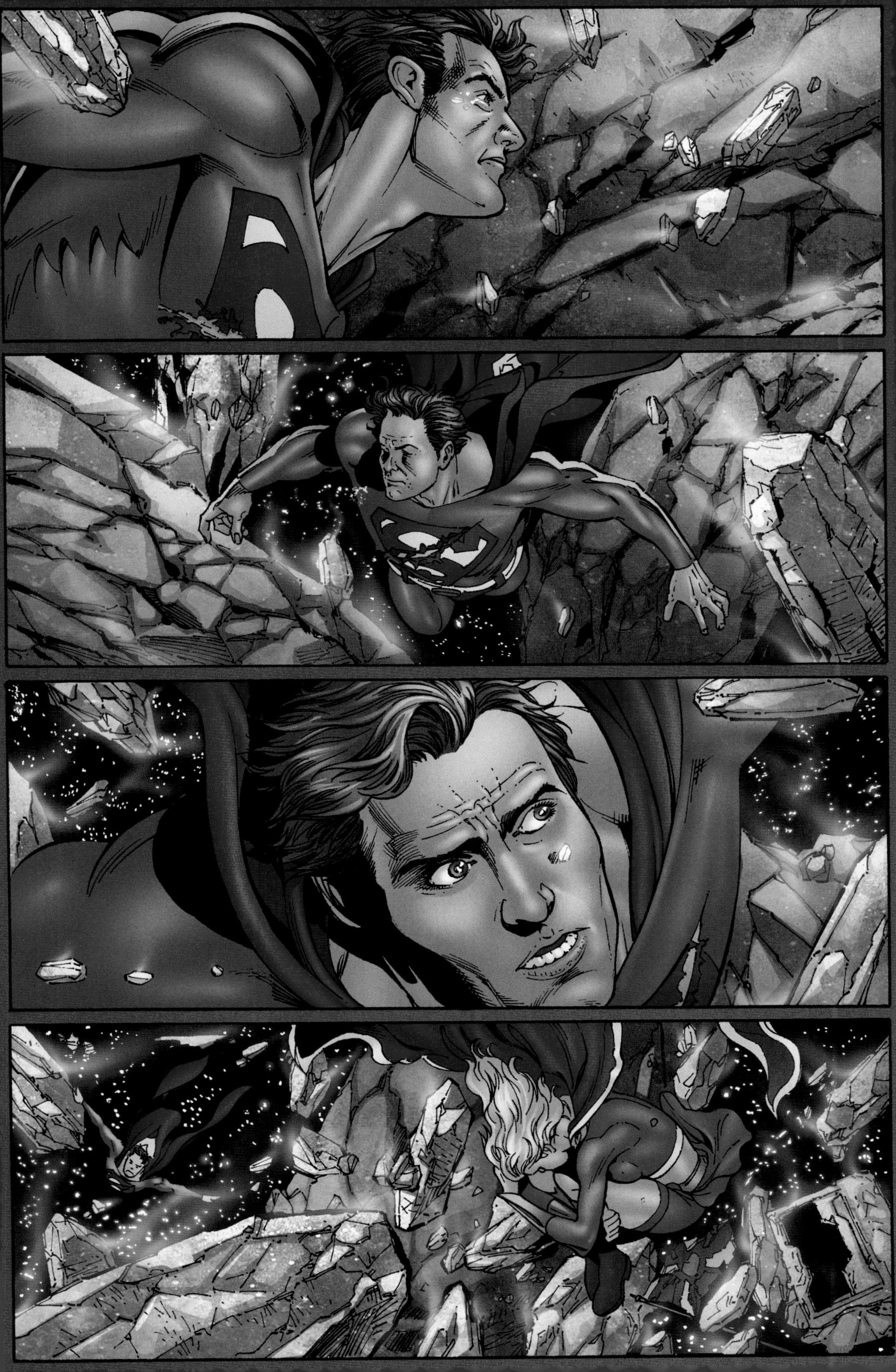

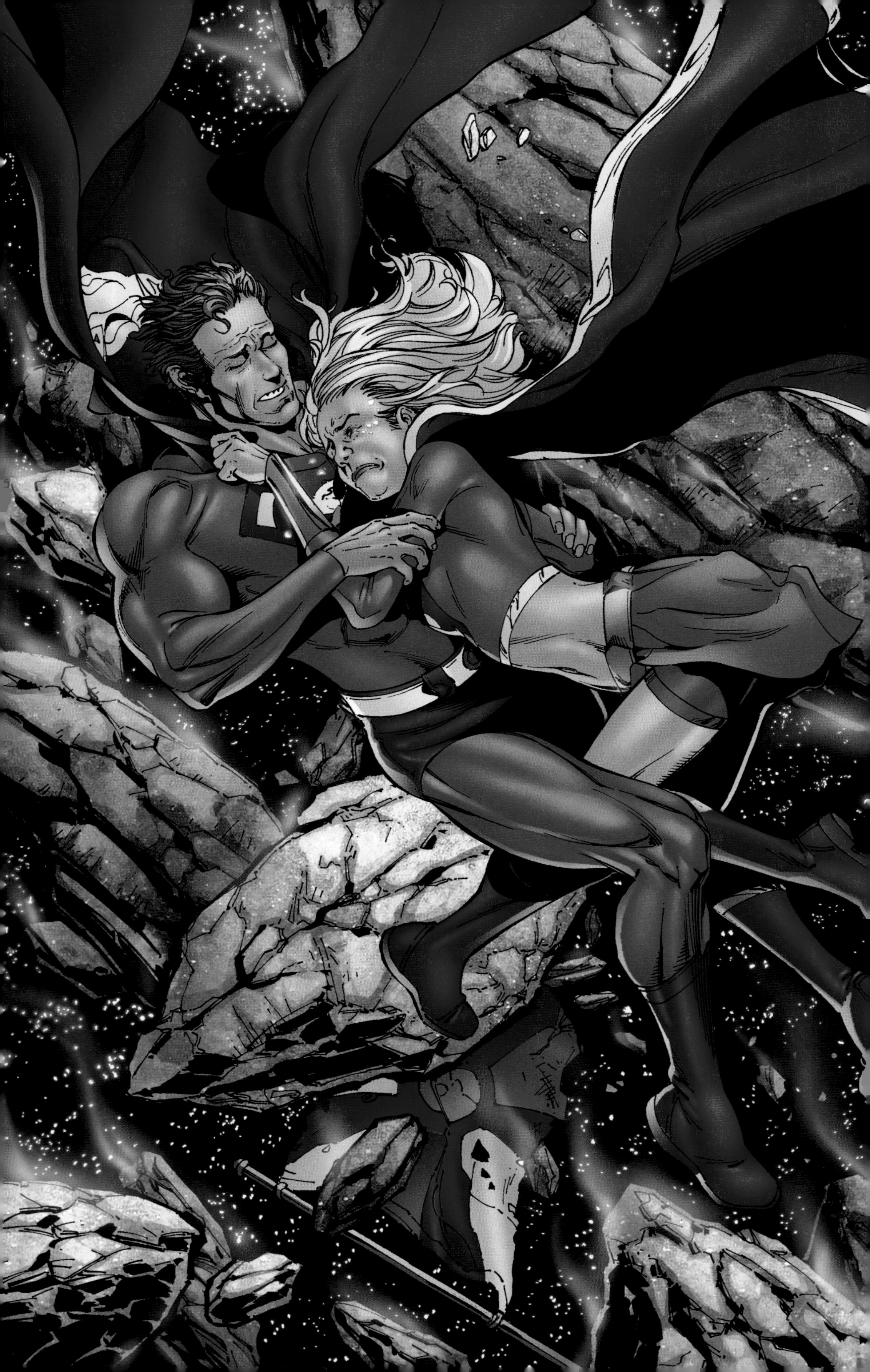

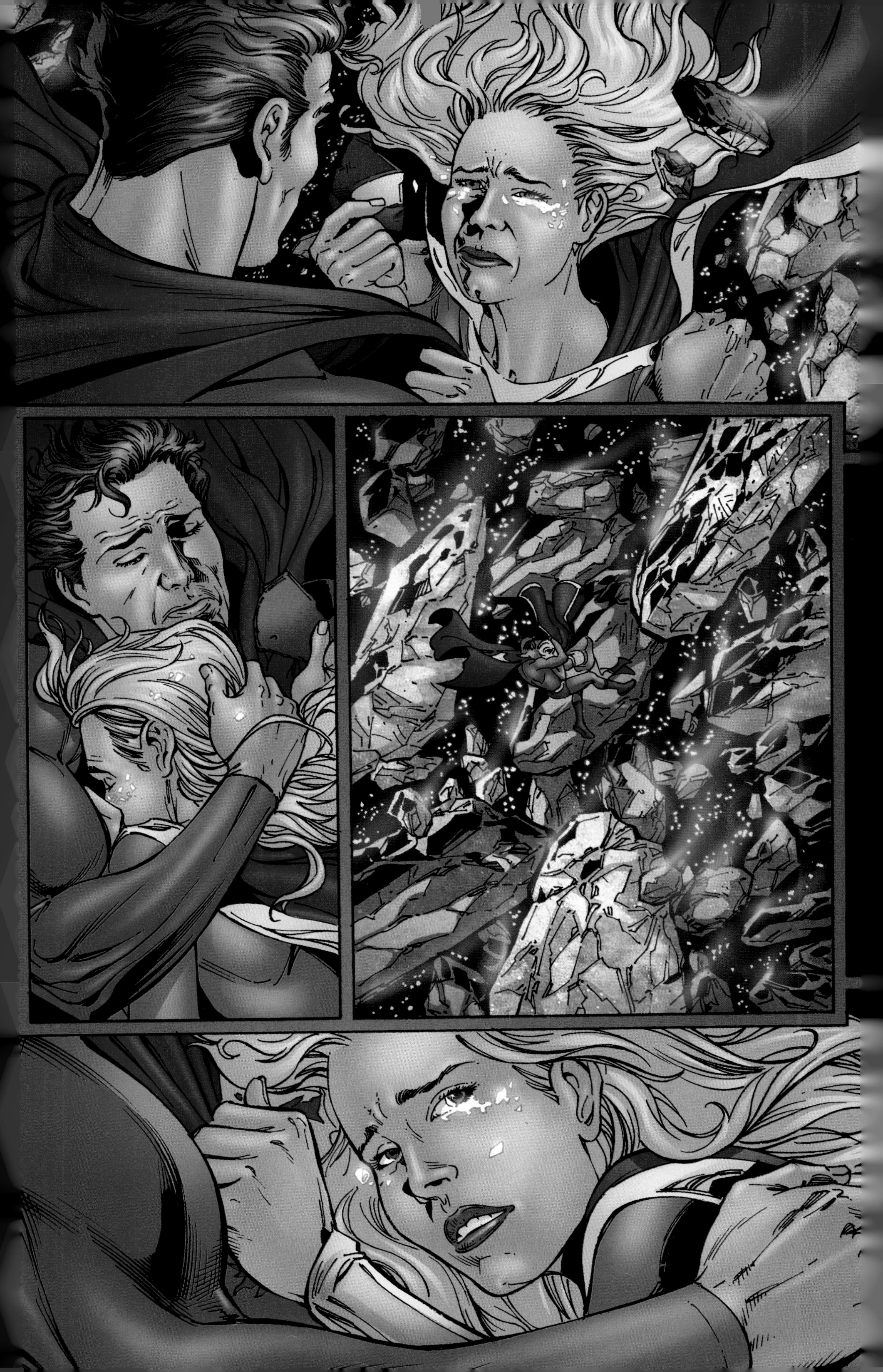

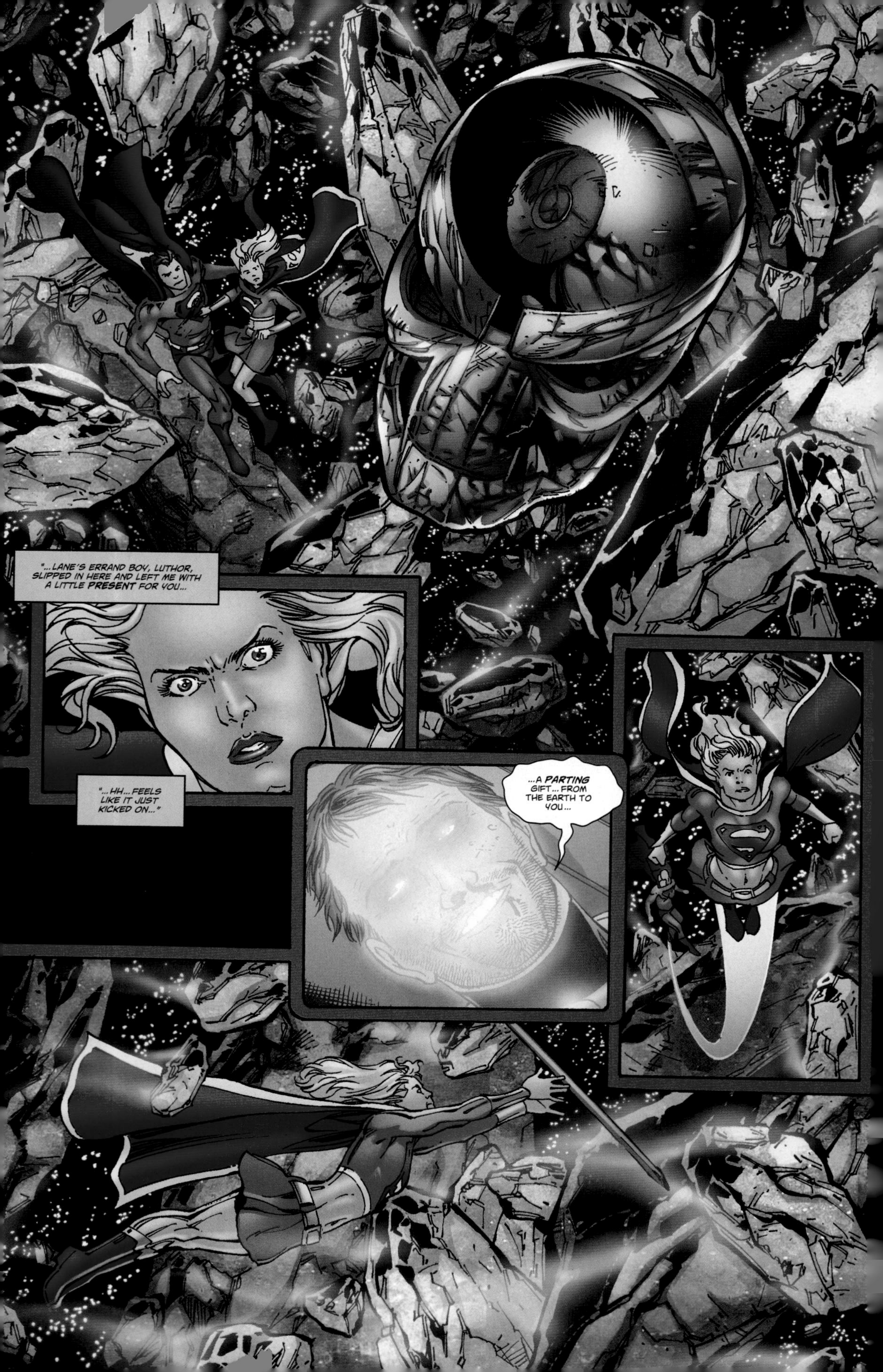
"...LANE'S ERRAND BOY, LUTHOR, SLIPPED IN HERE AND LEFT ME WITH A LITTLE PRESENT FOR YOU...
"...HH...FEELS LIKE IT JUST KICKED ON..."
...A PARTING GIFT... FROM THE EARTH TO YOU...

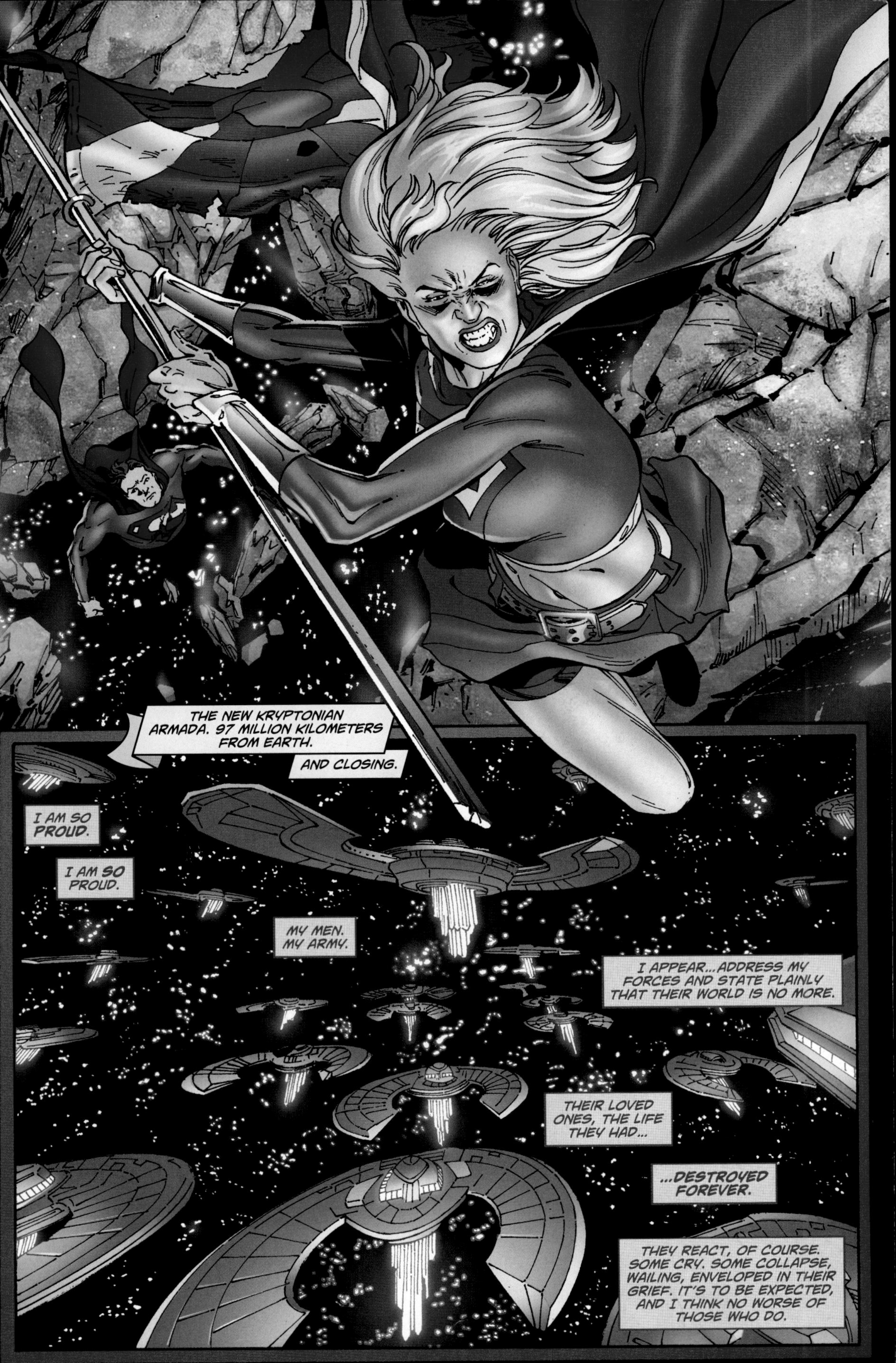
THE NEW KRYPTONIAN ARMADA. 97 MILLION KILOMETERS FROM EARTH.
AND CLOSING.
I AM SO PROUD.
I AM SO PROUD.
MY MEN. MY ARMY.
I APPEAR...ADDRESS MY FORCES AND STATE PLAINLY THAT THEIR WORLD IS NO MORE.
THEIR LOVED ONES, THE LIFE THEY HAD...
...DESTROYED FOREVER.
THEY REACT, OF COURSE. SOME CRY. SOME COLLAPSE, WAILING, ENVELOPED IN THEIR GRIEF. IT'S TO BE EXPECTED, AND I THINK NO WORSE OF THOSE WHO DO.

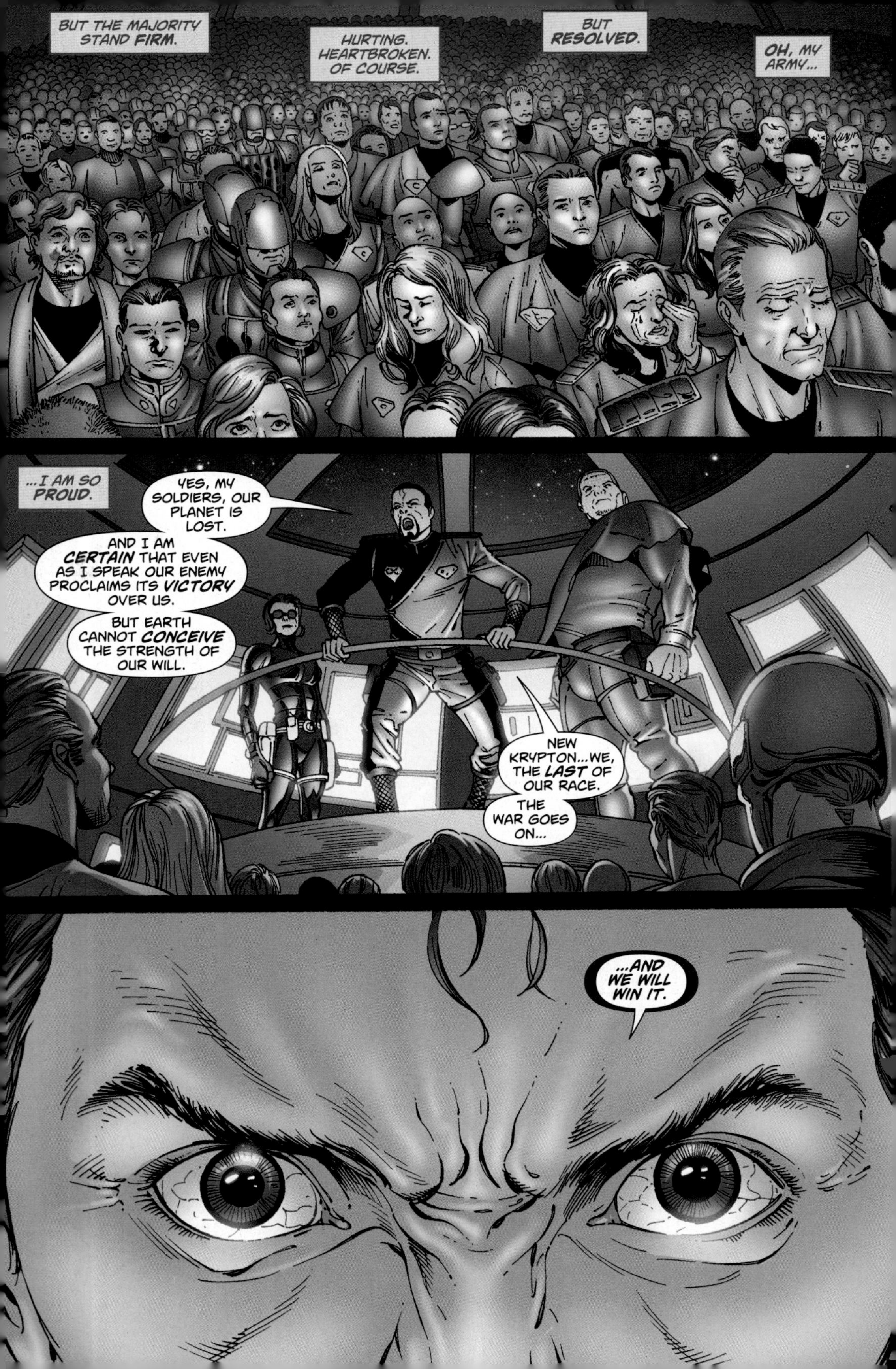
BUT THE MAJORITY STAND FIRM.
HURTING. HEARTBROKEN. OF COURSE.
BUT RESOLVED.
OH, MY ARMY...
...I AM SO PROUD.
YES, MY SOLDIERS, OUR PLANET IS LOST.
AND I AM CERTAIN THAT EVEN AS I SPEAK OUR ENEMY PROCLAIMS ITS VICTORY OVER US.
BUT EARTH CANNOT CONCEIVE THE STRENGTH OF OUR WILL.
NEW KRYPTON...WE, THE LAST OF OUR RACE.
THE WAR GOES ON...
...AND WE WILL WIN IT.

PART 2: THE BATTLE FOR MARS Cover by EDDY BARROWS, J.P. MAYER & ROD REIS

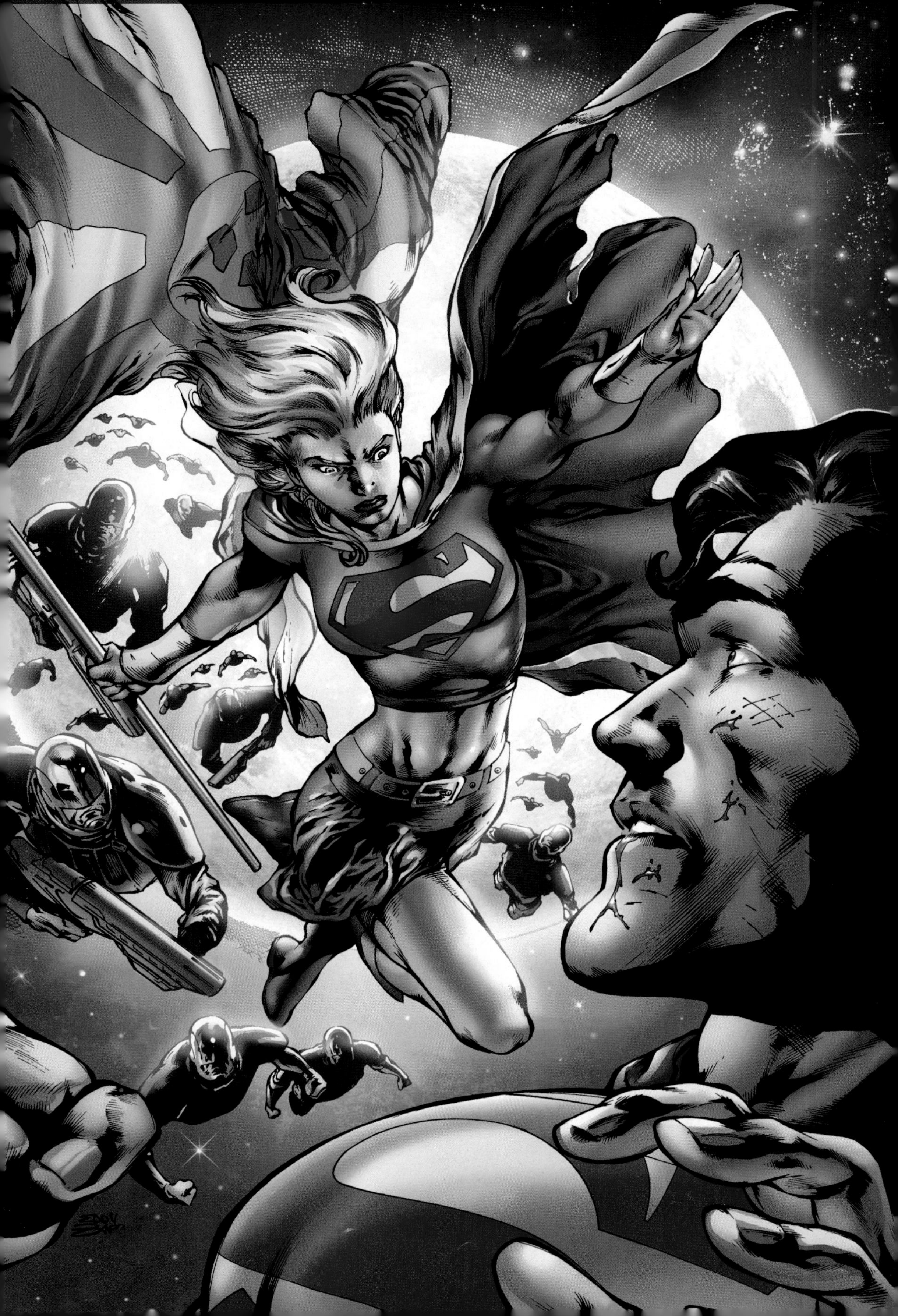

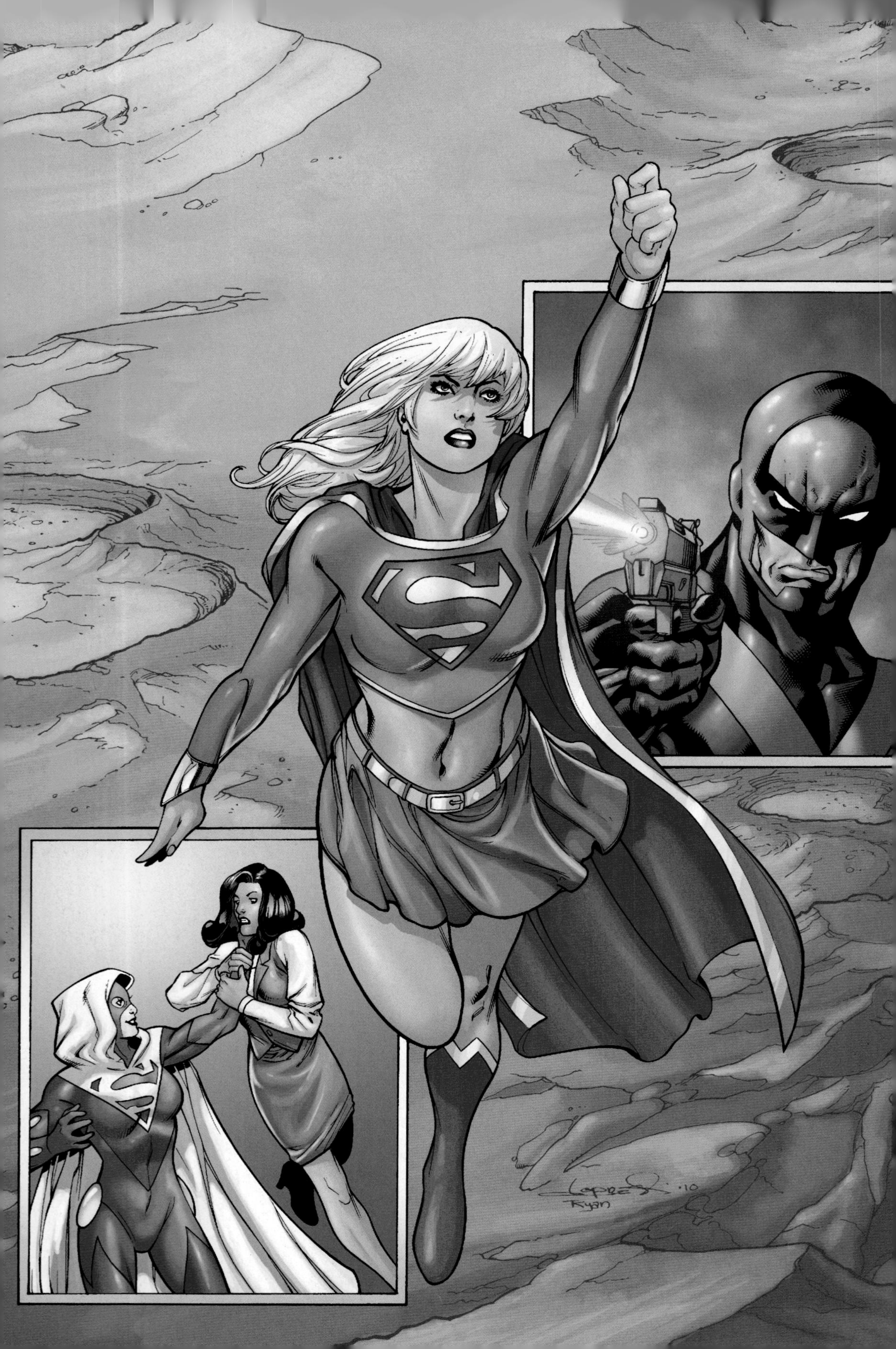

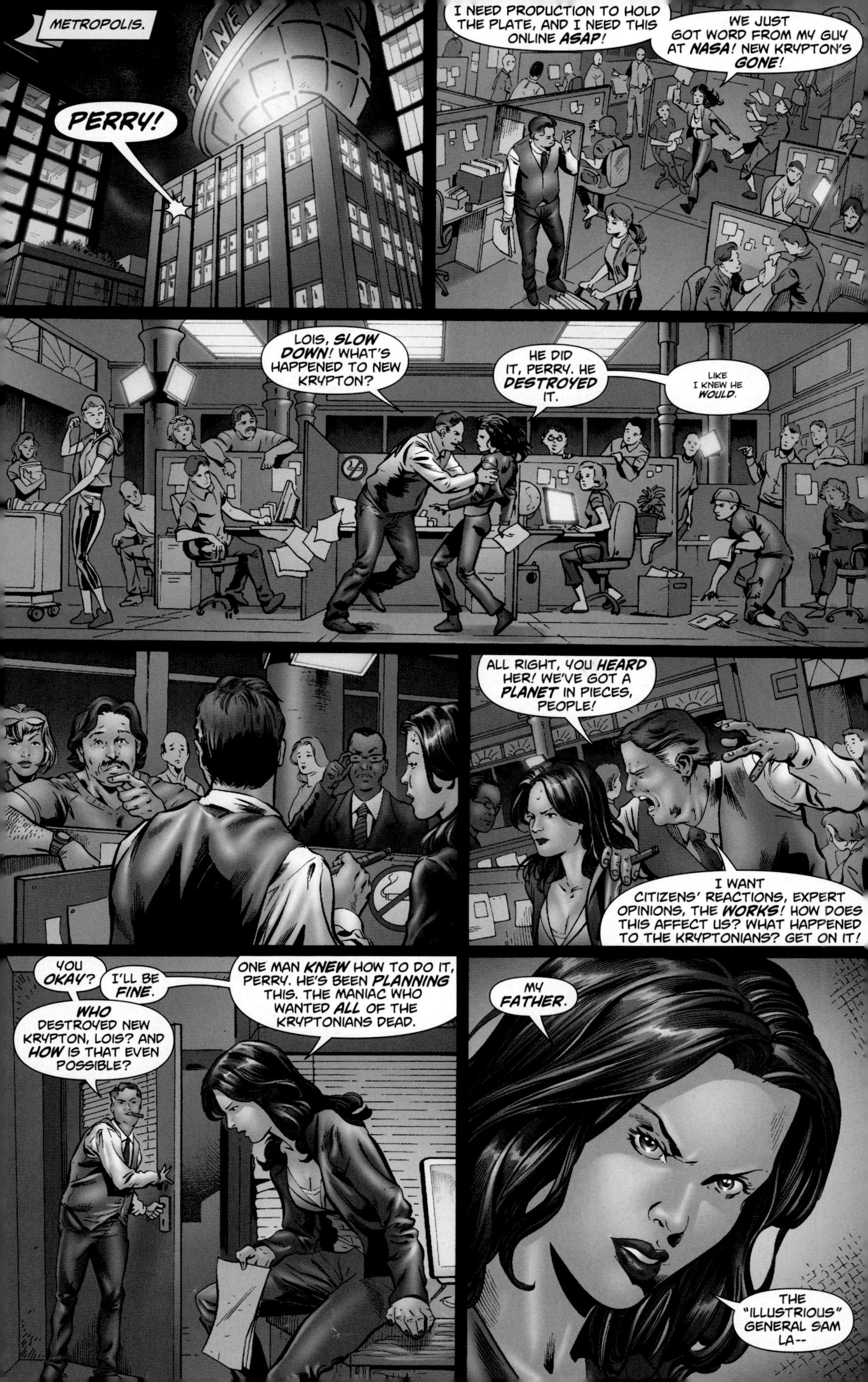
METROPOLIS.
PERRY!
I NEED PRODUCTION TO HOLD THE PLATE, AND I NEED THIS ONLINE ASAP!
WE JUST GOT WORD FROM MY GUY AT NASA! NEW KRYPTON'S GONE!
LOIS, SLOW DOWN! WHAT'S HAPPENED TO NEW KRYPTON?
HE DID IT, PERRY. HE DESTROYED IT.
LIKE I KNEW HE WOULD.
ALL RIGHT, YOU HEARD HER! WE'VE GOT A PLANET IN PIECES, PEOPLE!
I WANT CITIZENS' REACTIONS, EXPERT OPINIONS, THE WORKS! HOW DOES THIS AFFECT US? WHAT HAPPENED TO THE KRYPTONIANS? GET ON IT!
YOU OKAY?
I'LL BE FINE.
WHO DESTROYED NEW KRYPTON, LOIS? AND HOW IS THAT EVEN POSSIBLE?
ONE MAN KNEW HOW TO DO IT, PERRY. HE'S BEEN PLANNING THIS. THE MANIAC WHO WANTED ALL OF THE KRYPTONIANS DEAD.
MY FATHER.
THE "ILLUSTRIOUS" GENERAL SAM LA--

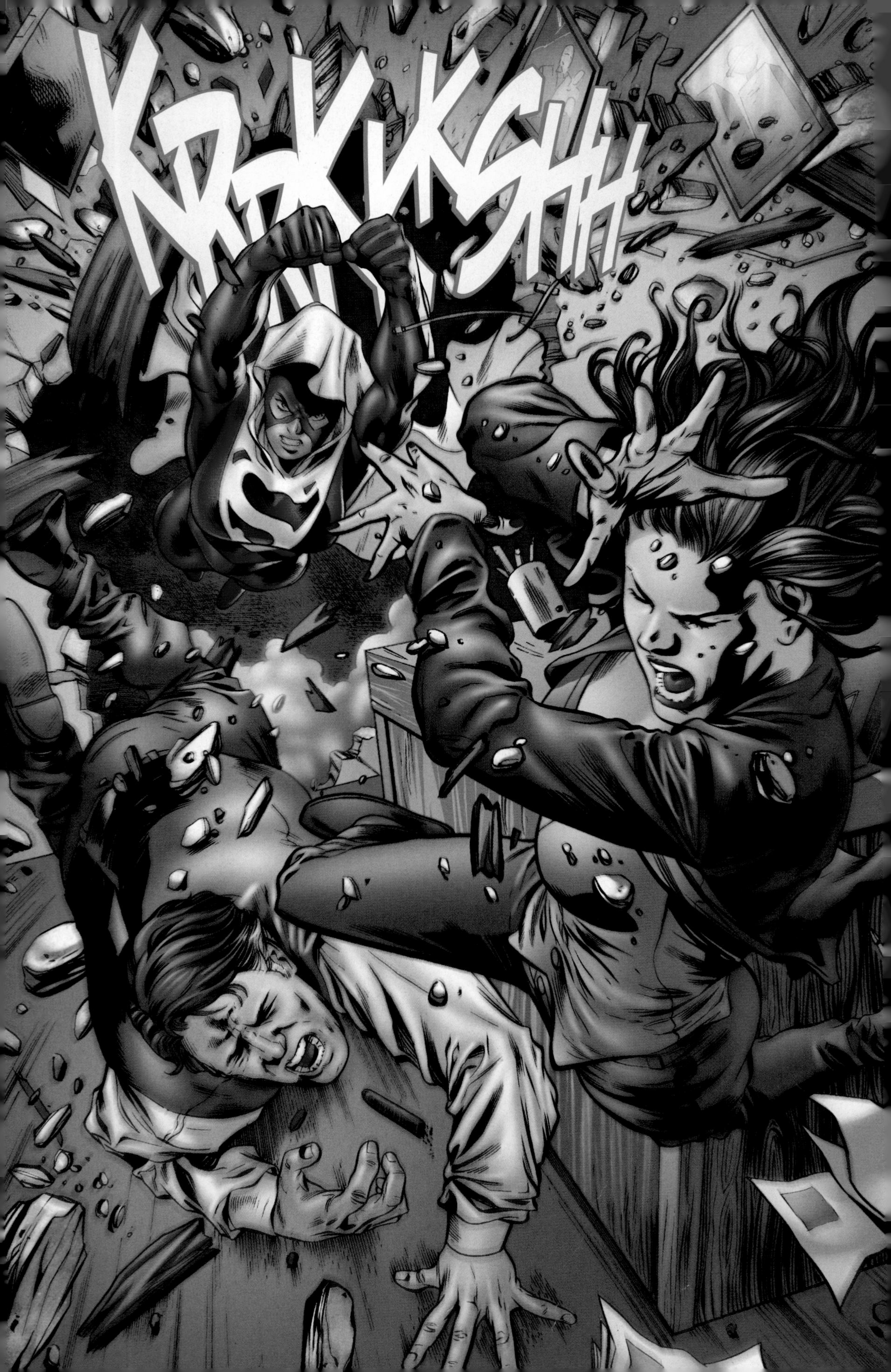
KRRKKSHH

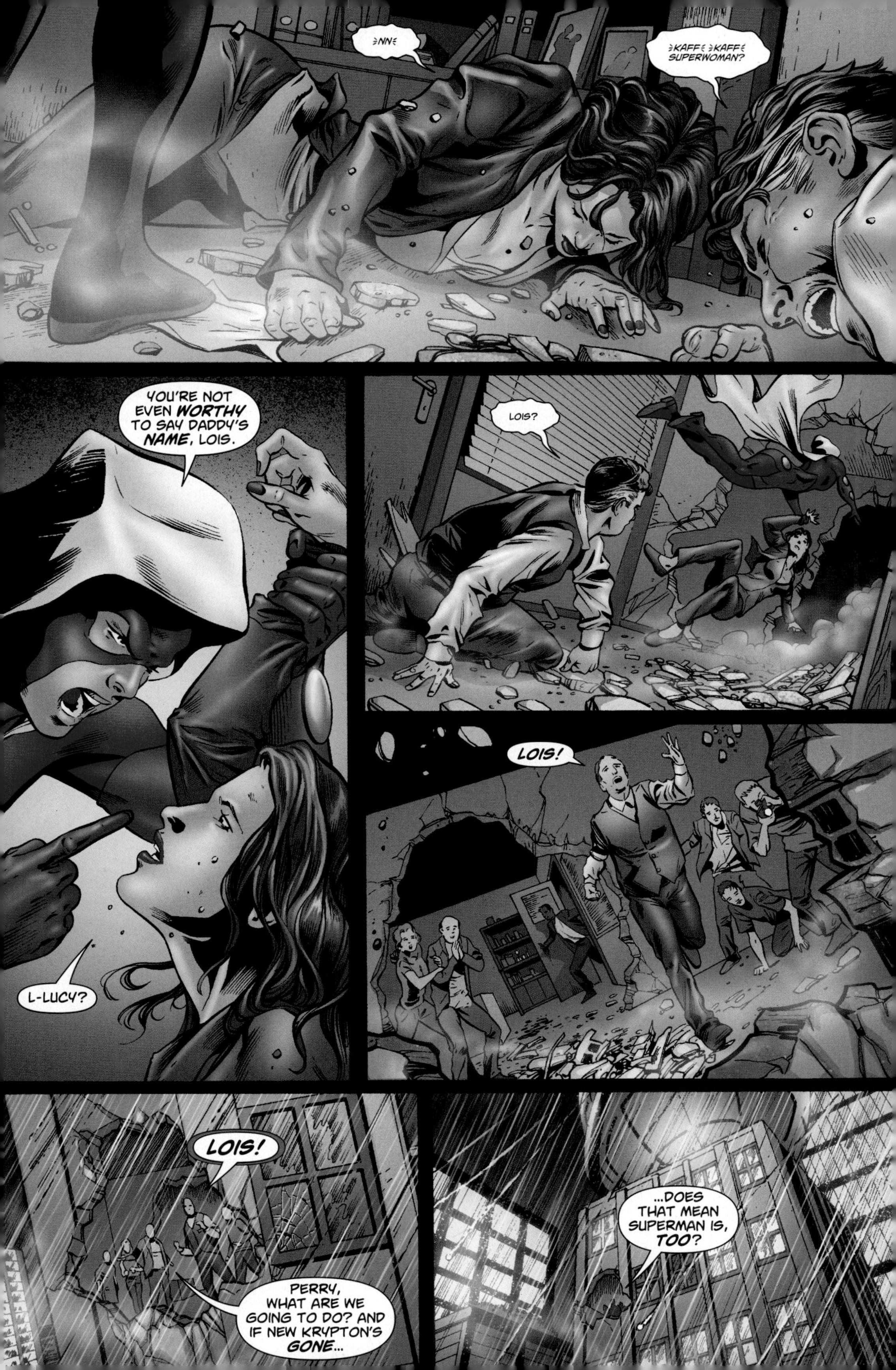
NN
KAFF KAFF SUPERWOMAN?
YOU'RE NOT EVEN WORTHY TO SAY DADDY'S NAME, LOIS.
L-LUCY?
LOIS?
LOIS!
LOIS!
PERRY, WHAT ARE WE GOING TO DO? AND IF NEW KRYPTON'S GONE...
...DOES THAT MEAN SUPERMAN IS, TOO?

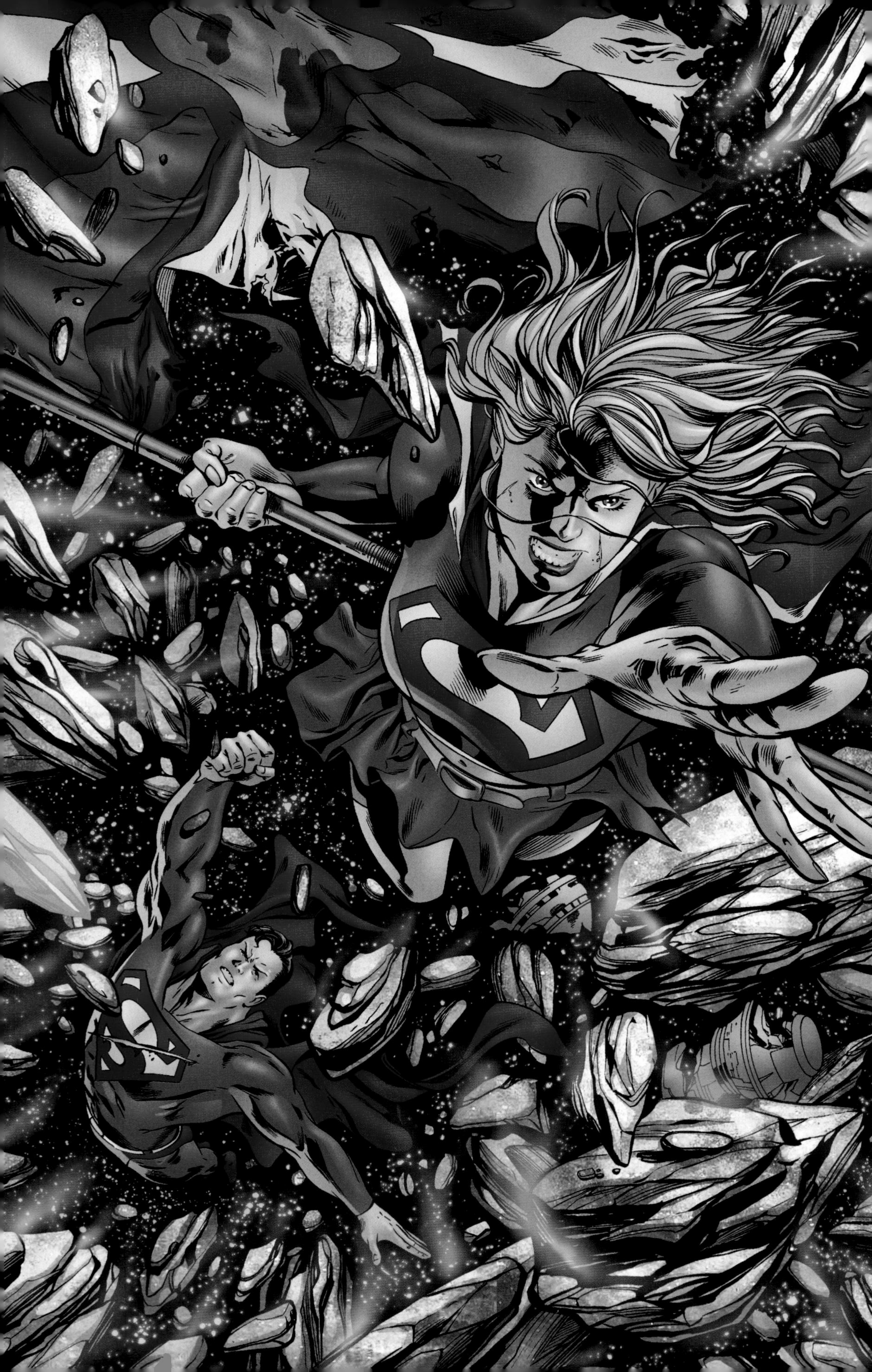

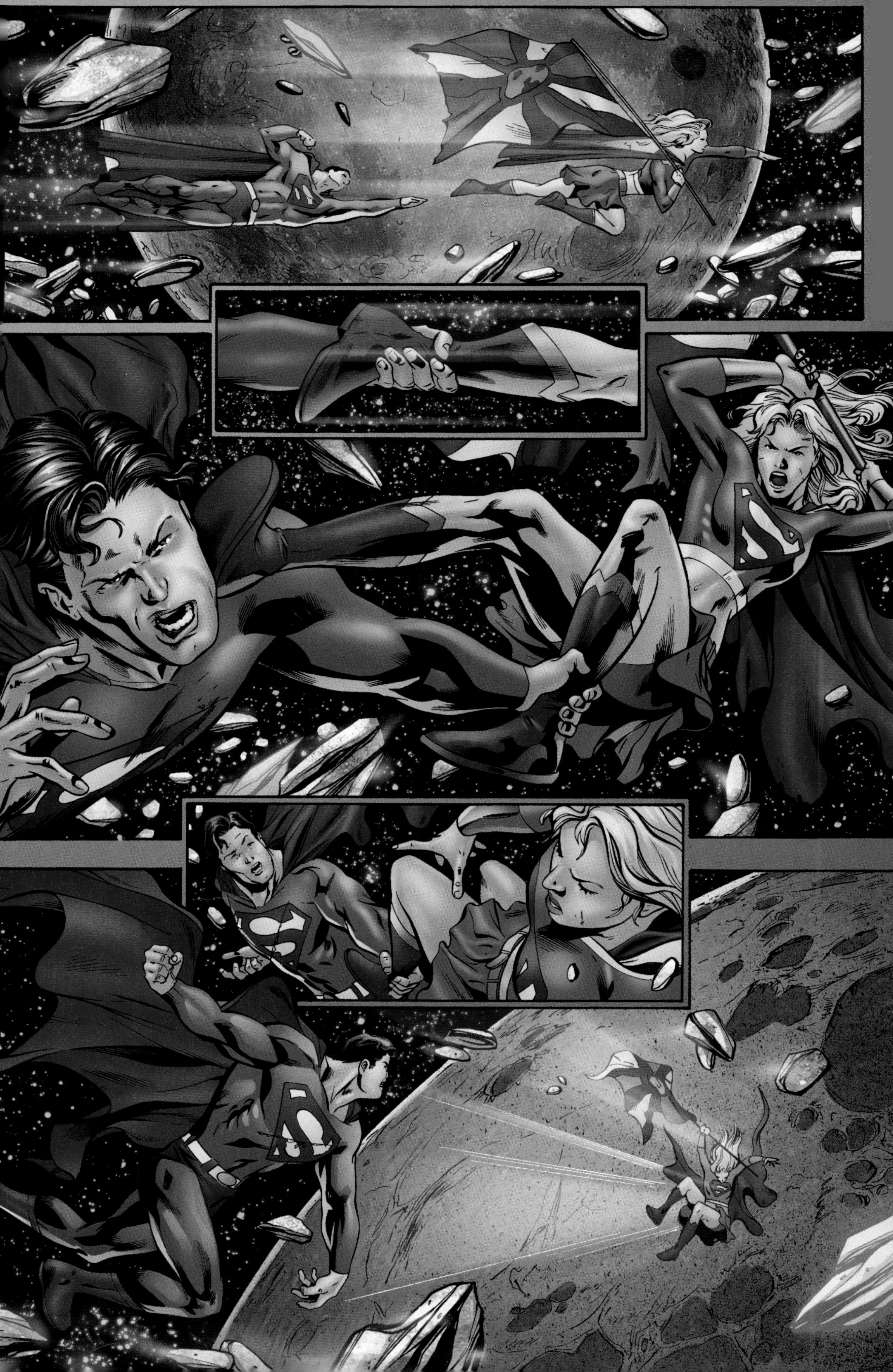

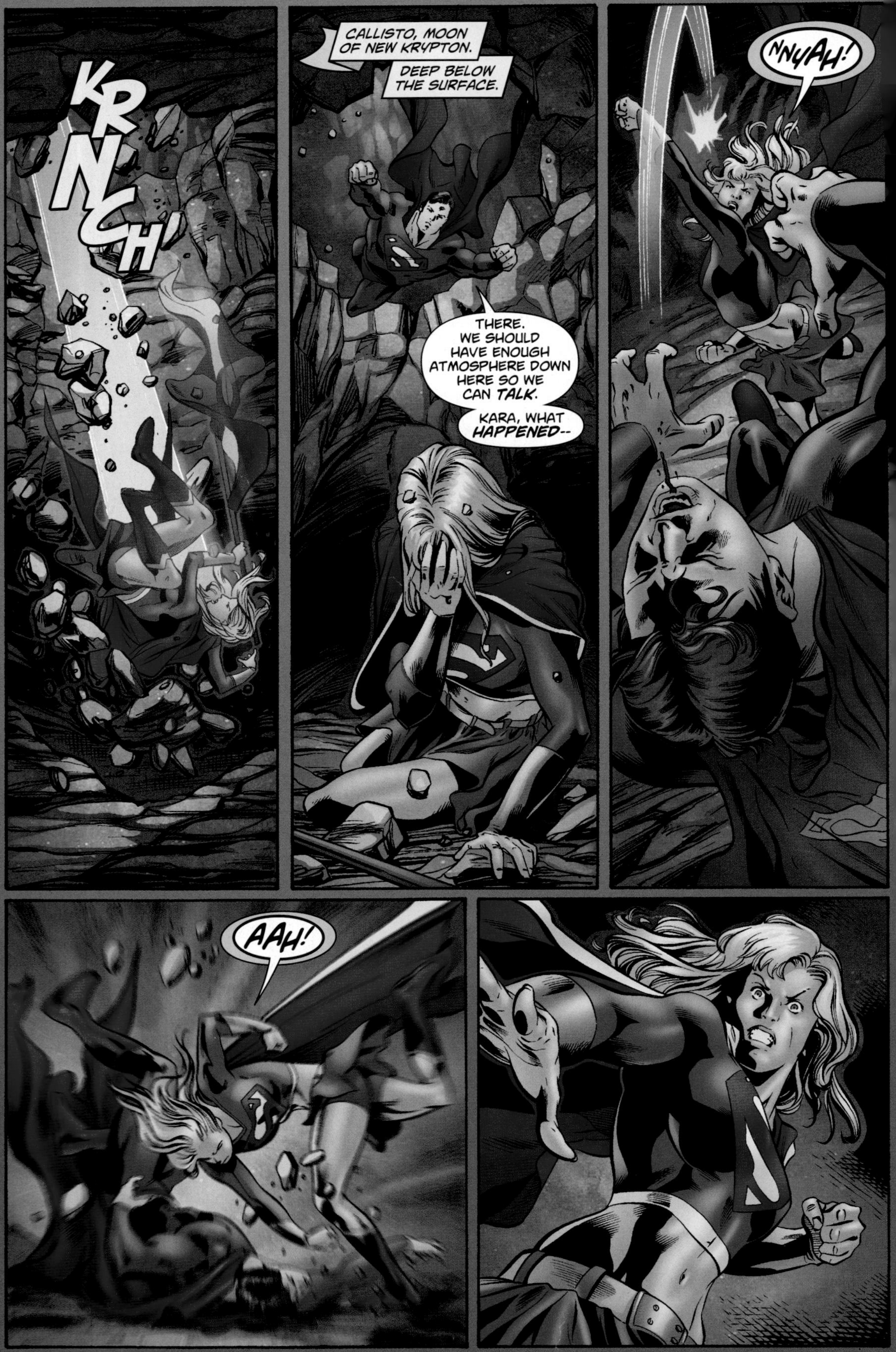

KRNCH!
CALLISTO, MOON OF NEW KRYPTON.
DEEP BELOW THE SURFACE.
THERE. WE SHOULD HAVE ENOUGH ATMOSPHERE DOWN HERE SO WE CAN TALK.
KARA, WHAT HAPPENED--
NNYAH!
AAH!

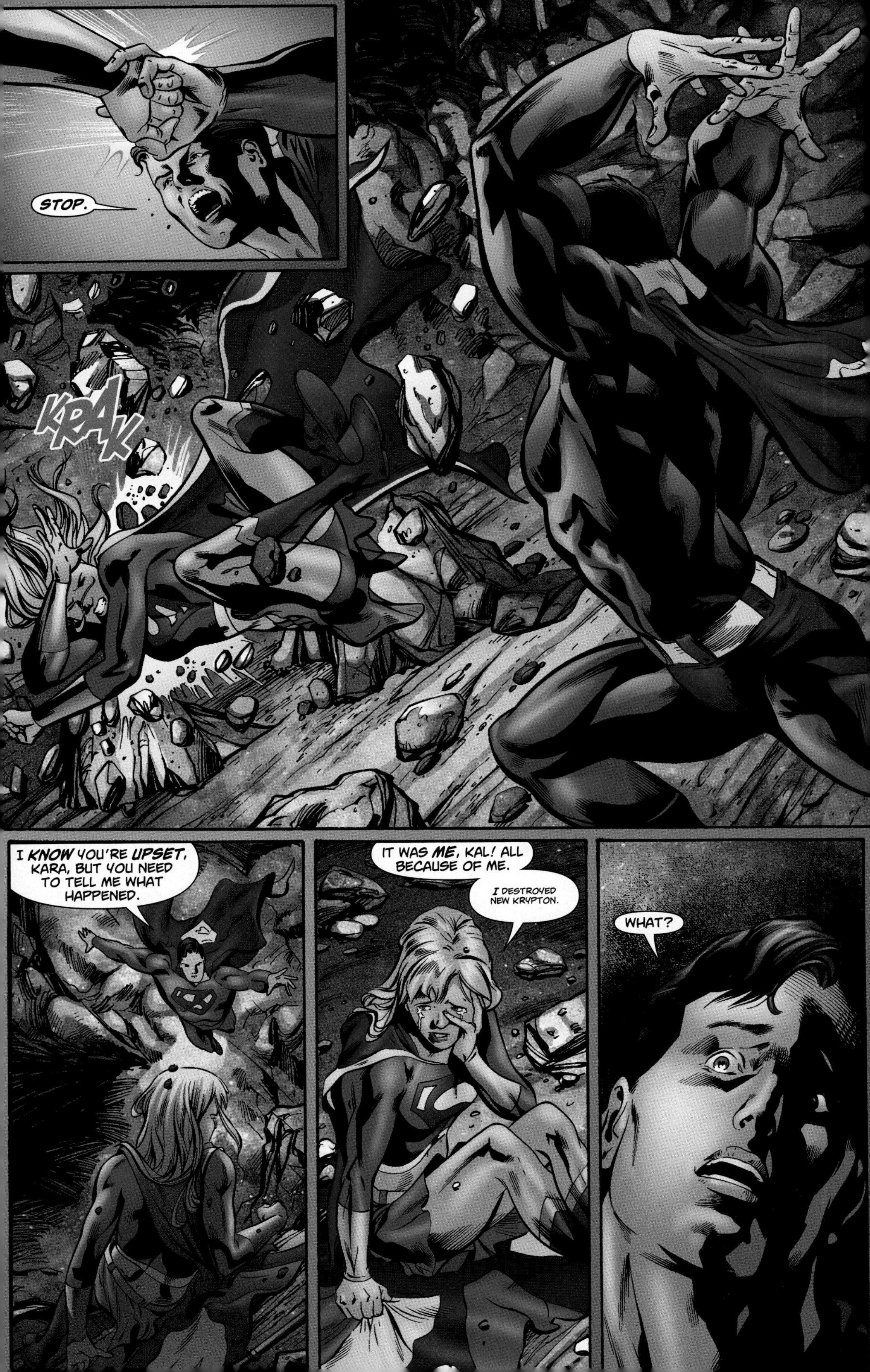
STOP.
KRAK
I KNOW YOU'RE UPSET, KARA, BUT YOU NEED TO TELL ME WHAT HAPPENED.
IT WAS ME, KAL! ALL BECAUSE OF ME.
I DESTROYED NEW KRYPTON.
WHAT?

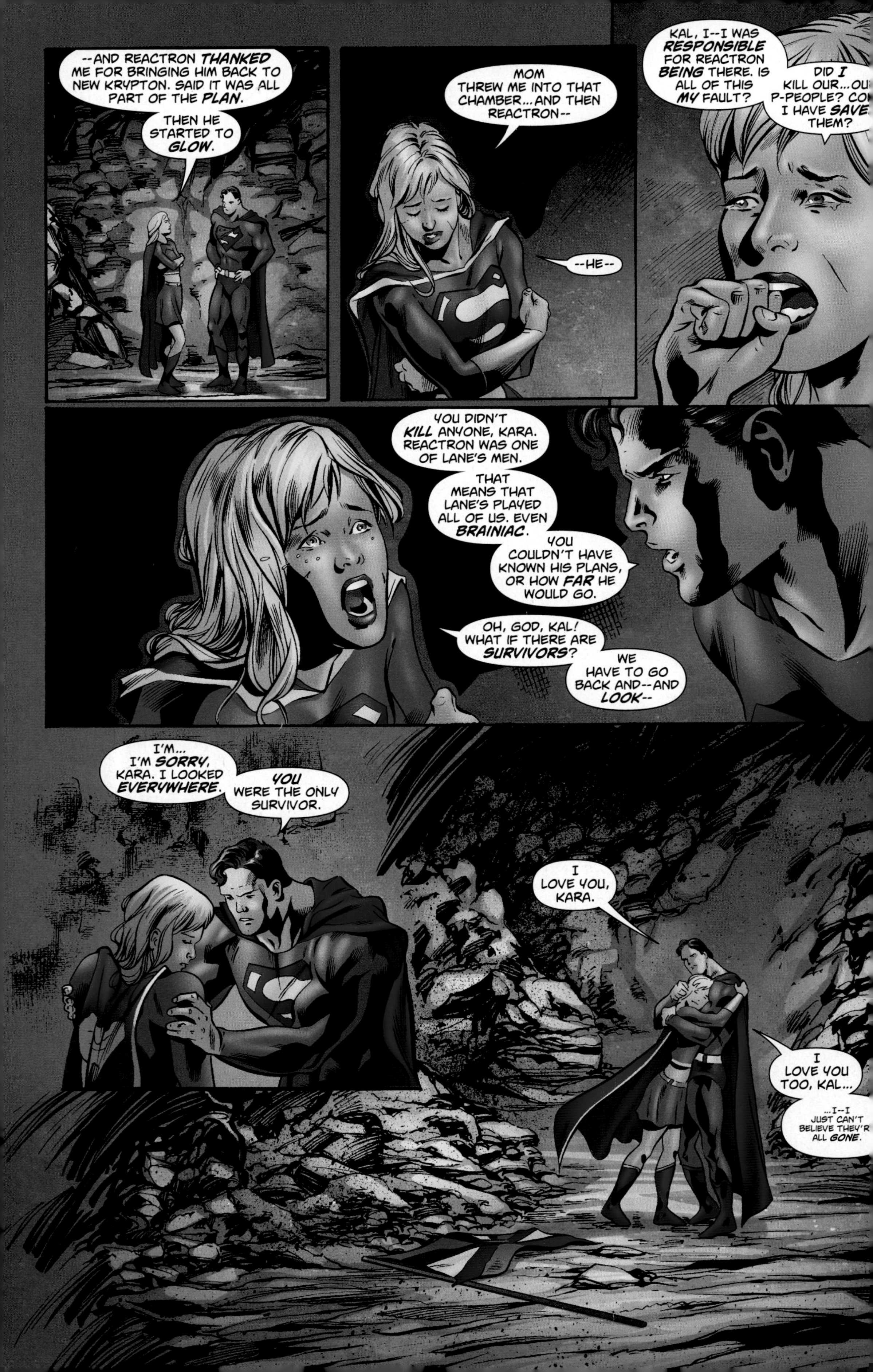
--AND REACTRON THANKED ME FOR BRINGING HIM BACK TO NEW KRYPTON. SAID IT WAS ALL PART OF THE PLAN.
THEN HE STARTED TO GLOW.
MOM THREW ME INTO THAT CHAMBER... AND THEN REACTRON--
--HE--
KAL, I--I WAS RESPONSIBLE FOR REACTRON BEING THERE. IS ALL OF THIS MY FAULT?
DID I KILL OUR... OU P-PEOPLE? CO I HAVE SAVE THEM?
YOU DIDN'T KILL ANYONE, KARA. REACTRON WAS ONE OF LANE'S MEN.
THAT MEANS THAT LANE'S PLAYED ALL OF US. EVEN BRAINIAC.
YOU COULDN'T HAVE KNOWN HIS PLANS, OR HOW FAR HE WOULD GO.
OH, GOD, KAL! WHAT IF THERE ARE SURVIVORS?
WE HAVE TO GO BACK AND--AND LOOK--
I'M... I'M SORRY, KARA. I LOOKED EVERYWHERE.
YOU WERE THE ONLY SURVIVOR.
I LOVE YOU, KARA.
I LOVE YOU TOO, KAL...
...I--I JUST CAN'T BELIEVE THEY'R ALL GONE.

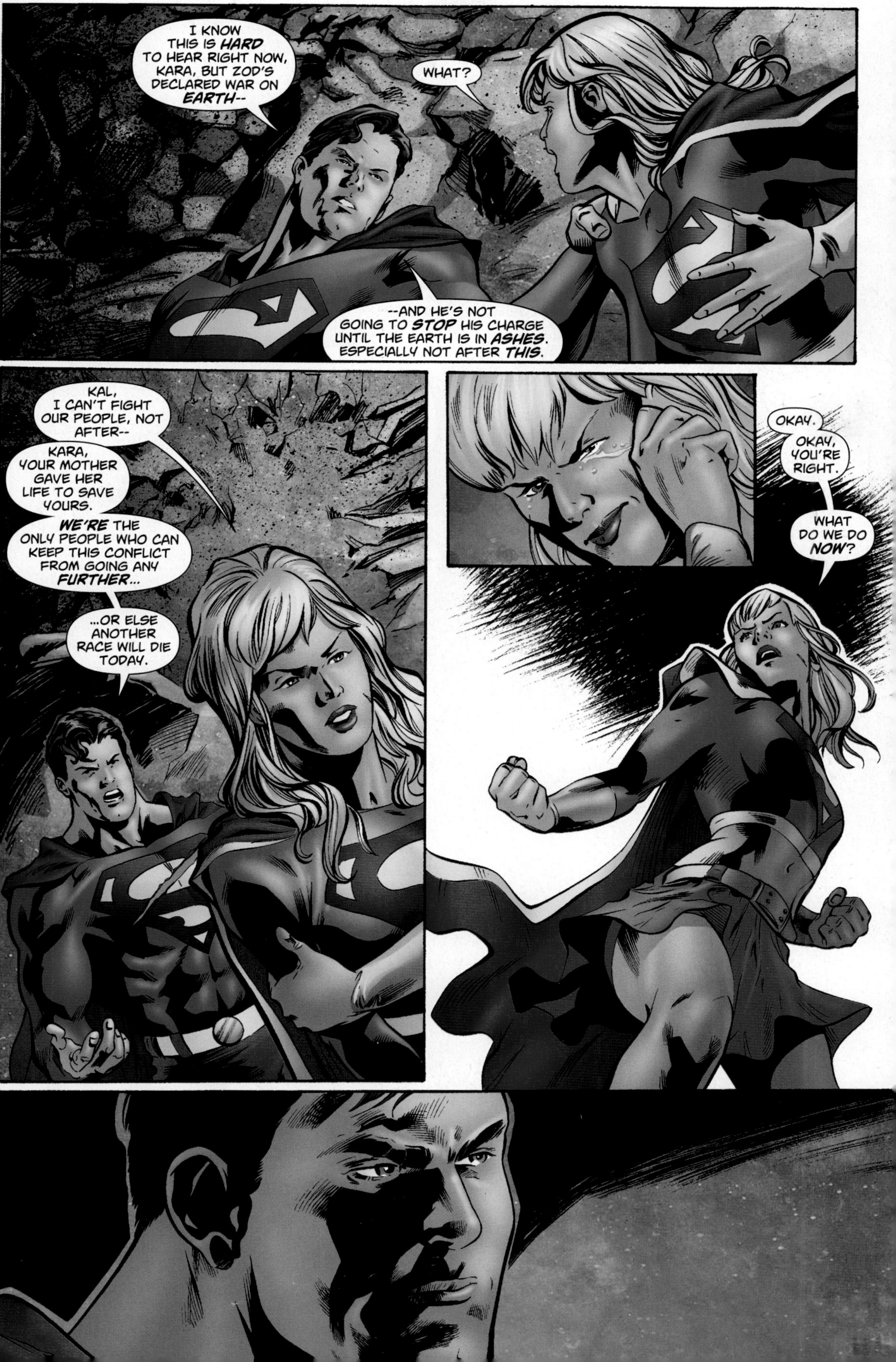

I KNOW THIS IS HARD TO HEAR RIGHT NOW, KARA, BUT ZOD'S DECLARED WAR ON EARTH--
WHAT?
--AND HE'S NOT GOING TO STOP HIS CHARGE UNTIL THE EARTH IS IN ASHES. ESPECIALLY NOT AFTER THIS.
KAL, I CAN'T FIGHT OUR PEOPLE, NOT AFTER--
KARA, YOUR MOTHER GAVE HER LIFE TO SAVE YOURS.
WE'RE THE ONLY PEOPLE WHO CAN KEEP THIS CONFLICT FROM GOING ANY FURTHER...
...OR ELSE ANOTHER RACE WILL DIE TODAY.
OKAY.
OKAY, YOU'RE RIGHT.
WHAT DO WE DO NOW?

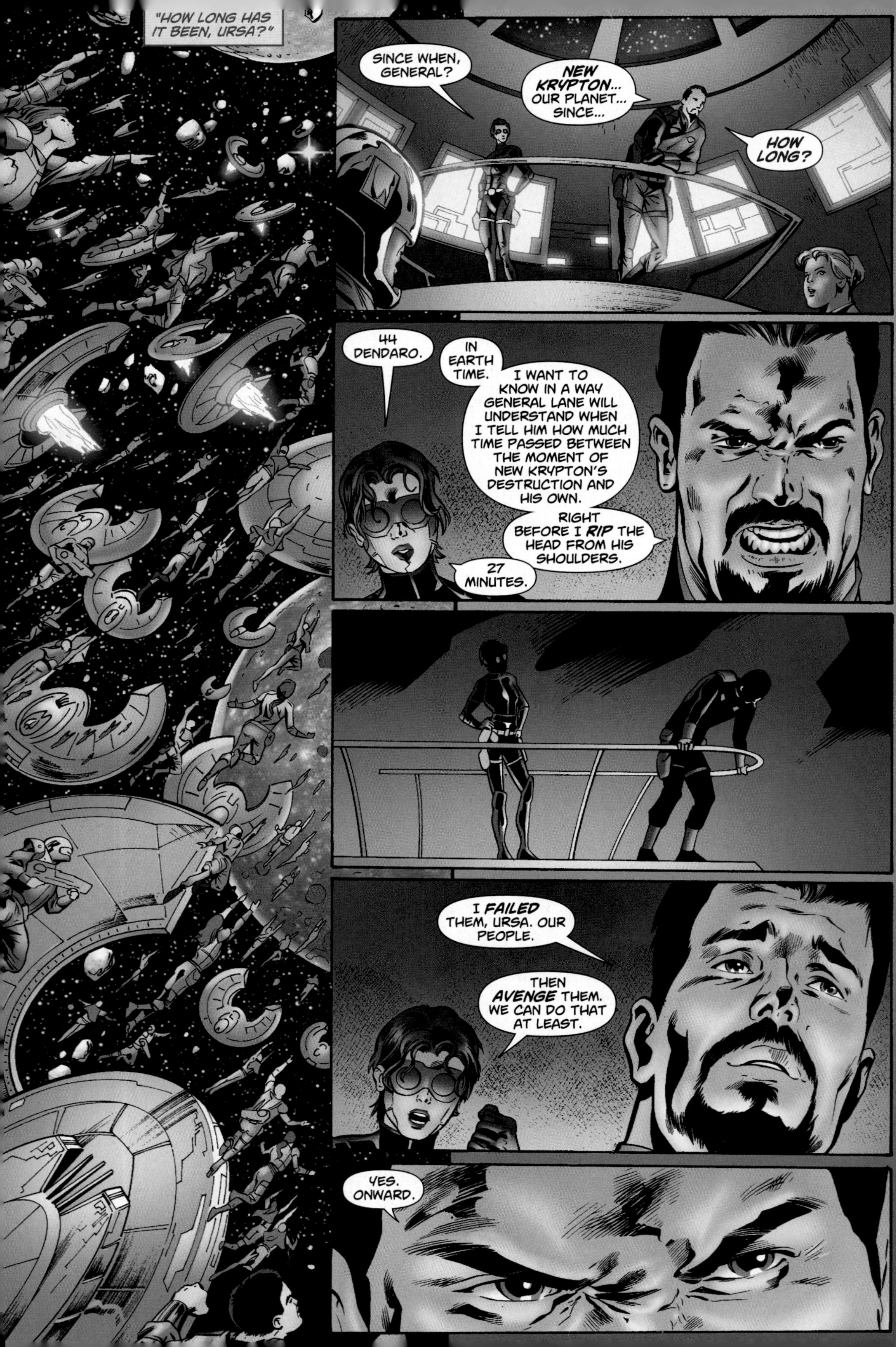
"HOW LONG HAS IT BEEN, URSA?"
SINCE WHEN, GENERAL?
NEW KRYPTON... OUR PLANET... SINCE...
HOW LONG?
44 DENDARO.
IN EARTH TIME.
I WANT TO KNOW IN A WAY GENERAL LANE WILL UNDERSTAND WHEN I TELL HIM HOW MUCH TIME PASSED BETWEEN THE MOMENT OF NEW KRYPTON'S DESTRUCTION AND HIS OWN.
RIGHT BEFORE I RIP THE HEAD FROM HIS SHOULDERS.
27 MINUTES.
I FAILED THEM, URSA. OUR PEOPLE.
THEN AVENGE THEM. WE CAN DO THAT AT LEAST.
YES. ONWARD.

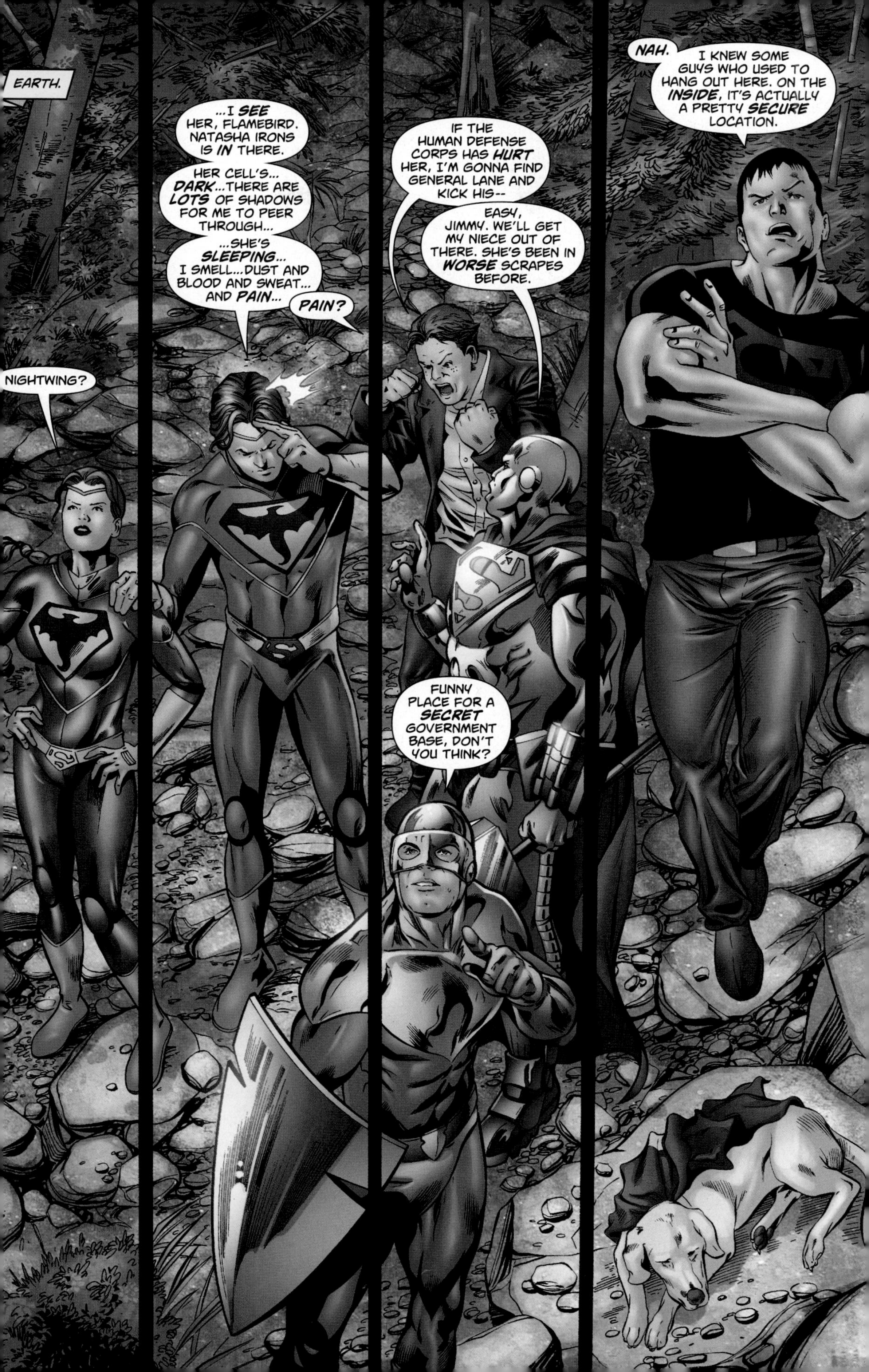
EARTH.
NIGHTWING?
...I SEE HER, FLAMEBIRD. NATASHA IRONS IS IN THERE.
HER CELL'S... DARK...THERE ARE LOTS OF SHADOWS FOR ME TO PEER THROUGH...
...SHE'S SLEEPING... I SMELL...DUST AND BLOOD AND SWEAT... AND PAIN...
PAIN?
IF THE HUMAN DEFENSE CORPS HAS HURT HER, I'M GONNA FIND GENERAL LANE AND KICK HIS--
EASY, JIMMY. WE'LL GET MY NIECE OUT OF THERE. SHE'S BEEN IN WORSE SCRAPES BEFORE.
FUNNY PLACE FOR A SECRET GOVERNMENT BASE, DON'T YOU THINK?
NAH.
I KNEW SOME GUYS WHO USED TO HANG OUT HERE. ON THE INSIDE, IT'S ACTUALLY A PRETTY SECURE LOCATION.

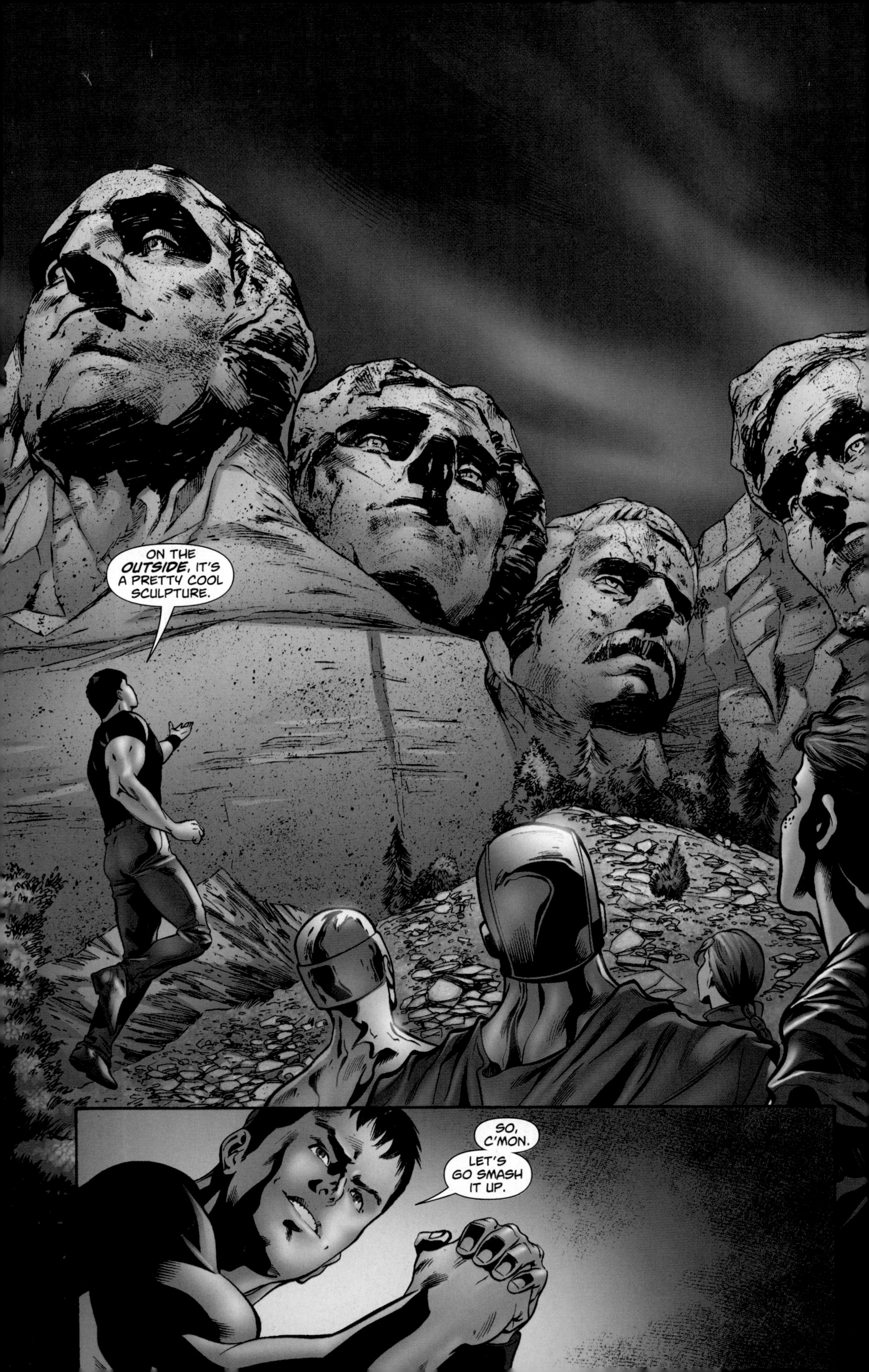
ON THE OUTSIDE, IT'S A PRETTY COOL SCULPTURE.
SO, C'MON. LET'S GO SMASH IT UP.

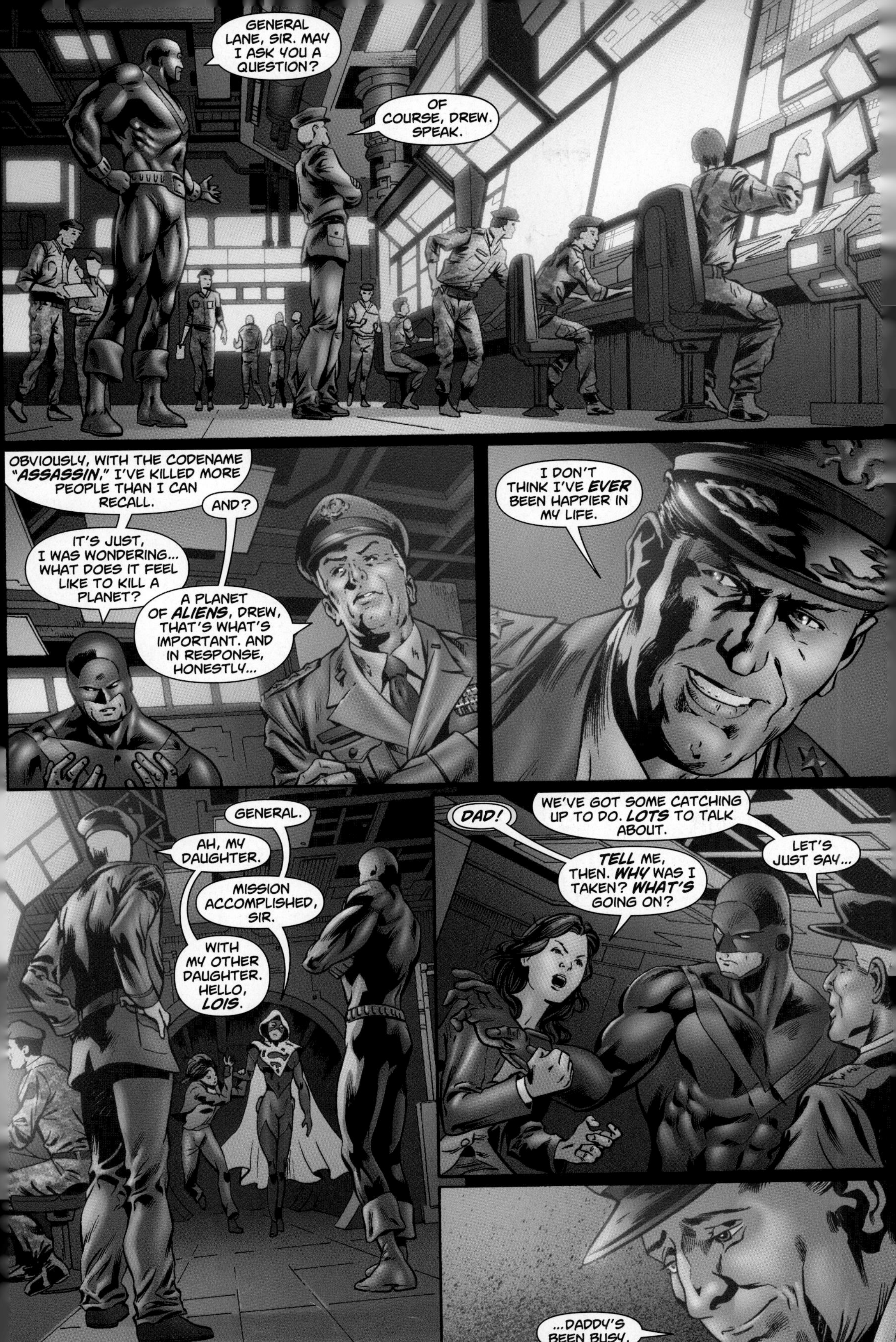
GENERAL LANE, SIR. MAY I ASK YOU A QUESTION?
OF COURSE, DREW. SPEAK.
OBVIOUSLY, WITH THE CODENAME "ASSASSIN," I'VE KILLED MORE PEOPLE THAN I CAN RECALL.
AND?
IT'S JUST, I WAS WONDERING... WHAT DOES IT FEEL LIKE TO KILL A PLANET?
A PLANET OF ALIENS, DREW, THAT'S WHAT'S IMPORTANT. AND IN RESPONSE, HONESTLY...
I DON'T THINK I'VE EVER BEEN HAPPIER IN MY LIFE.
GENERAL.
AH, MY DAUGHTER.
MISSION ACCOMPLISHED, SIR.
WITH MY OTHER DAUGHTER. HELLO, LOIS.
DAD!
WE'VE GOT SOME CATCHING UP TO DO. LOTS TO TALK ABOUT.
TELL ME, THEN. WHY WAS I TAKEN? WHAT'S GOING ON?
LET'S JUST SAY...
...DADDY'S BEEN BUSY.

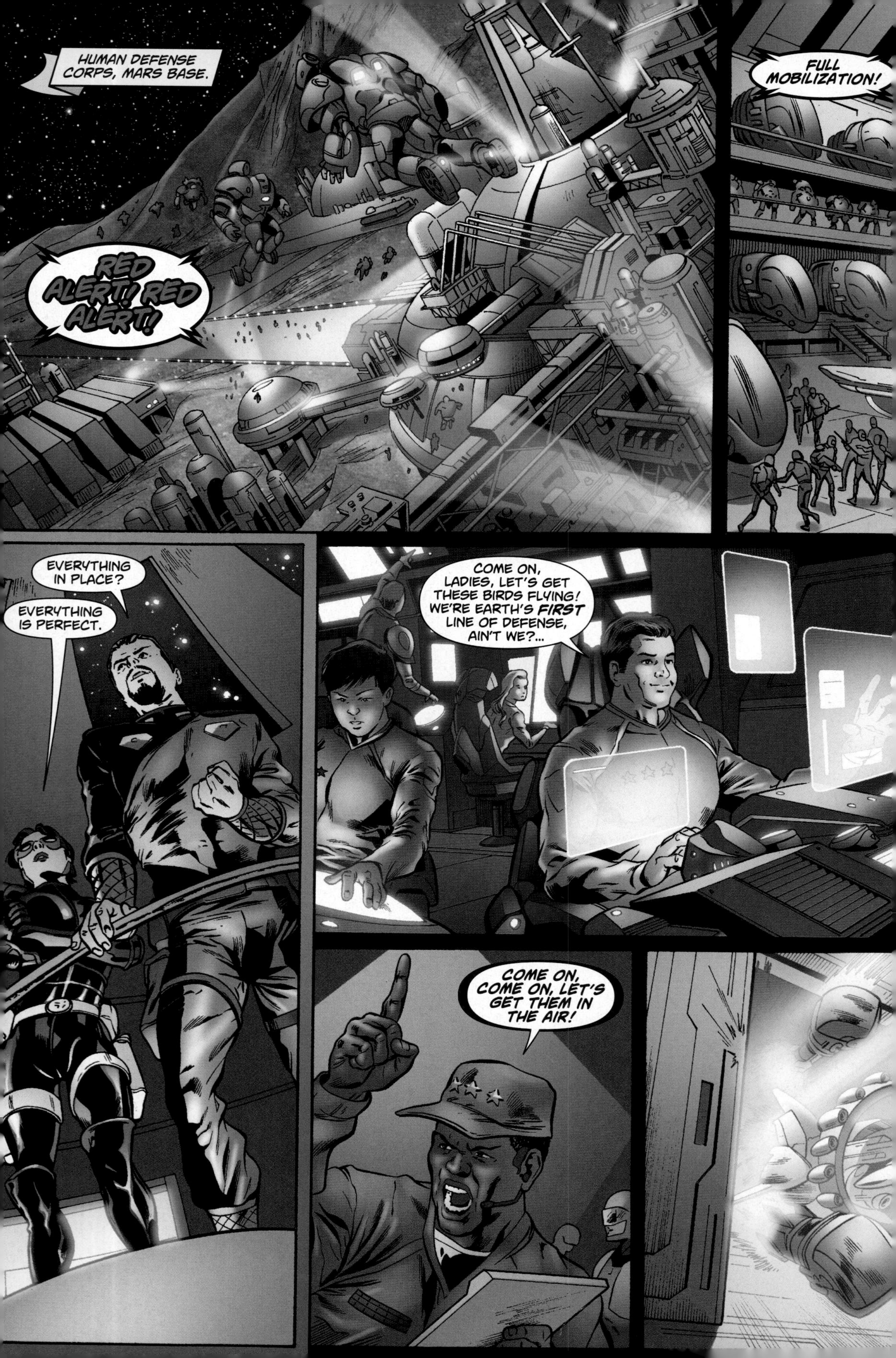
HUMAN DEFENSE CORPS, MARS BASE.
RED ALERT! RED ALERT!
FULL MOBILIZATION!
EVERYTHING IN PLACE?
EVERYTHING IS PERFECT.
COME ON, LADIES, LET'S GET THESE BIRDS FLYING! WE'RE EARTH'S FIRST LINE OF DEFENSE, AIN'T WE?...
COME ON, COME ON, LET'S GET THEM IN THE AIR!

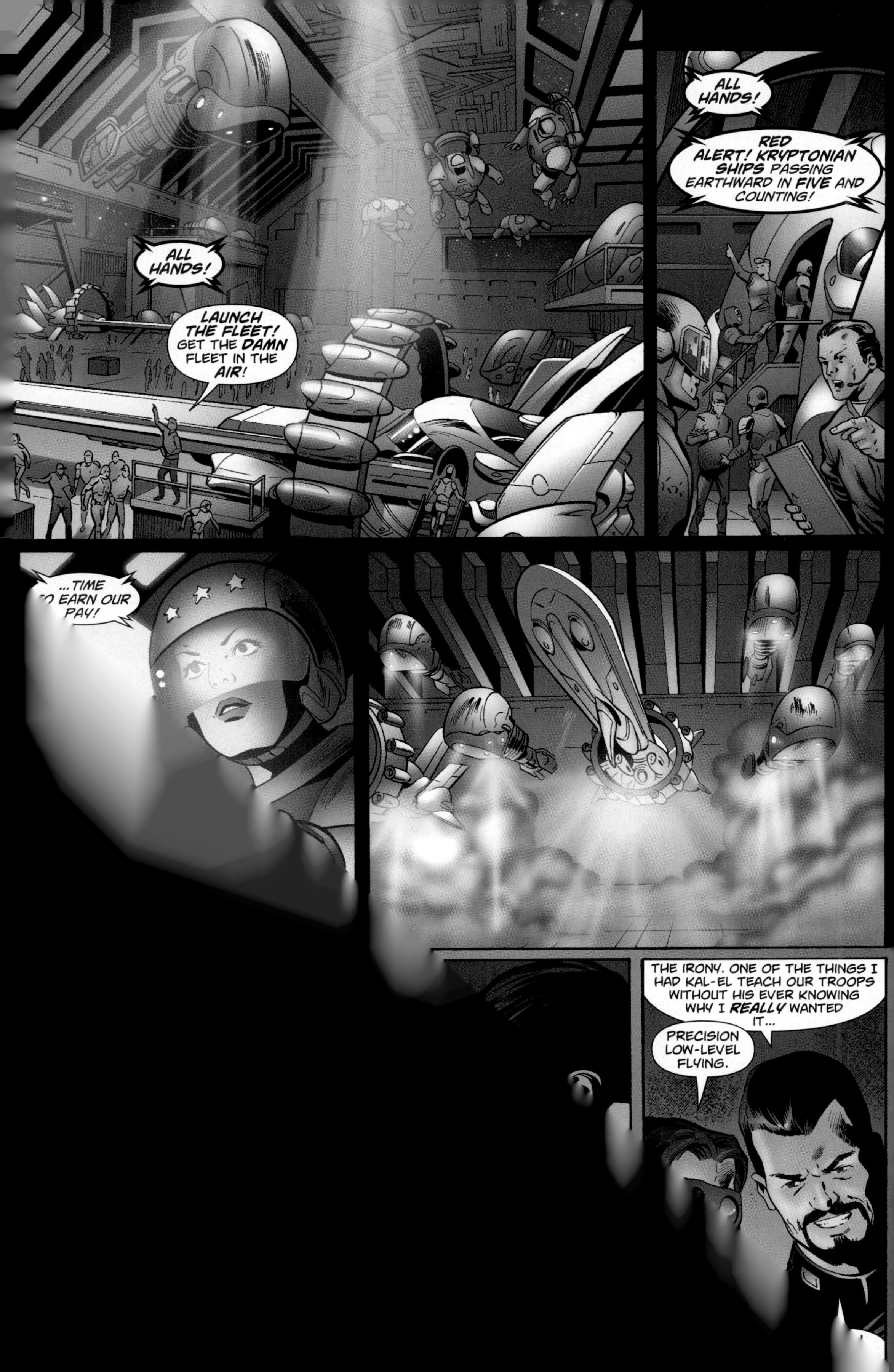
ALL HANDS!
LAUNCH THE FLEET! GET THE DAMN FLEET IN THE AIR!
ALL HANDS!
RED ALERT! KRYPTONIAN SHIPS PASSING EARTHWARD IN FIVE AND COUNTING!
...TIME TO EARN OUR PAY!
THE IRONY. ONE OF THE THINGS I HAD KAL-EL TEACH OUR TROOPS WITHOUT HIS EVER KNOWING WHY I REALLY WANTED IT...
PRECISION LOW-LEVEL FLYING.

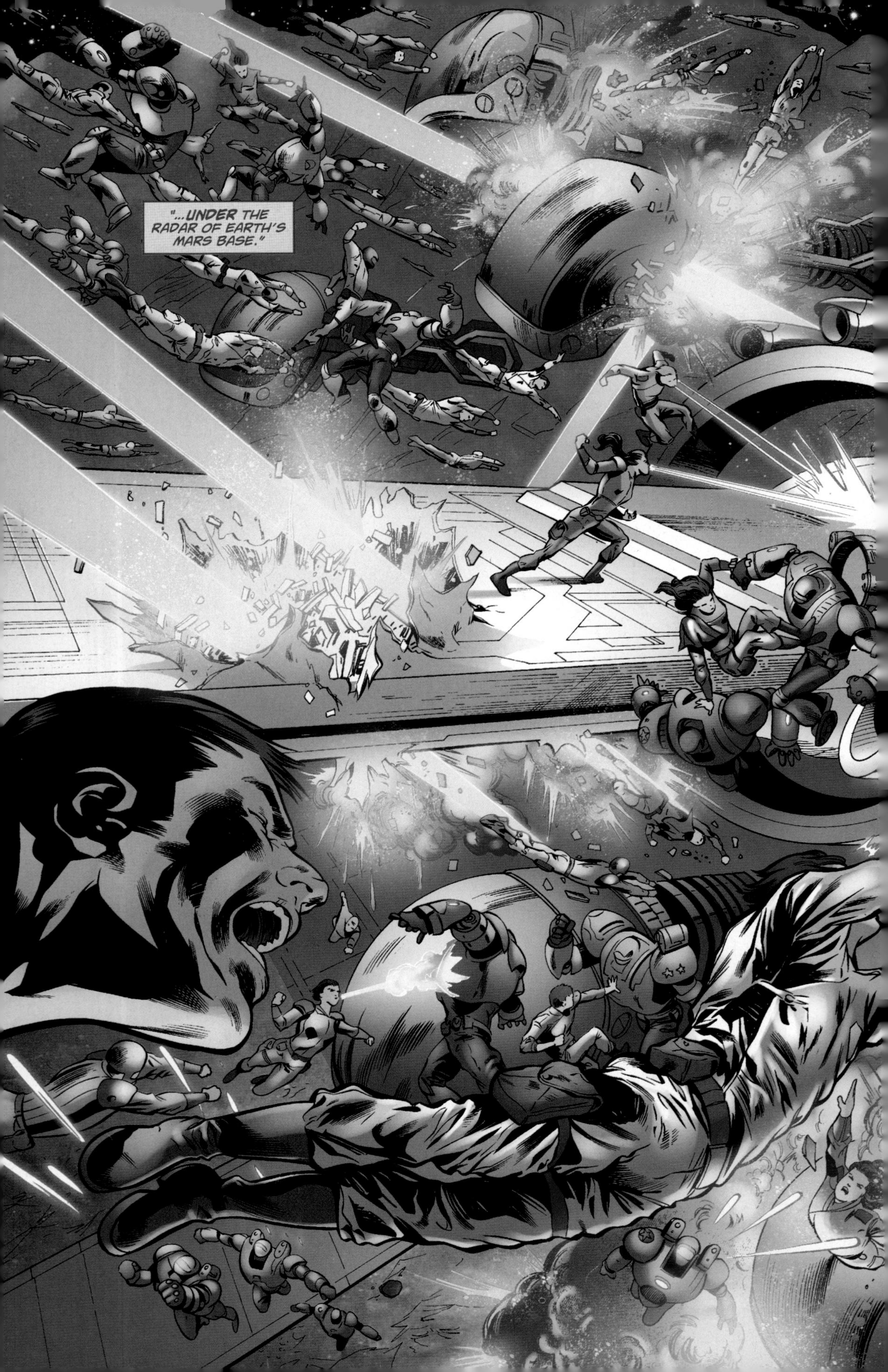
"...UNDER THE RADAR OF EARTH'S MARS BASE."

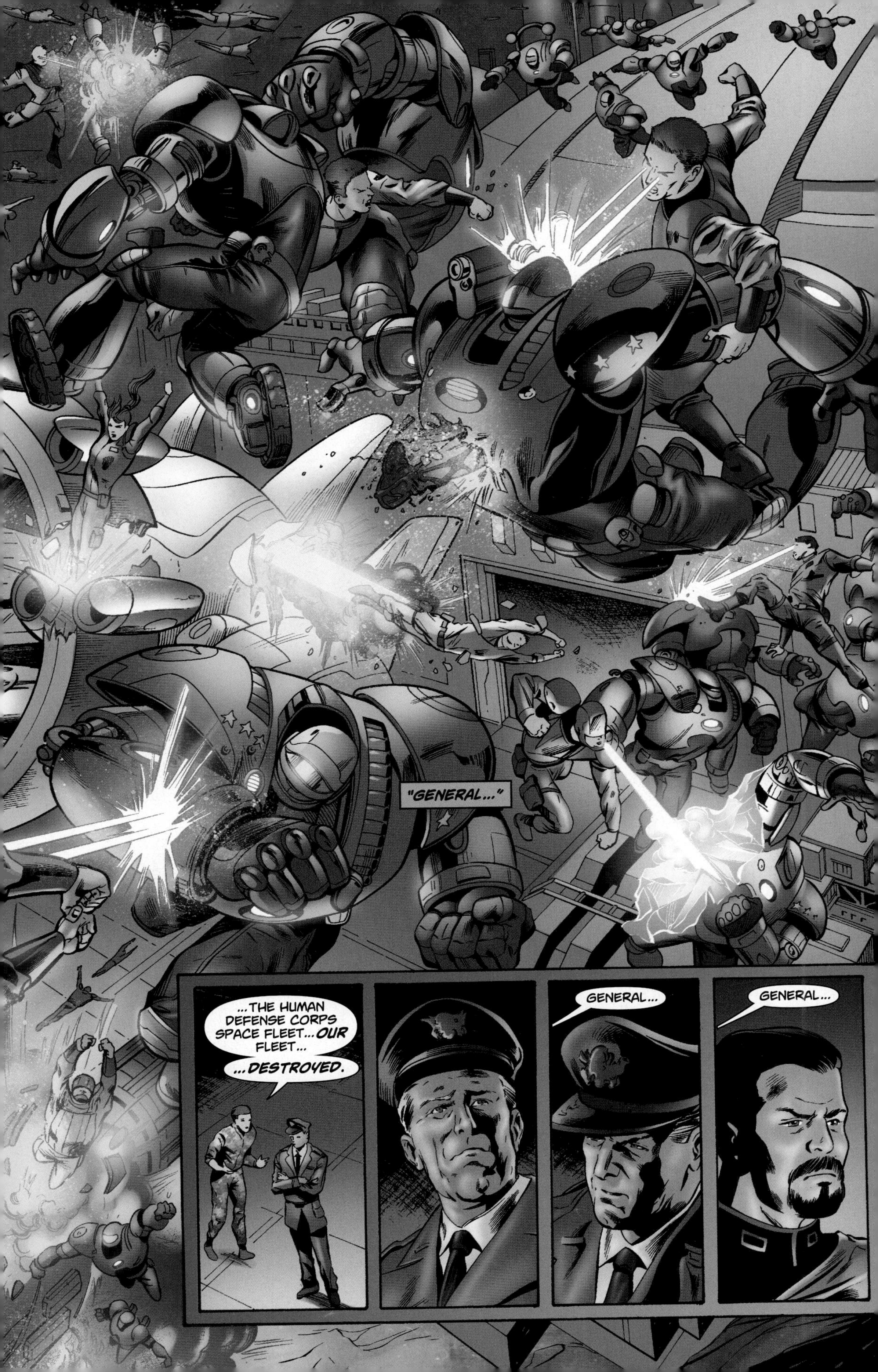

"GENERAL..."
...THE HUMAN DEFENSE CORPS SPACE FLEET... OUR FLEET...
...DESTROYED.
GENERAL...
GENERAL...

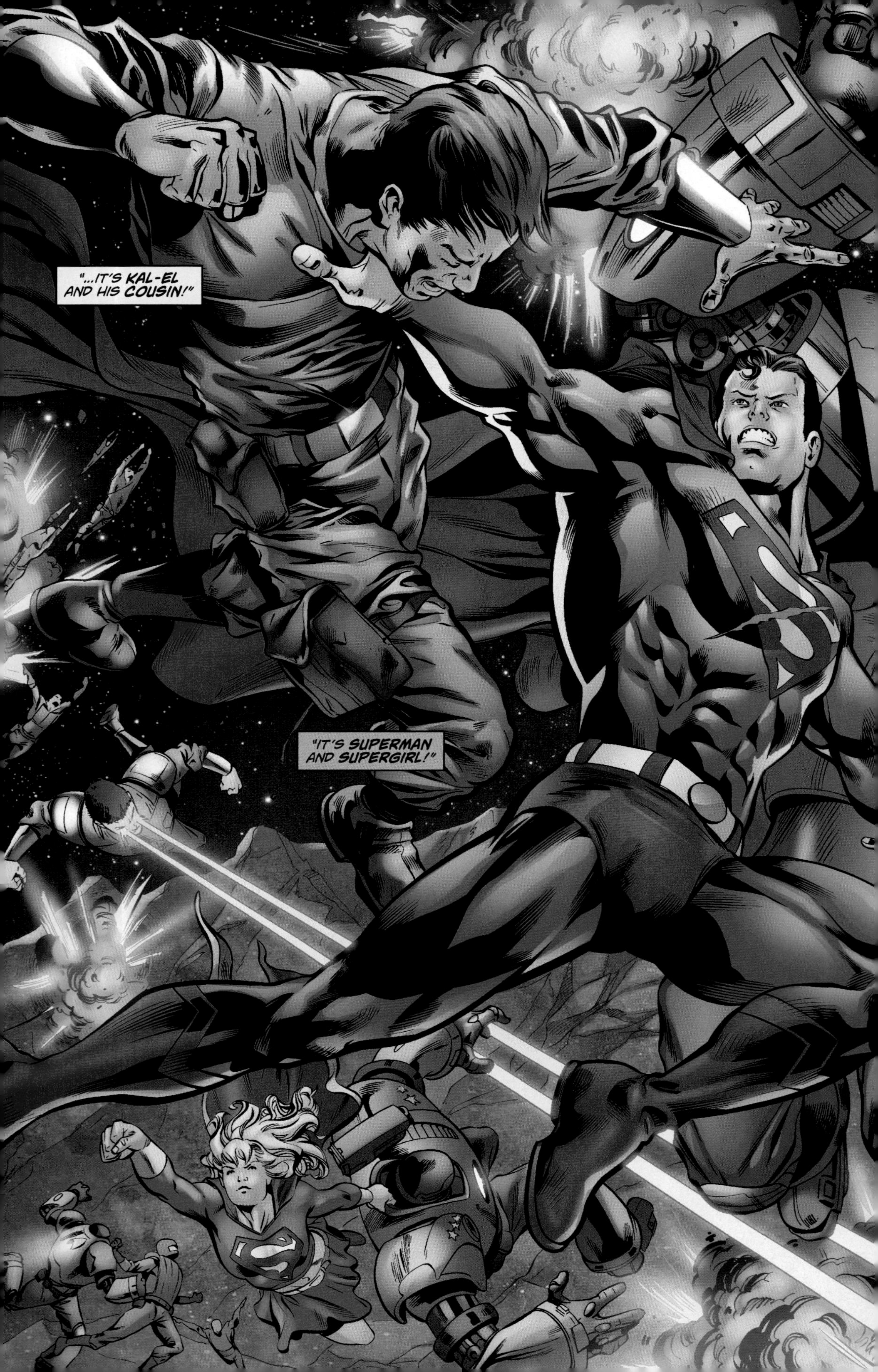
"...IT'S KAL-EL AND HIS COUSIN!"
"IT'S SUPERMAN AND SUPERGIRL!"

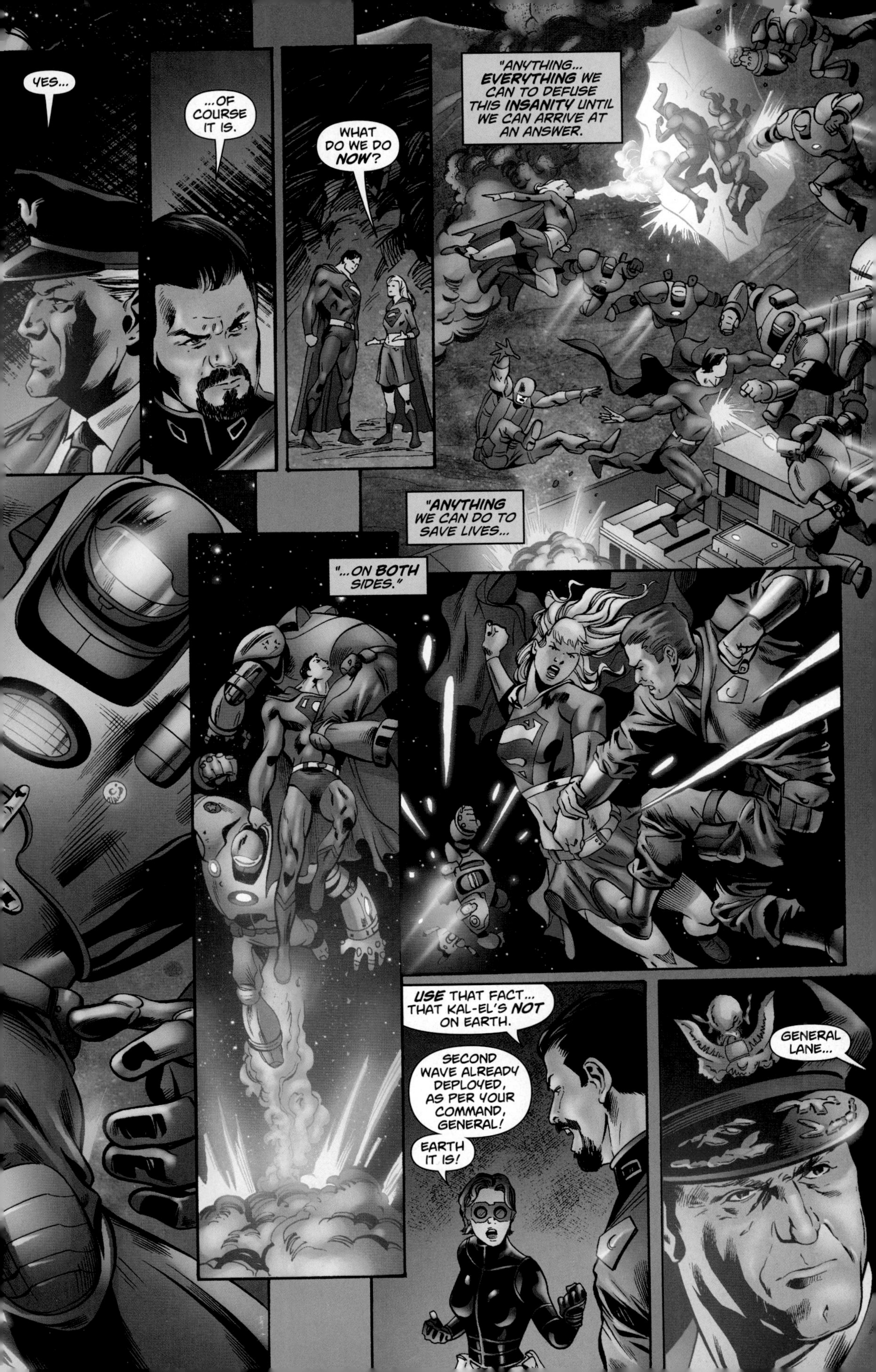
YES...
...OF COURSE IT IS.
WHAT DO WE DO NOW?
"ANYTHING... EVERYTHING WE CAN TO DEFUSE THIS INSANITY UNTIL WE CAN ARRIVE AT AN ANSWER.
"ANYTHING WE CAN DO TO SAVE LIVES...
"...ON BOTH SIDES."
USE THAT FACT... THAT KAL-EL'S NOT ON EARTH.
SECOND WAVE ALREADY DEPLOYED, AS PER YOUR COMMAND, GENERAL!
EARTH IT IS!
GENERAL LANE...

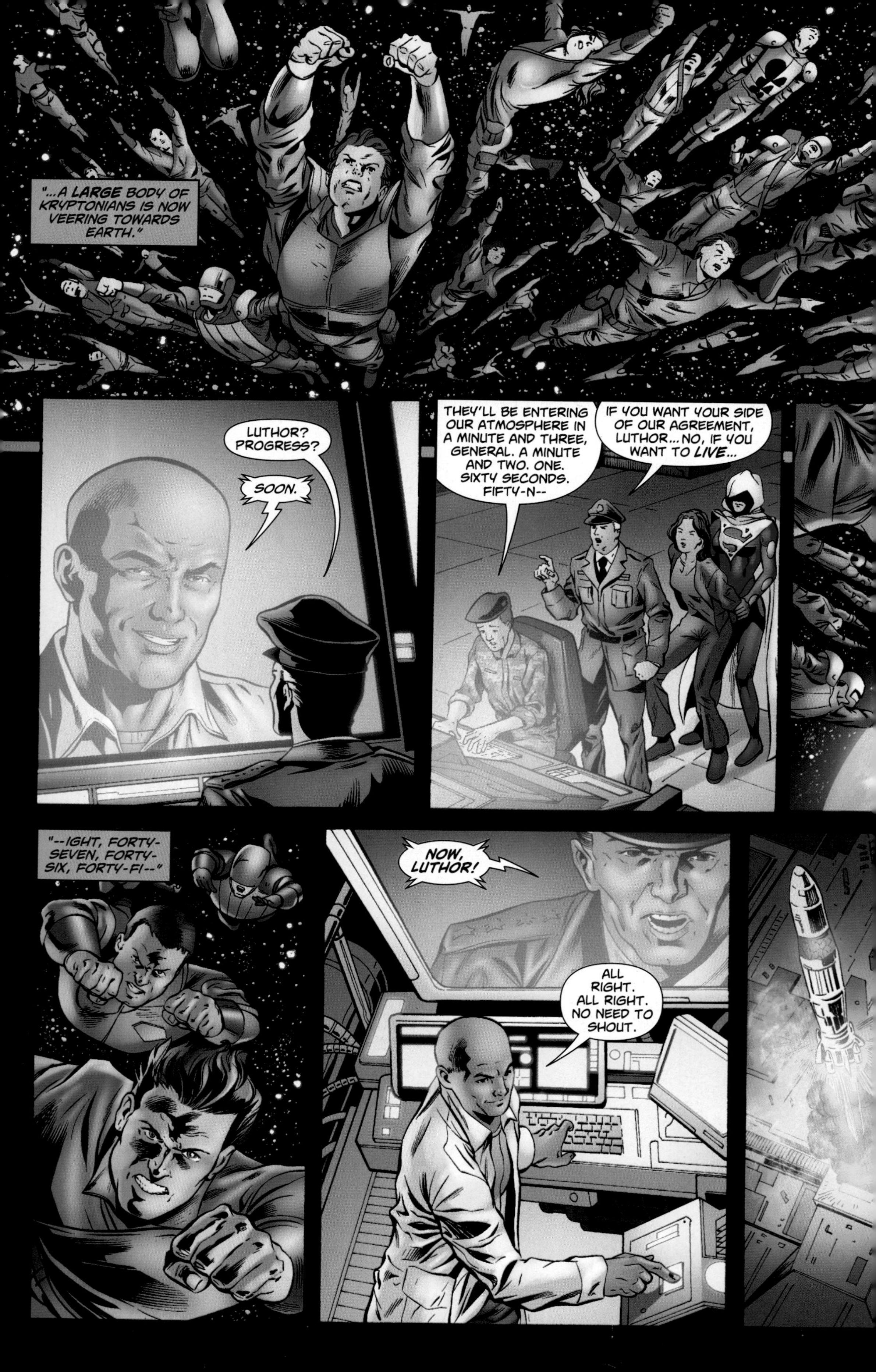
"...A LARGE BODY OF KRYPTONIANS IS NOW VEERING TOWARDS EARTH."
LUTHOR? PROGRESS?
SOON.
THEY'LL BE ENTERING OUR ATMOSPHERE IN A MINUTE AND THREE, GENERAL. A MINUTE AND TWO. ONE. SIXTY SECONDS. FIFTY-N--
IF YOU WANT YOUR SIDE OF OUR AGREEMENT, LUTHOR... NO, IF YOU WANT TO LIVE...
"--IGHT, FORTY-SEVEN, FORTY-SIX, FORTY-FI--"
NOW, LUTHOR!
ALL RIGHT. ALL RIGHT. NO NEED TO SHOUT.

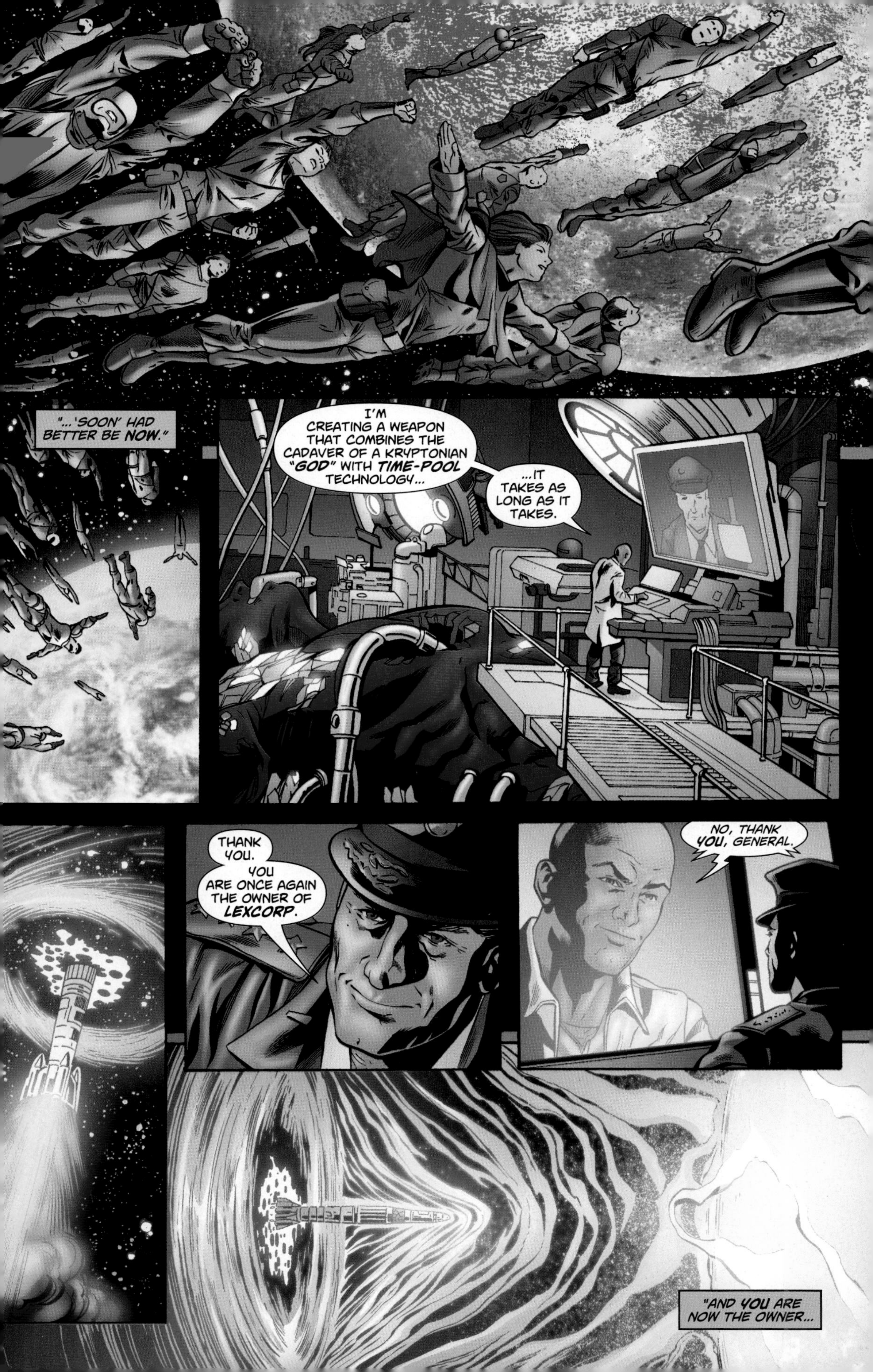
"...'SOON' HAD BETTER BE NOW."
I'M CREATING A WEAPON THAT COMBINES THE CADAVER OF A KRYPTONIAN "GOD" WITH TIME-POOL TECHNOLOGY...
...IT TAKES AS LONG AS IT TAKES.
THANK YOU.
YOU ARE ONCE AGAIN THE OWNER OF LEXCORP.
NO, THANK YOU, GENERAL.
"AND YOU ARE NOW THE OWNER...

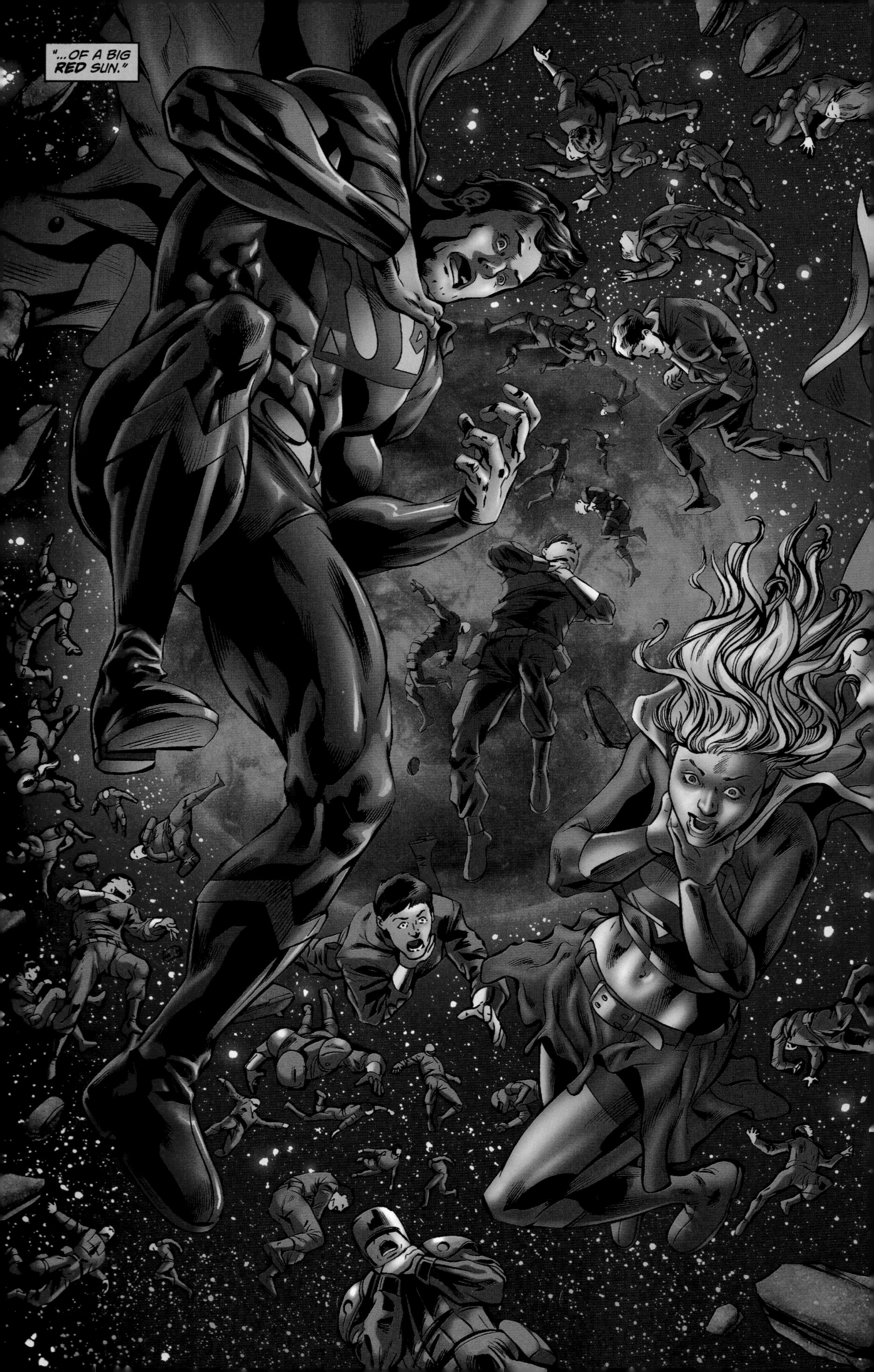
"...OF A BIG RED SUN."

PART 5: THE BATTLE FOR EARTH Cover by EDDY BARROWS, J.P. MAYER & ROD REIS

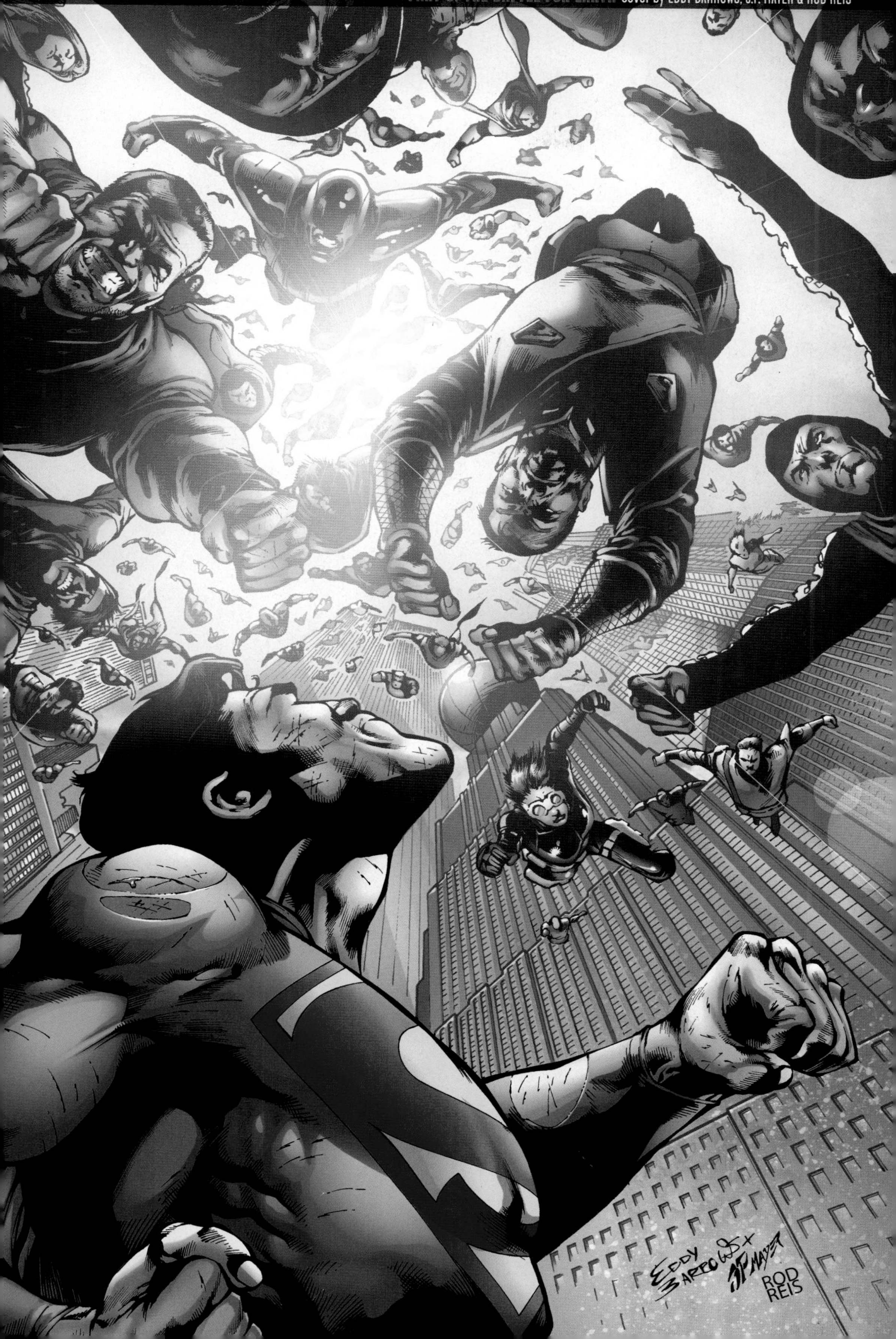
EDDY BARROWS + JP MAYER
ROD REIS

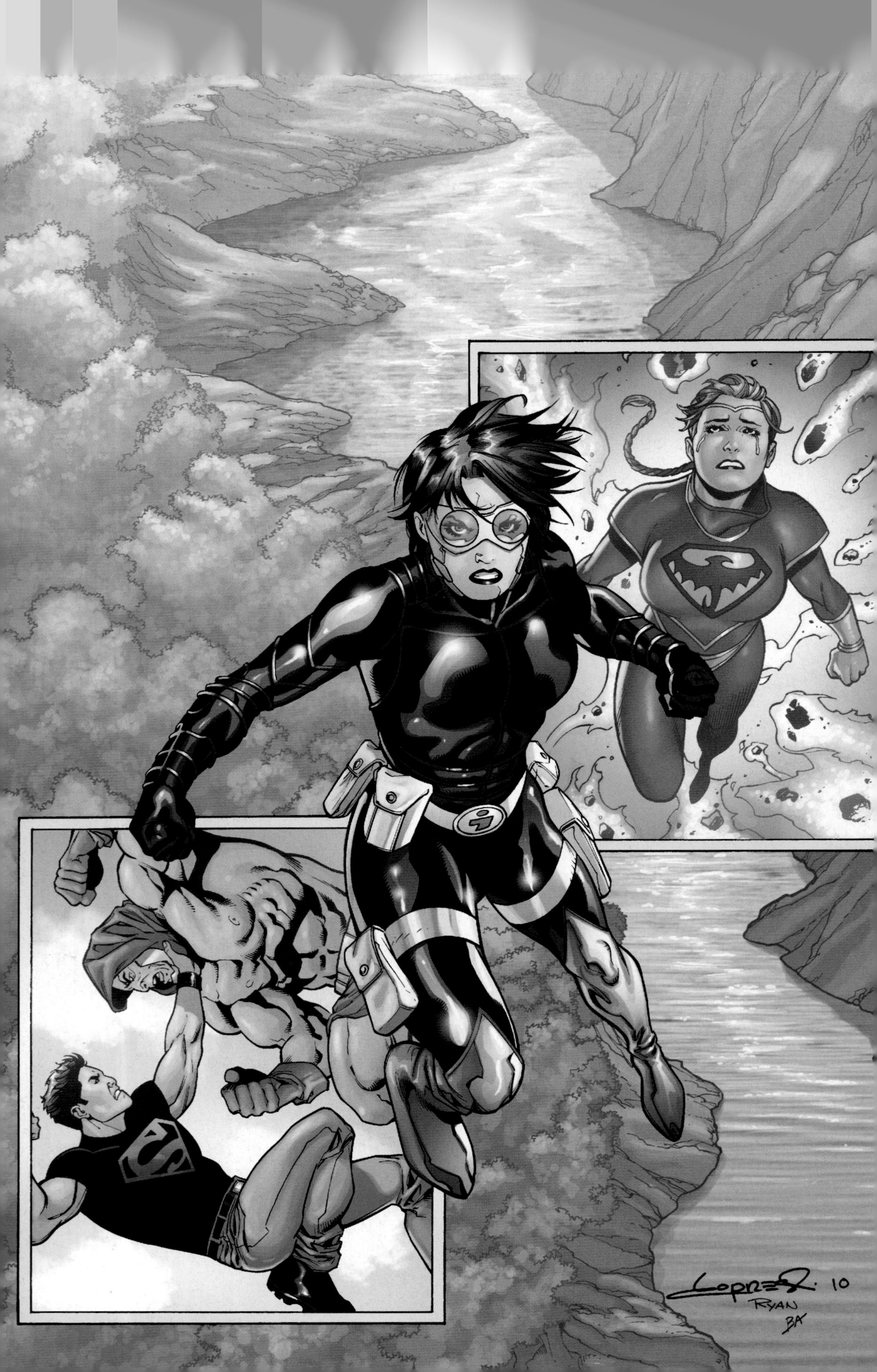
10
RYAN
BA

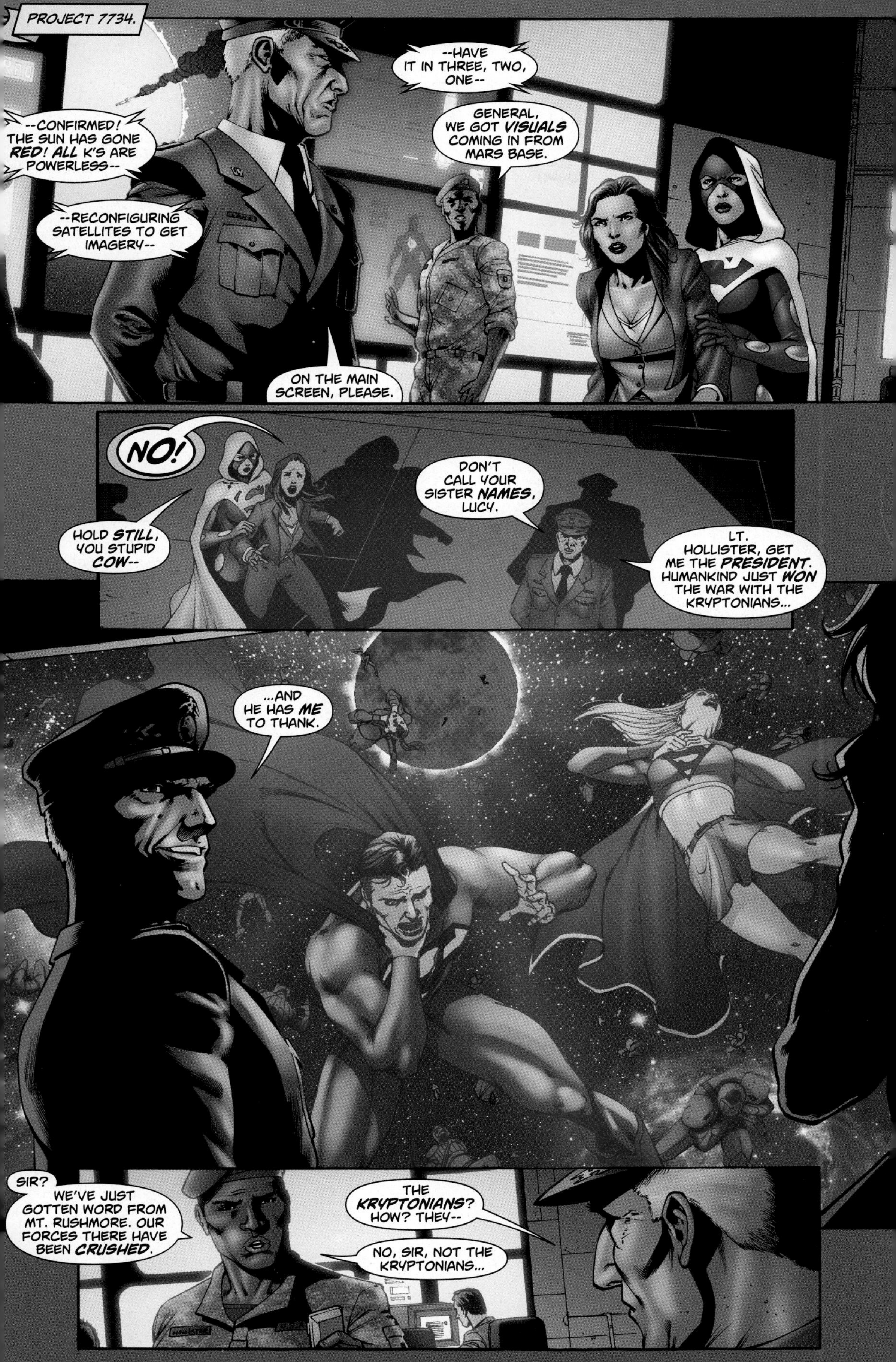
PROJECT 7734.
--CONFIRMED! THE SUN HAS GONE RED! ALL K'S ARE POWERLESS--
--RECONFIGURING SATELLITES TO GET IMAGERY--
--HAVE IT IN THREE, TWO, ONE--
GENERAL, WE GOT VISUALS COMING IN FROM MARS BASE.
ON THE MAIN SCREEN, PLEASE.
NO!
HOLD STILL, YOU STUPID COW--
DON'T CALL YOUR SISTER NAMES, LUCY.
LT. HOLLISTER, GET ME THE PRESIDENT. HUMANKIND JUST WON THE WAR WITH THE KRYPTONIANS...
...AND HE HAS ME TO THANK.
SIR? WE'VE JUST GOTTEN WORD FROM MT. RUSHMORE. OUR FORCES THERE HAVE BEEN CRUSHED.
THE KRYPTONIANS? HOW? THEY--
NO, SIR, NOT THE KRYPTONIANS...

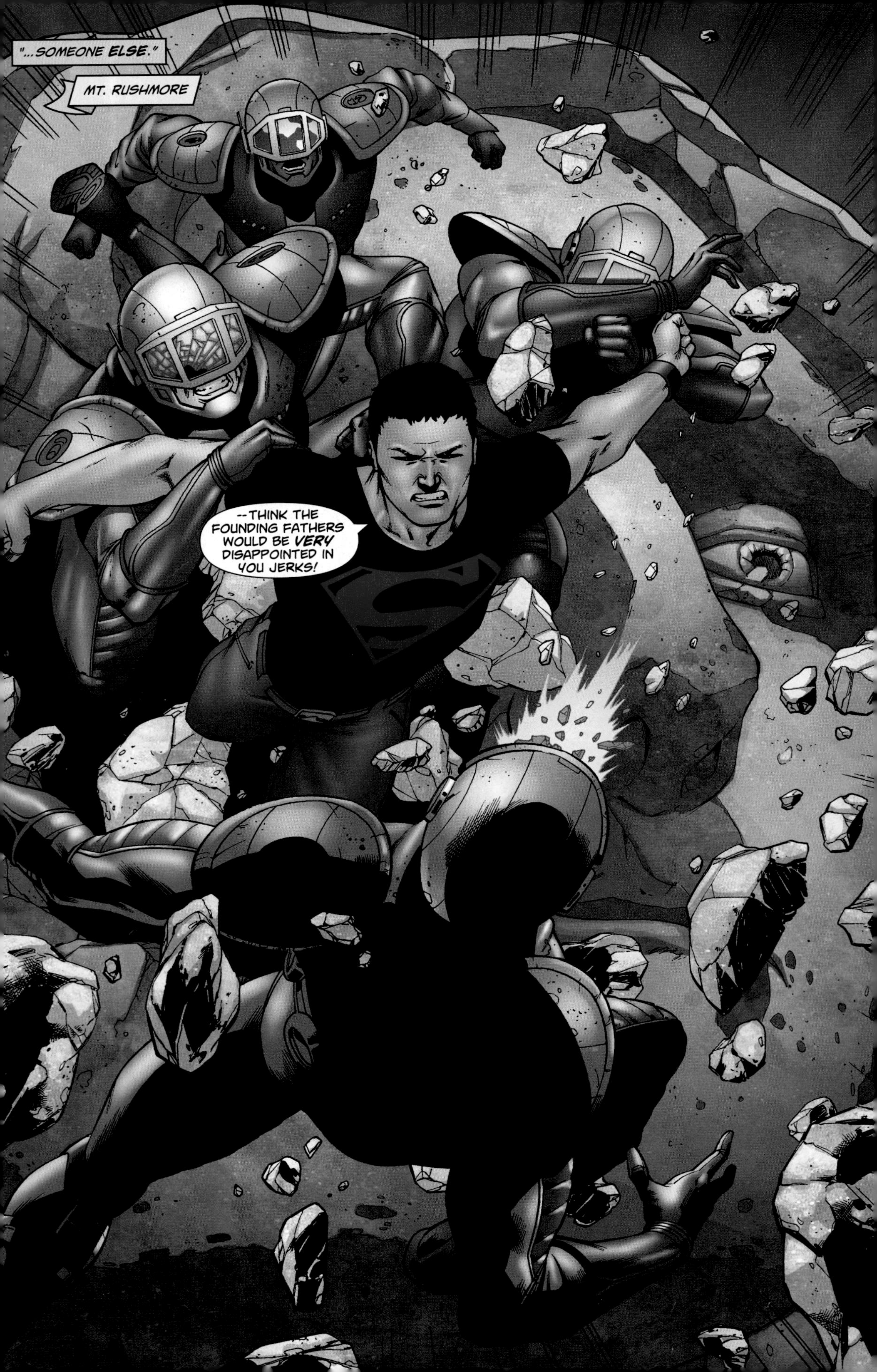
"...SOMEONE ELSE."
MT. RUSHMORE
--THINK THE FOUNDING FATHERS WOULD BE VERY DISAPPOINTED IN YOU JERKS!

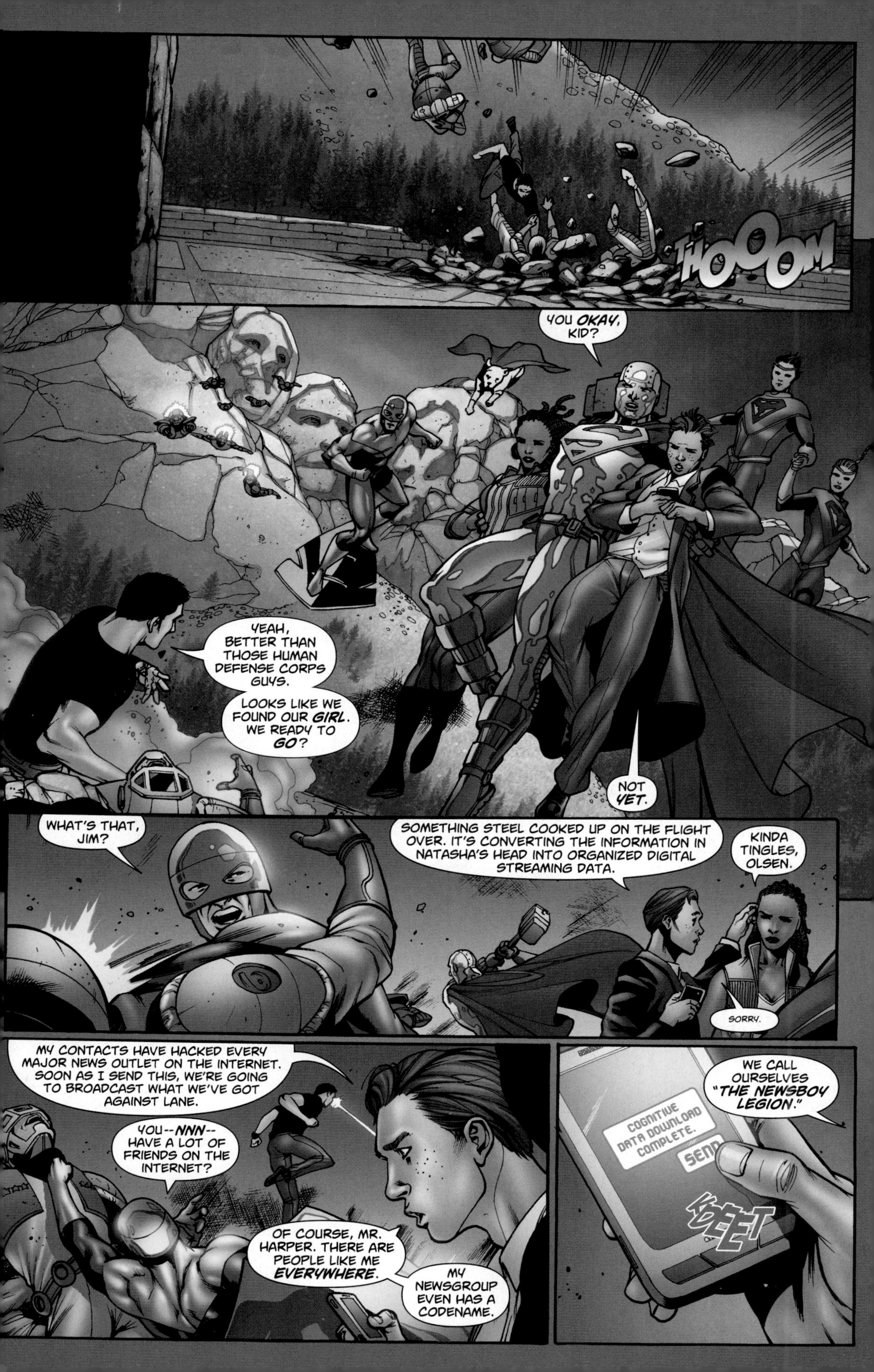
THOOOOM
YOU OKAY, KID?
YEAH, BETTER THAN THOSE HUMAN DEFENSE CORPS GUYS.
LOOKS LIKE WE FOUND OUR GIRL. WE READY TO GO?
NOT YET.
WHAT'S THAT, JIM?
SOMETHING STEEL COOKED UP ON THE FLIGHT OVER. IT'S CONVERTING THE INFORMATION IN NATASHA'S HEAD INTO ORGANIZED DIGITAL STREAMING DATA.
KINDA TINGLES, OLSEN.
SORRY.
MY CONTACTS HAVE HACKED EVERY MAJOR NEWS OUTLET ON THE INTERNET. SOON AS I SEND THIS, WE'RE GOING TO BROADCAST WHAT WE'VE GOT AGAINST LANE.
YOU--NNN--HAVE A LOT OF FRIENDS ON THE INTERNET?
OF COURSE, MR. HARPER. THERE ARE PEOPLE LIKE ME EVERYWHERE.
MY NEWSGROUP EVEN HAS A CODENAME.
WE CALL OURSELVES "THE NEWSBOY LEGION."
COGNITIVE DATA DOWNLOAD COMPLETE.
SEND
KBEET

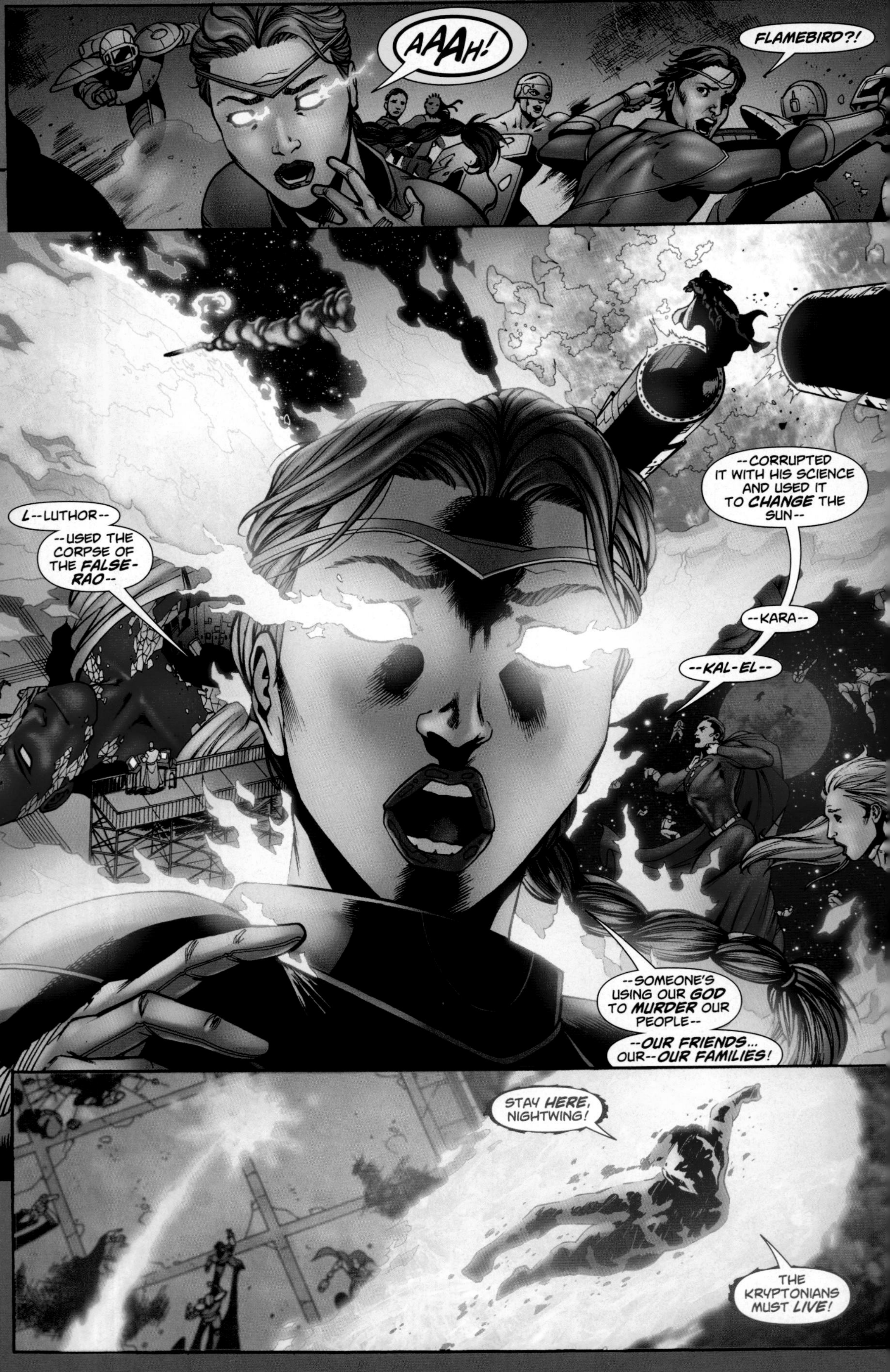
AAAH!
FLAMEBIRD?!
L--LUTHOR--
--USED THE CORPSE OF THE FALSE-RAO--
--CORRUPTED IT WITH HIS SCIENCE AND USED IT TO CHANGE THE SUN--
--KARA--
--KAL-EL--
--SOMEONE'S USING OUR GOD TO MURDER OUR PEOPLE--
--OUR FRIENDS... OUR--OUR FAMILIES!
STAY HERE, NIGHTWING!
THE KRYPTONIANS MUST LIVE!

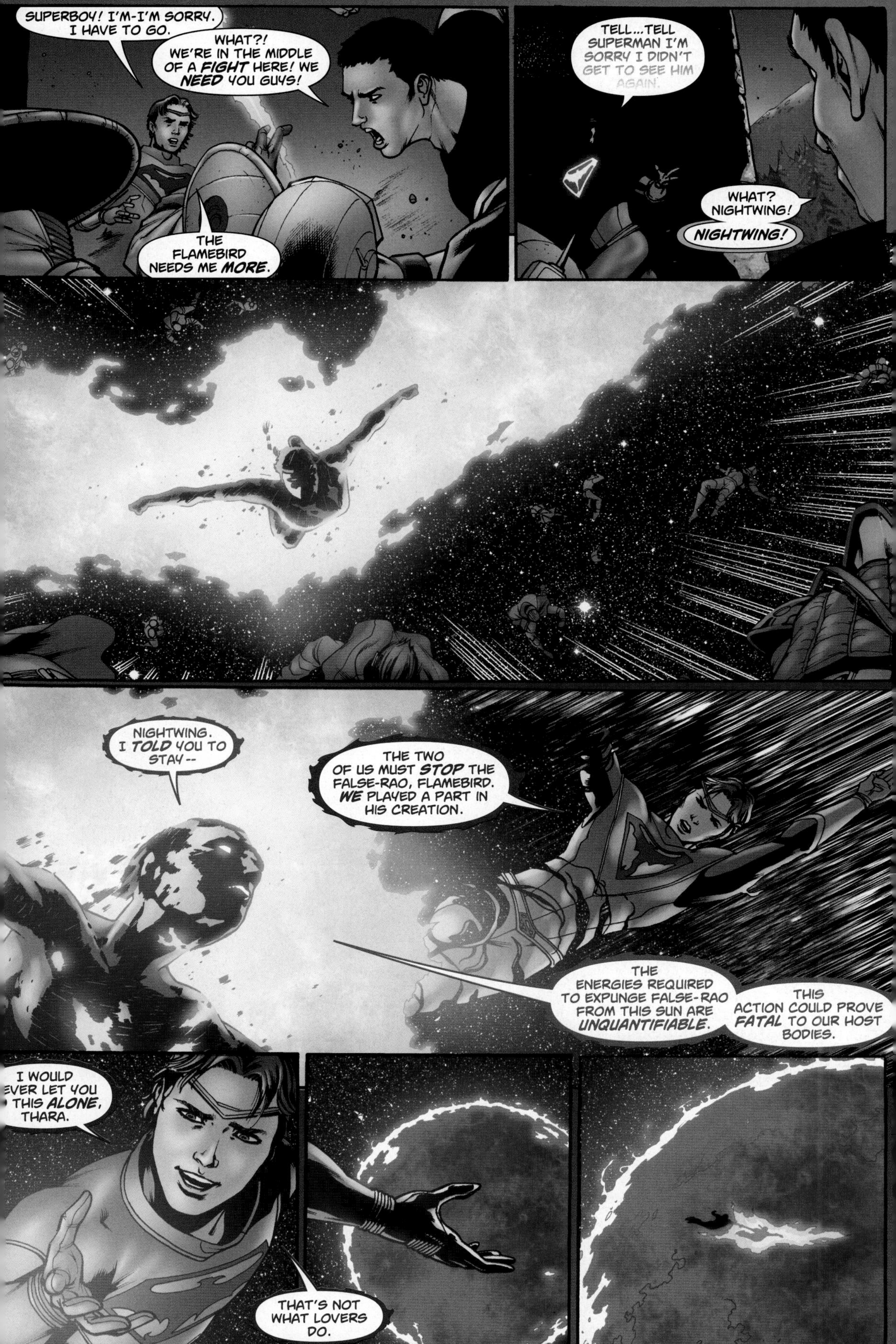

SUPERBOY! I'M-I'M SORRY. I HAVE TO GO.
WHAT?! WE'RE IN THE MIDDLE OF A FIGHT HERE! WE NEED YOU GUYS!
THE FLAMEBIRD NEEDS ME MORE.
TELL...TELL SUPERMAN I'M SORRY I DIDN'T GET TO SEE HIM AGAIN.
WHAT? NIGHTWING!
NIGHTWING!
NIGHTWING. I TOLD YOU TO STAY--
THE TWO OF US MUST STOP THE FALSE-RAO, FLAMEBIRD. WE PLAYED A PART IN HIS CREATION.
THE ENERGIES REQUIRED TO EXPUNGE FALSE-RAO FROM THIS SUN ARE UNQUANTIFIABLE.
THIS ACTION COULD PROVE FATAL TO OUR HOST BODIES.
I WOULD EVER LET YOU THIS ALONE, THARA.
THAT'S NOT WHAT LOVERS DO.

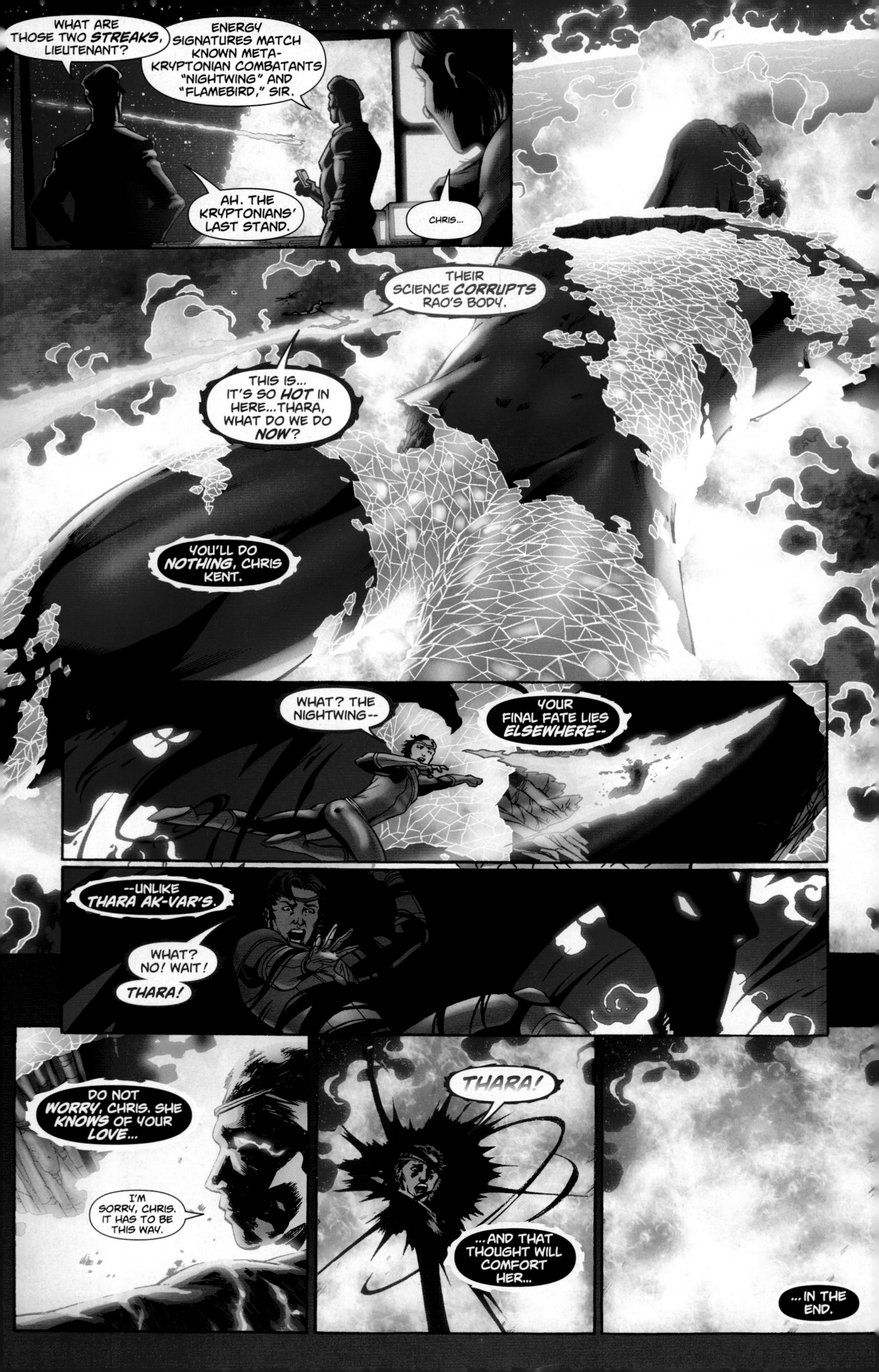
WHAT ARE THOSE TWO STREAKS, LIEUTENANT?
ENERGY SIGNATURES MATCH KNOWN META-KRYPTONIAN COMBATANTS "NIGHTWING" AND "FLAMEBIRD," SIR.
AH. THE KRYPTONIANS' LAST STAND.
CHRIS...
THEIR SCIENCE CORRUPTS RAO'S BODY.
THIS IS... IT'S SO HOT IN HERE...THARA, WHAT DO WE DO NOW?
YOU'LL DO NOTHING, CHRIS KENT.
WHAT? THE NIGHTWING--
YOUR FINAL FATE LIES ELSEWHERE--
--UNLIKE THARA AK-VAR'S.
WHAT? NO! WAIT!
THARA!
DO NOT WORRY, CHRIS. SHE KNOWS OF YOUR LOVE...
I'M SORRY, CHRIS. IT HAS TO BE THIS WAY.
THARA!
...AND THAT THOUGHT WILL COMFORT HER...
...IN THE END.

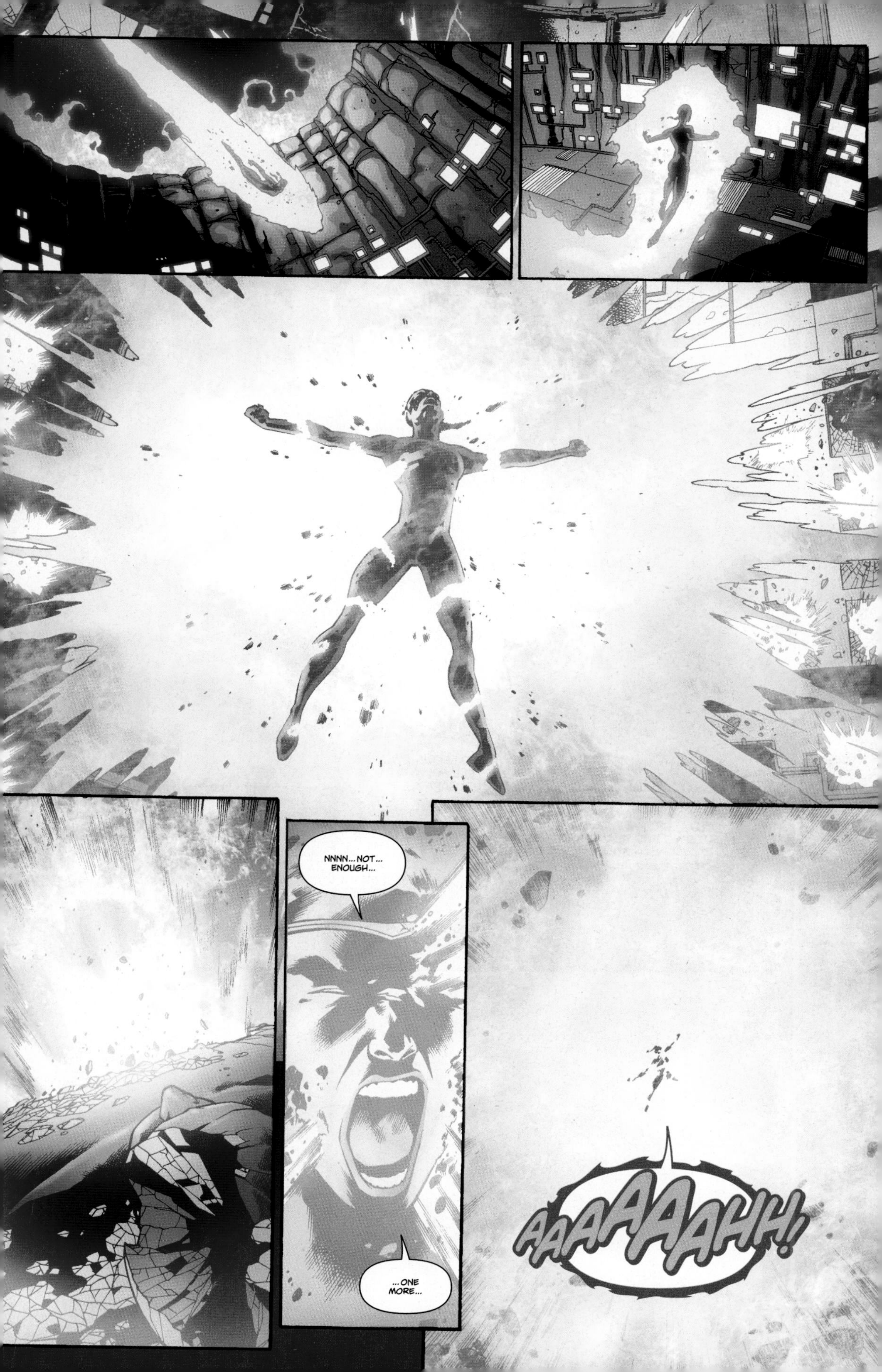
NNNN... NOT... ENOUGH...
...ONE MORE...
AAAAAAAHH!

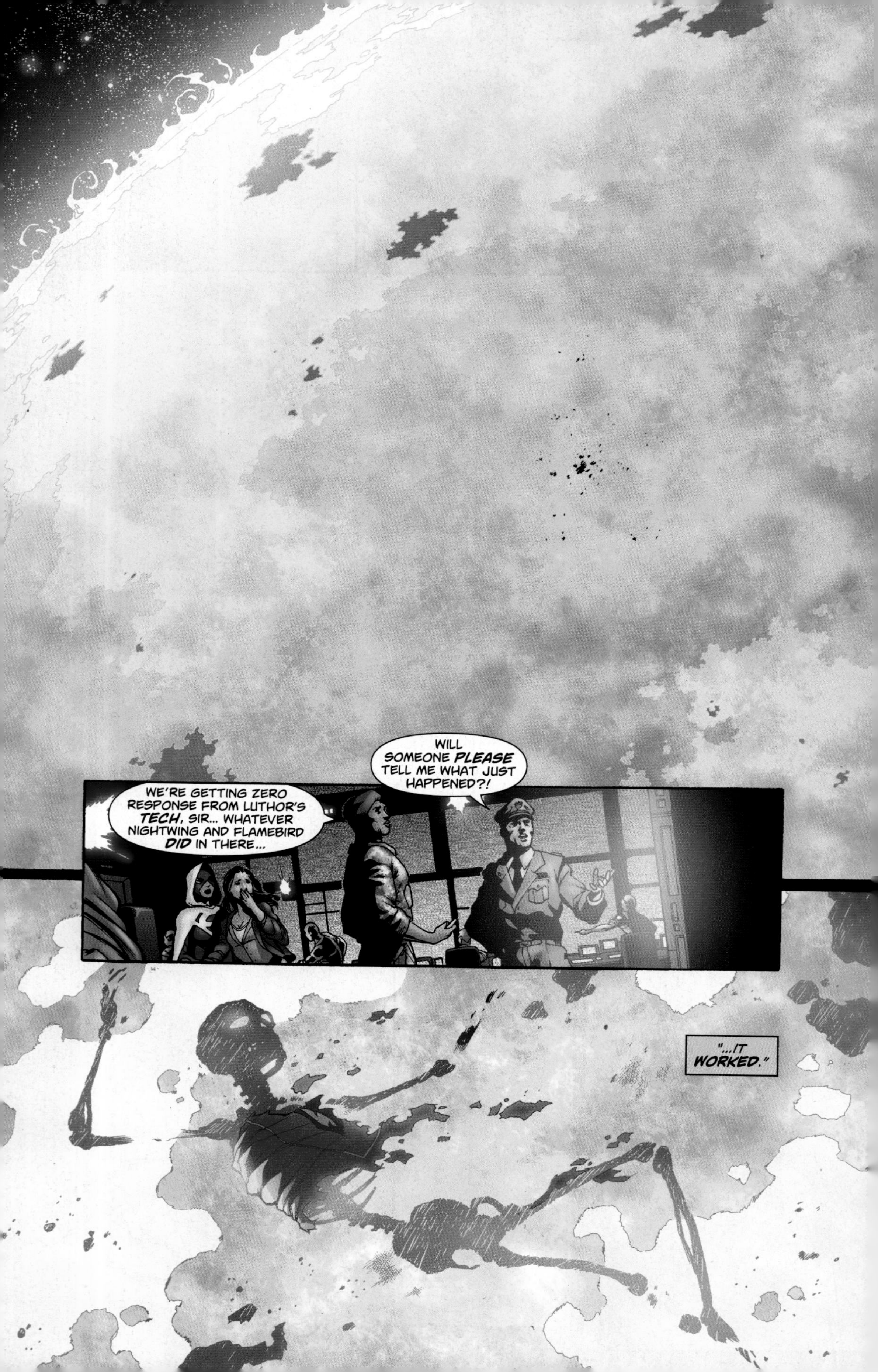
WILL SOMEONE PLEASE TELL ME WHAT JUST HAPPENED?!
WE'RE GETTING ZERO RESPONSE FROM LUTHOR'S TECH, SIR... WHATEVER NIGHTWING AND FLAMEBIRD DID IN THERE...
"...IT WORKED."

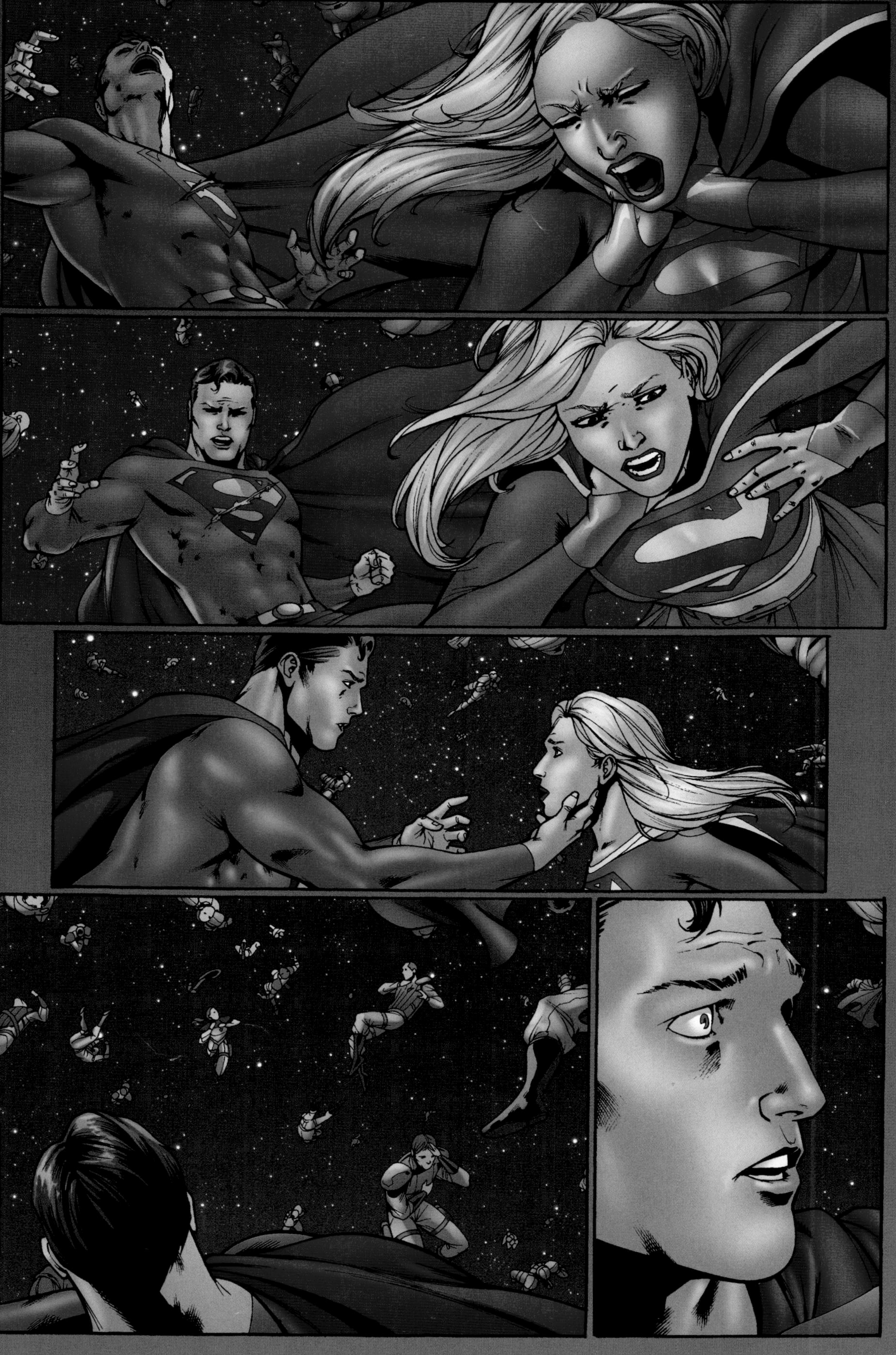

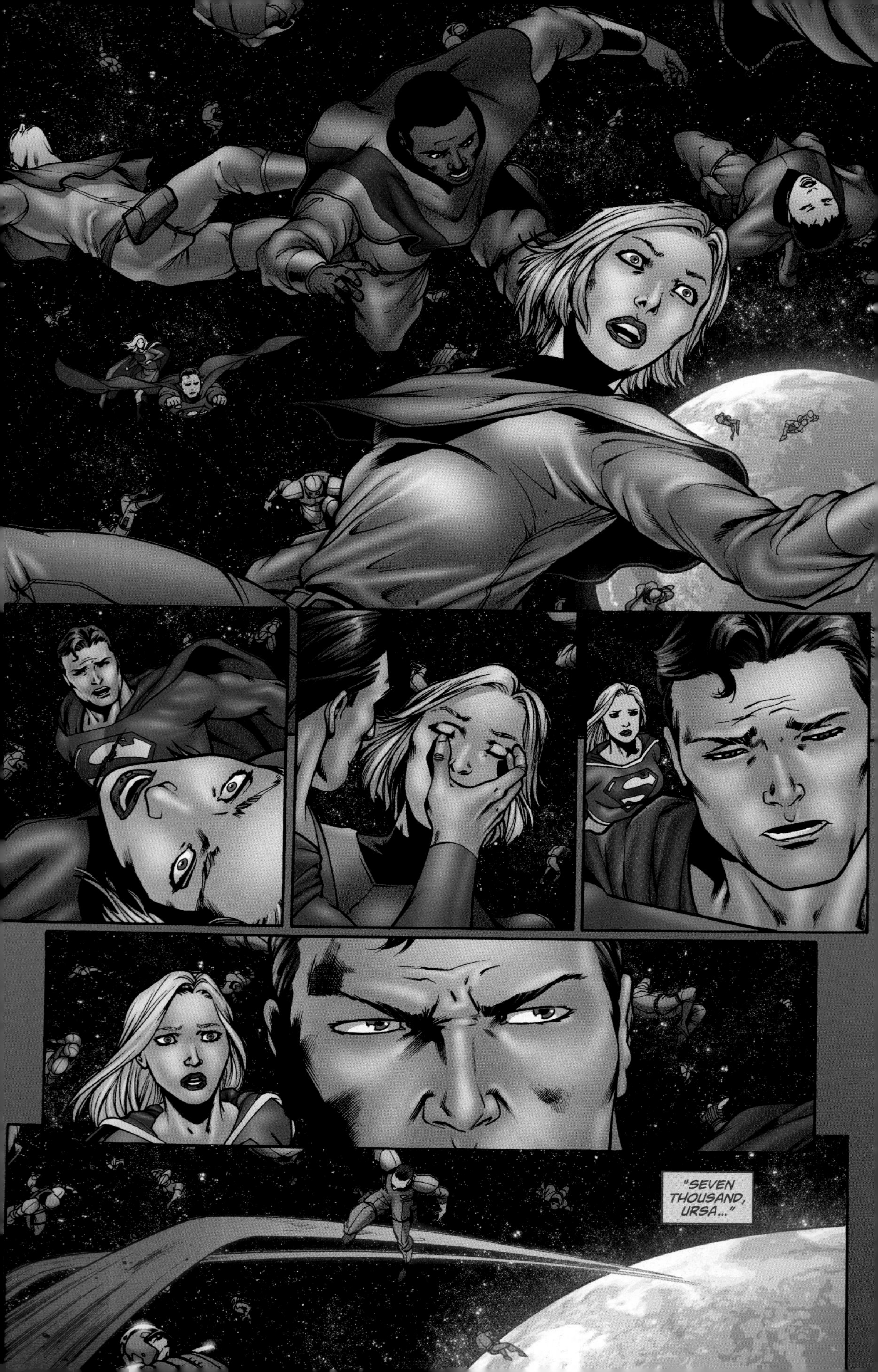
"SEVEN THOUSAND, URSA..."

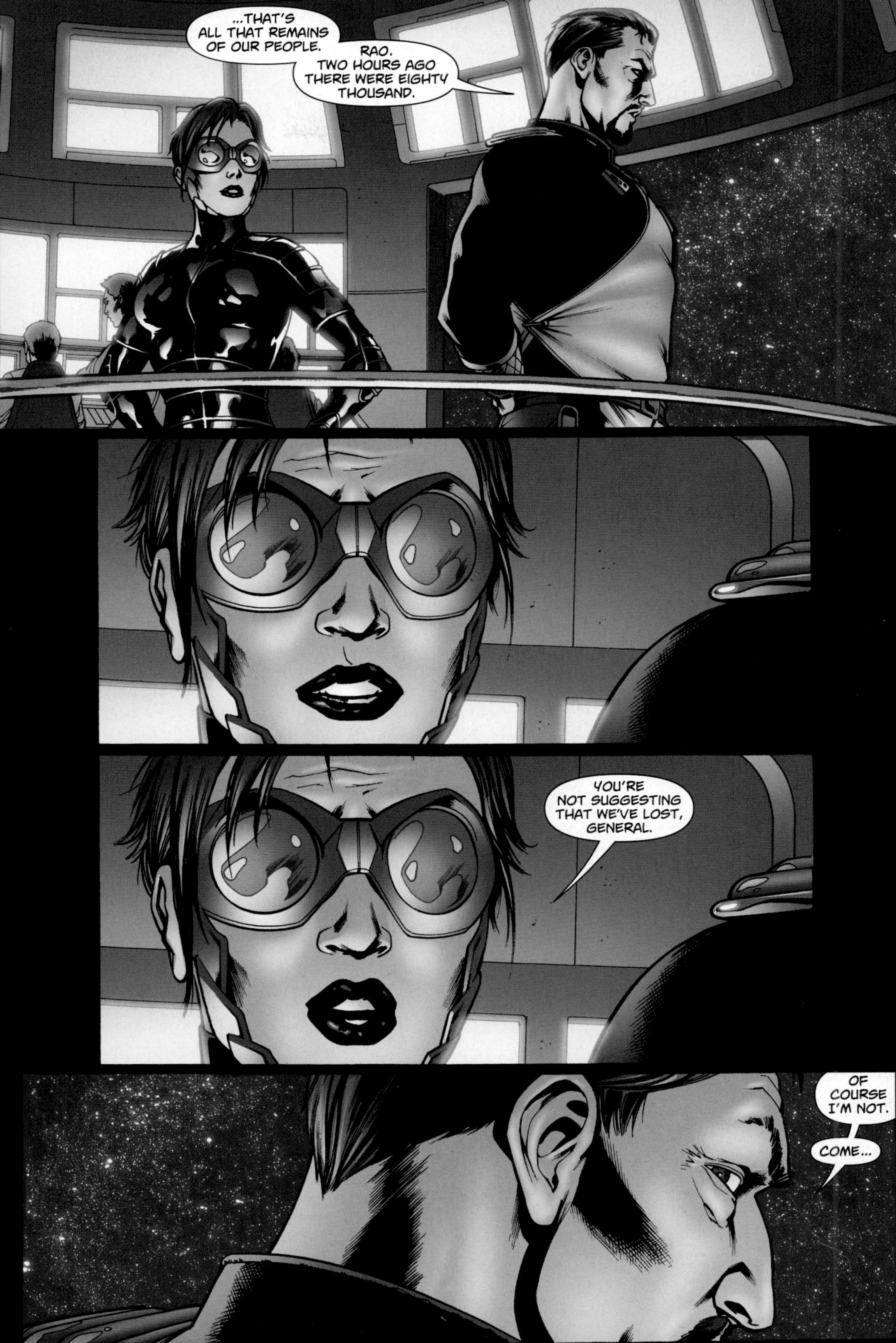
...THAT'S ALL THAT REMAINS OF OUR PEOPLE.
RAO. TWO HOURS AGO THERE WERE EIGHTY THOUSAND.
YOU'RE NOT SUGGESTING THAT WE'VE LOST, GENERAL.
OF COURSE I'M NOT.
COME...

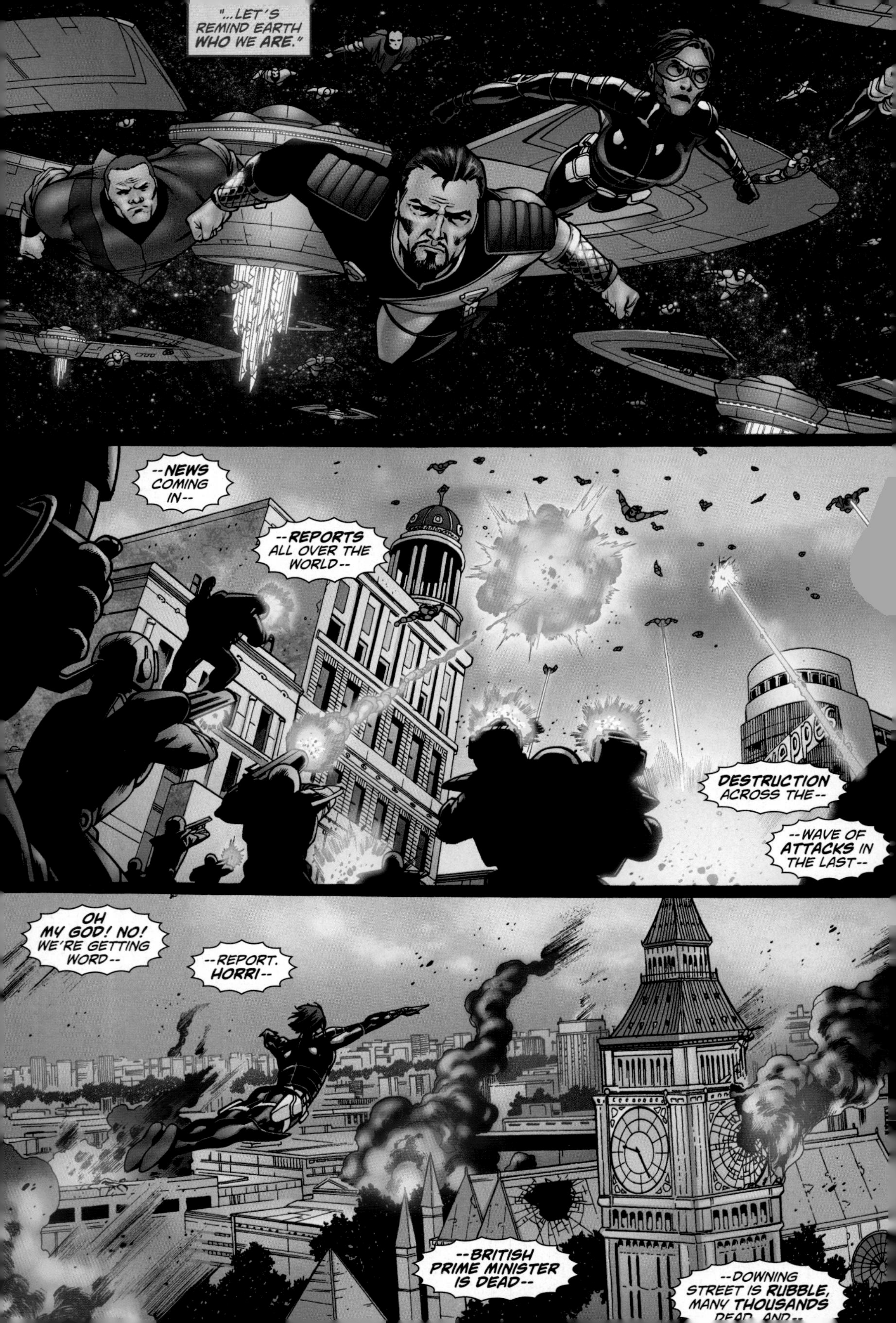
"...LET'S REMIND EARTH WHO WE ARE."
--NEWS COMING IN--
--REPORTS ALL OVER THE WORLD--
DESTRUCTION ACROSS THE--
--WAVE OF ATTACKS IN THE LAST--
OH MY GOD! NO! WE'RE GETTING WORD--
--REPORT. HORRI--
--BRITISH PRIME MINISTER IS DEAD--
--DOWNING STREET IS RUBBLE, MANY THOUSANDS DEAD, AND--

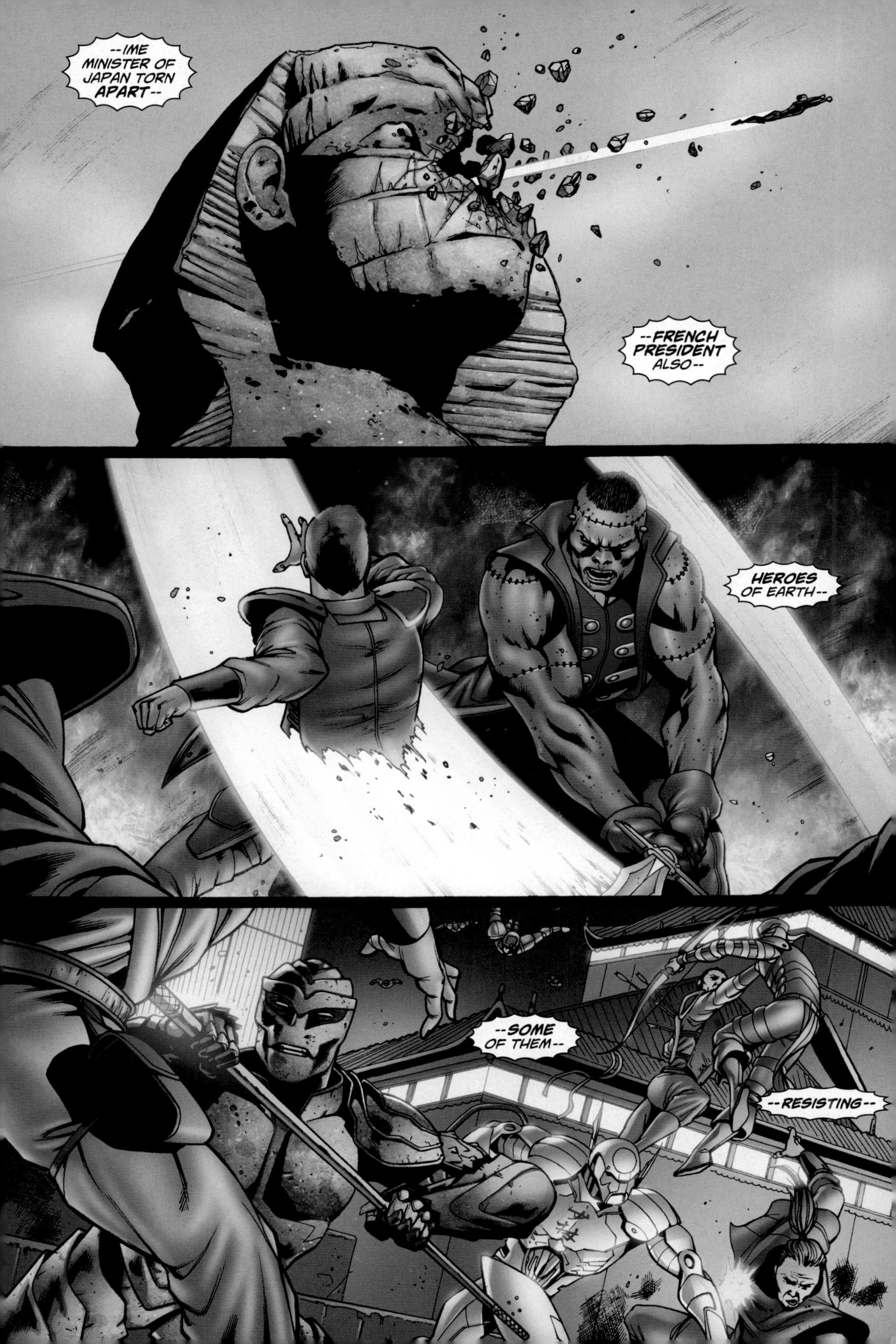
--IME MINISTER OF JAPAN TORN APART--
--FRENCH PRESIDENT ALSO--
HEROES OF EARTH--
--SOME OF THEM--
--RESISTING--

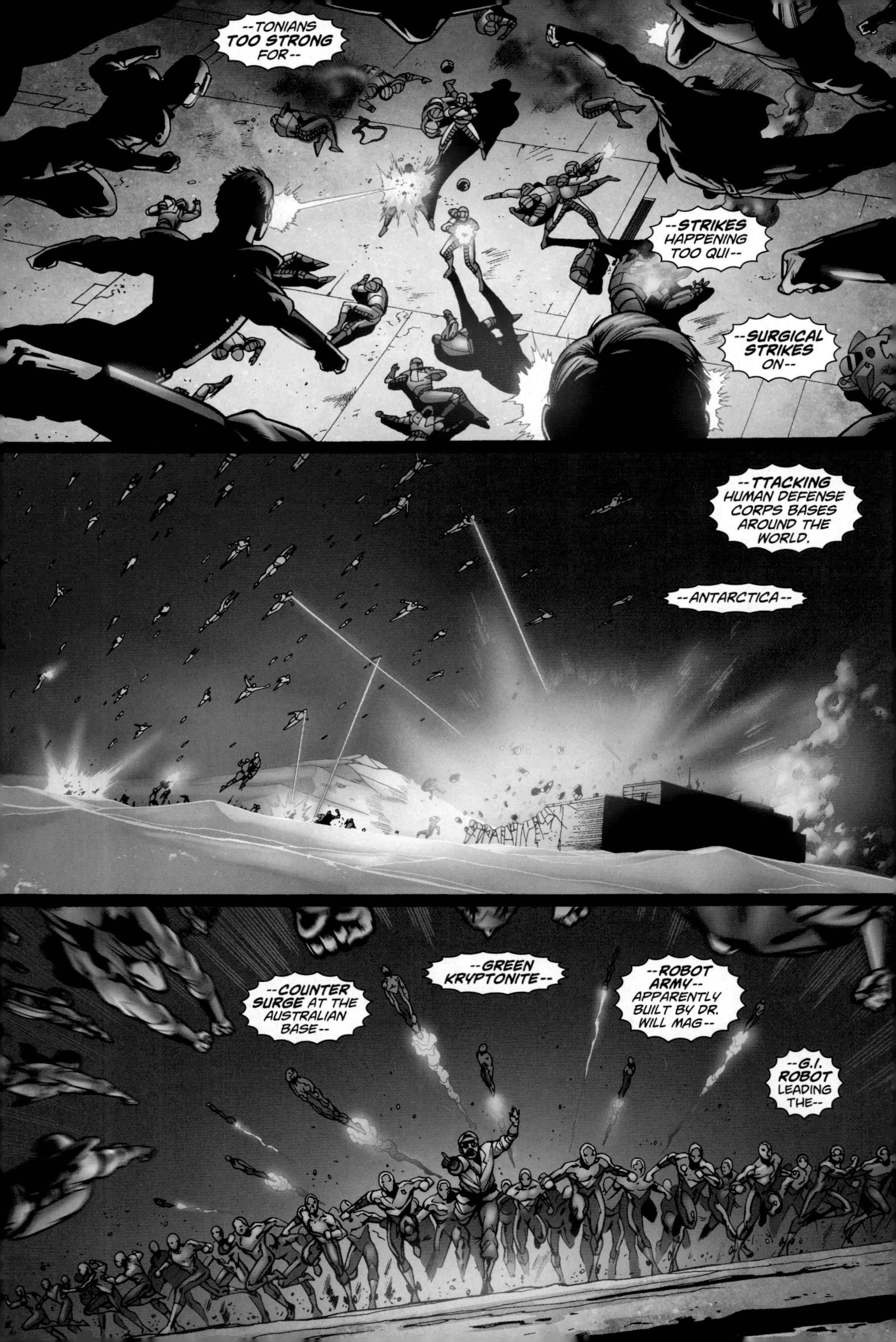
--TONIANS TOO STRONG FOR--
--STRIKES HAPPENING TOO QUI--
--SURGICAL STRIKES ON--
--TTACKING HUMAN DEFENSE CORPS BASES AROUND THE WORLD.
--ANTARCTICA--
--COUNTER SURGE AT THE AUSTRALIAN BASE--
--GREEN KRYPTONITE--
--ROBOT ARMY-- APPARENTLY BUILT BY DR. WILL MAG--
--G.I. ROBOT LEADING THE--

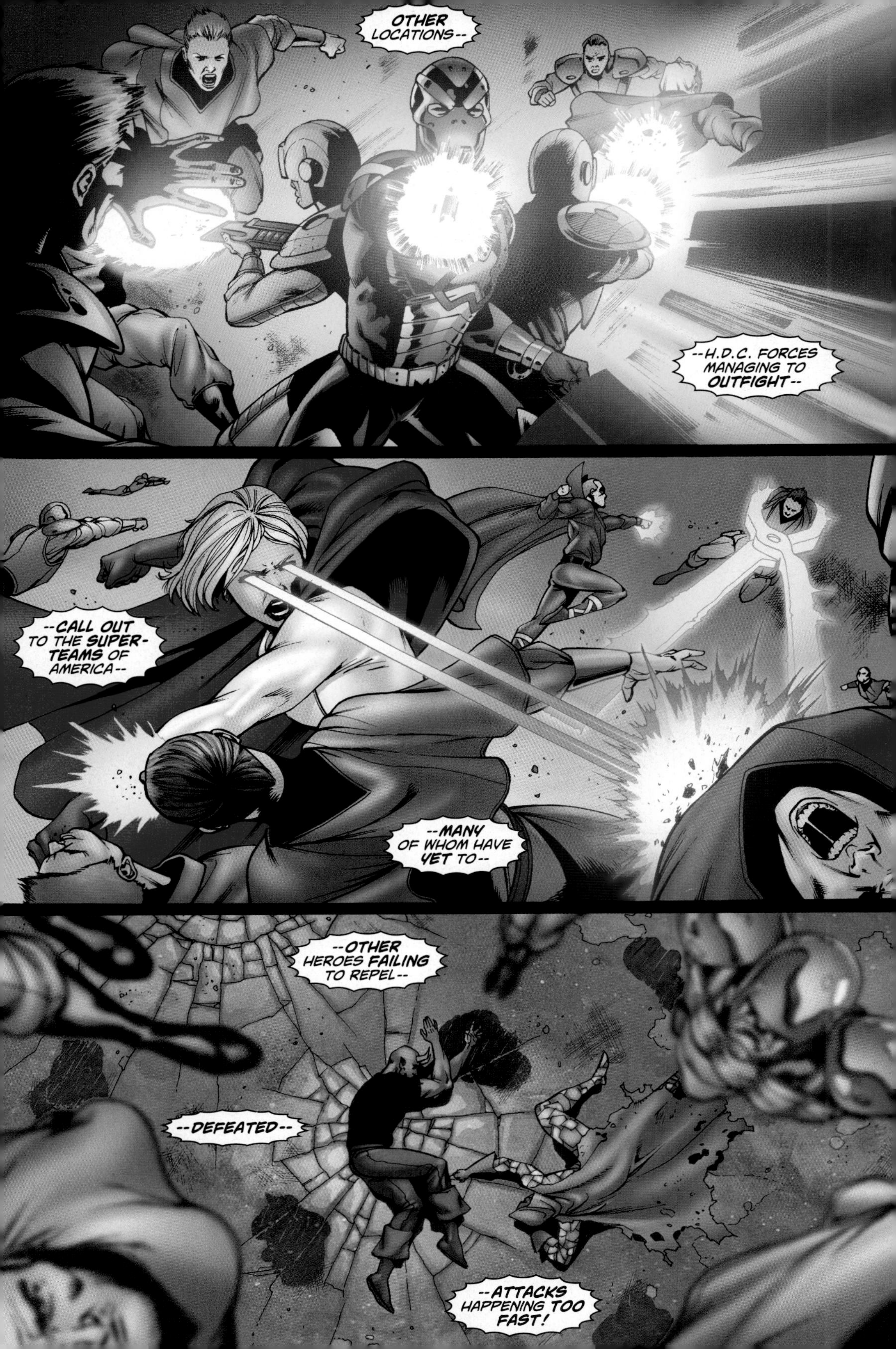
OTHER LOCATIONS--
--H.D.C. FORCES MANAGING TO OUTFIGHT--
--CALL OUT TO THE SUPER-TEAMS OF AMERICA--
--MANY OF WHOM HAVE YET TO--
--OTHER HEROES FAILING TO REPEL--
--DEFEATED--
--ATTACKS HAPPENING TOO FAST!

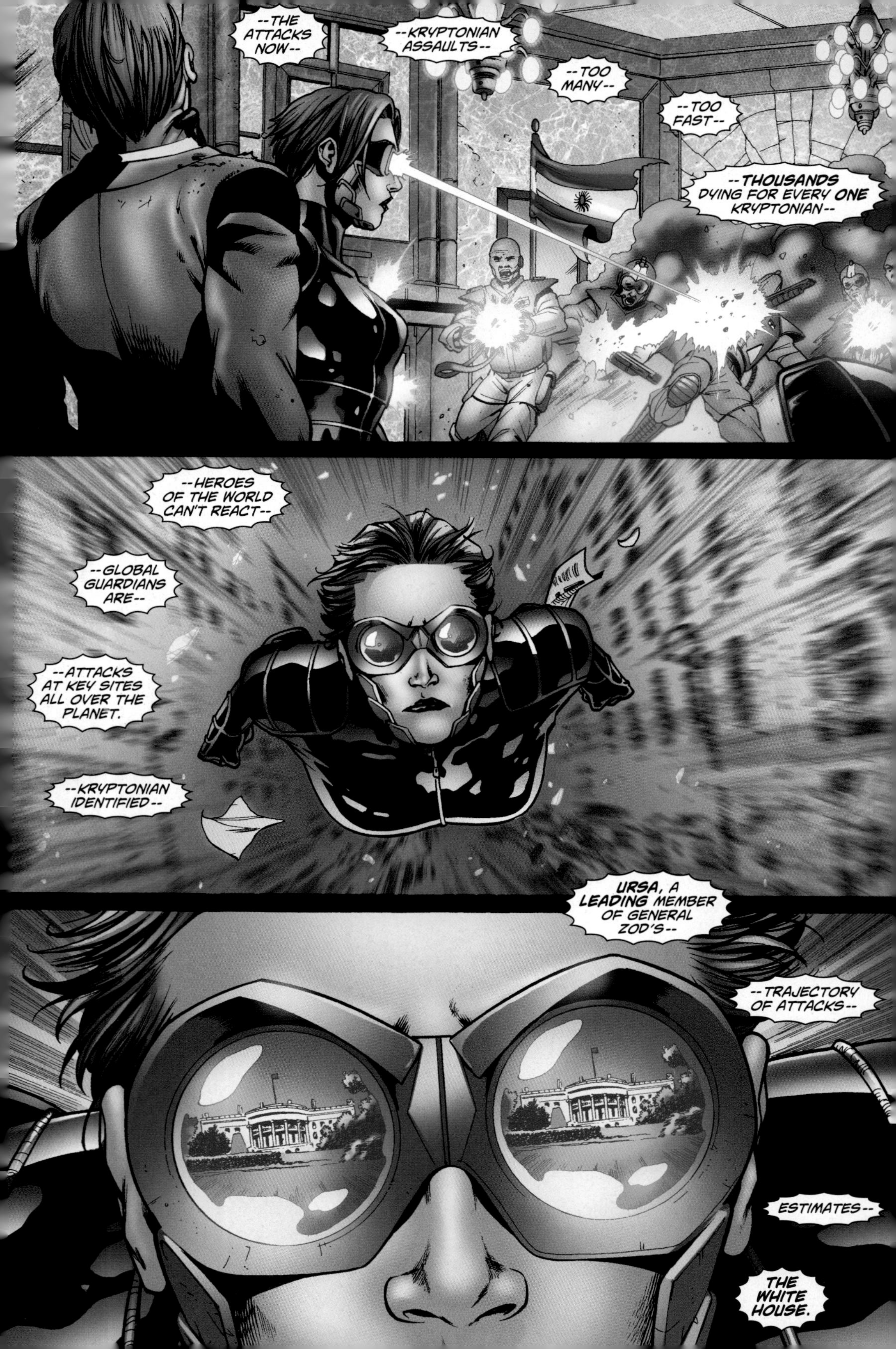

--THE ATTACKS NOW--
--KRYPTONIAN ASSAULTS--
--TOO MANY--
--TOO FAST--
--THOUSANDS DYING FOR EVERY ONE KRYPTONIAN--
--HEROES OF THE WORLD CAN'T REACT--
--GLOBAL GUARDIANS ARE--
--ATTACKS AT KEY SITES ALL OVER THE PLANET.
--KRYPTONIAN IDENTIFIED--
URSA, A LEADING MEMBER OF GENERAL ZOD'S--
--TRAJECTORY OF ATTACKS--
ESTIMATES--
THE WHITE HOUSE.

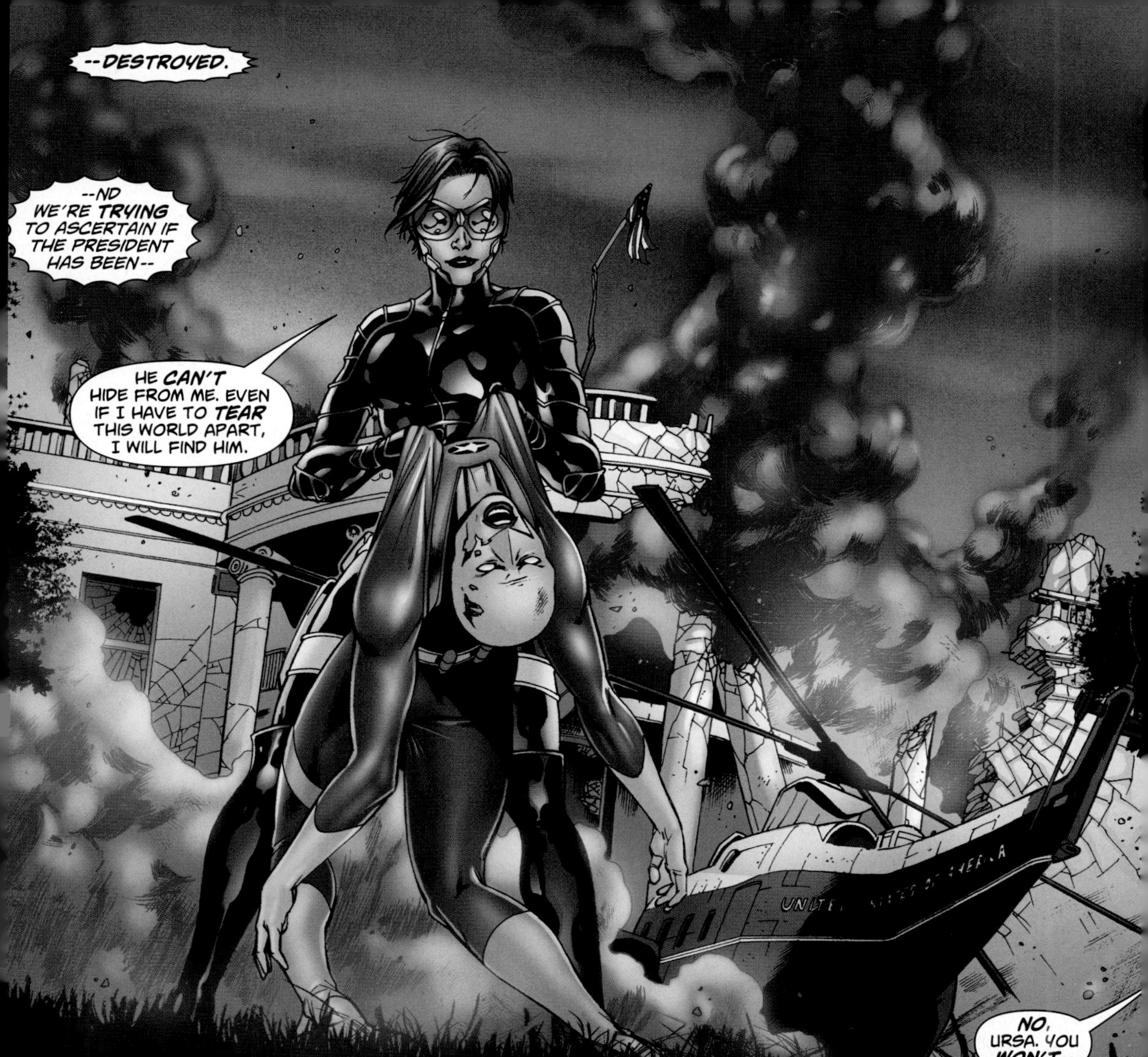
--DESTROYED.
--ND WE'RE TRYING TO ASCERTAIN IF THE PRESIDENT HAS BEEN--
HE CAN'T HIDE FROM ME. EVEN IF I HAVE TO TEAR THIS WORLD APART, I WILL FIND HIM.
NO, URSA. YOU WON'T--
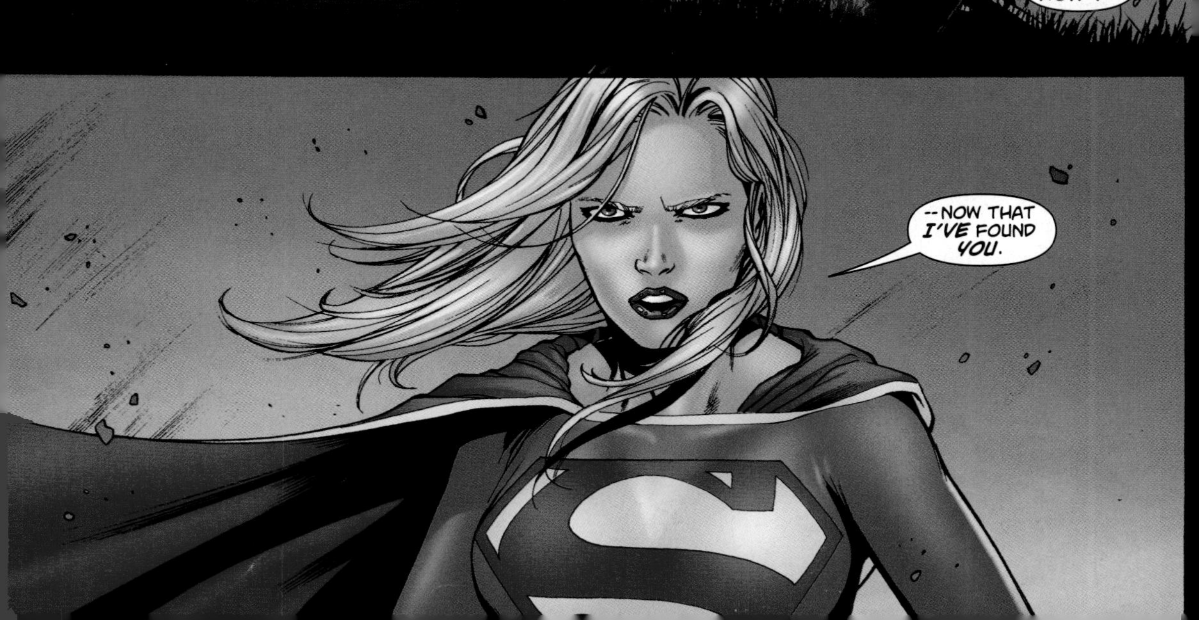
--NOW THAT I'VE FOUND YOU.

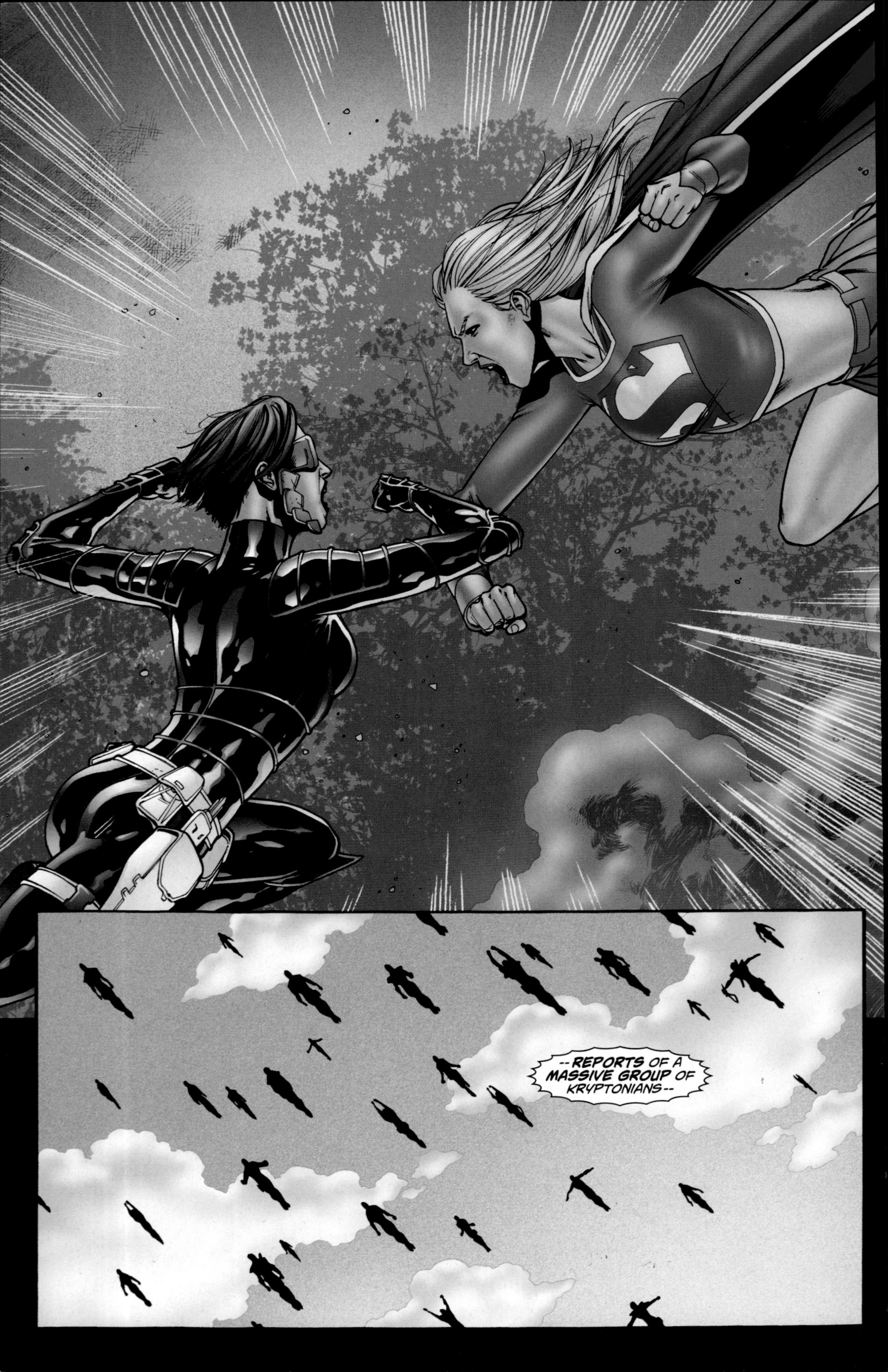
--REPORTS OF A MASSIVE GROUP OF KRYPTONIANS--

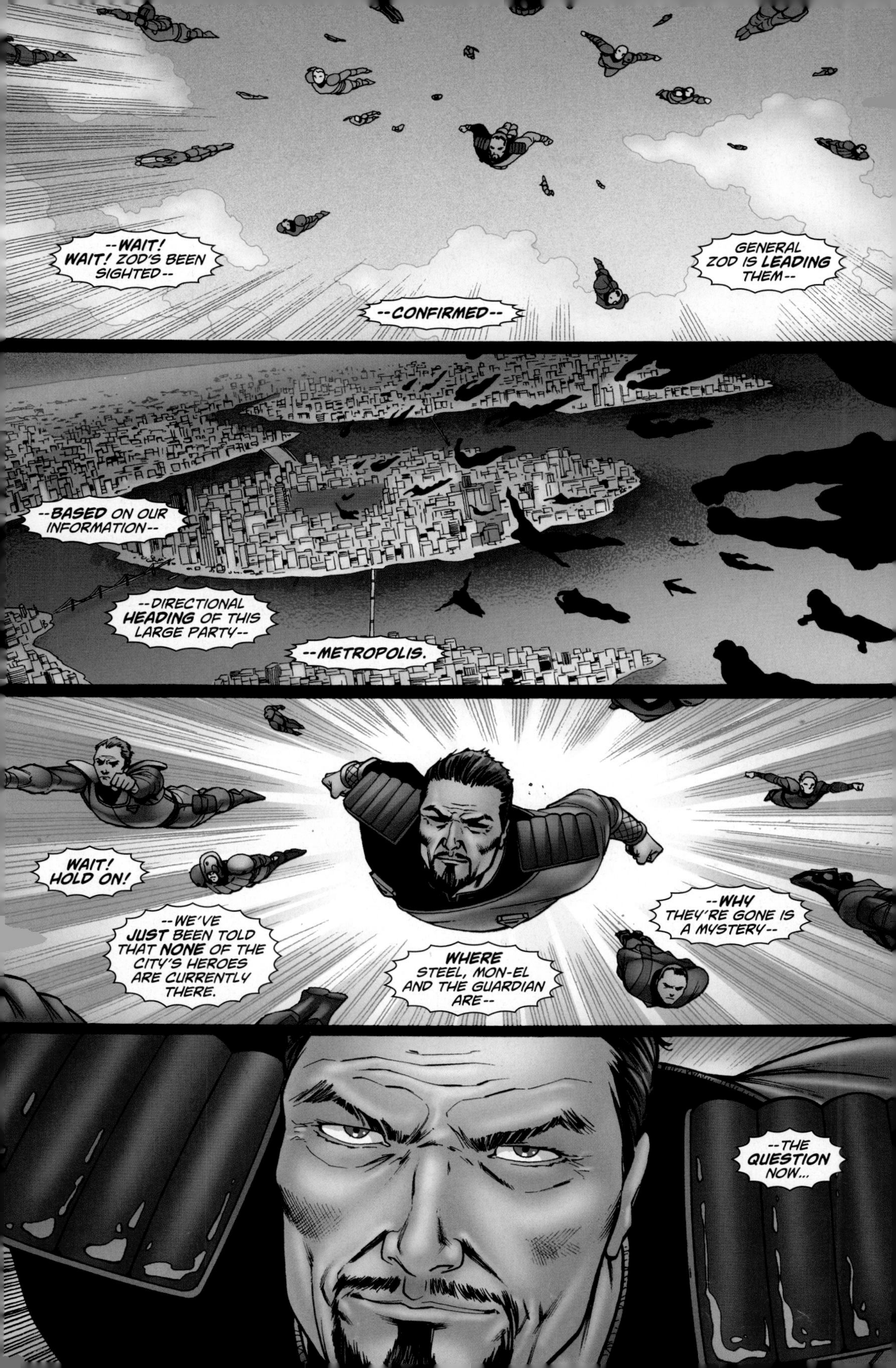
--WAIT! WAIT! ZOD'S BEEN SIGHTED--
--CONFIRMED--
GENERAL ZOD IS LEADING THEM--
--BASED ON OUR INFORMATION--
--DIRECTIONAL HEADING OF THIS LARGE PARTY--
--METROPOLIS.
WAIT! HOLD ON!
--WE'VE JUST BEEN TOLD THAT NONE OF THE CITY'S HEROES ARE CURRENTLY THERE.
WHERE STEEL, MON-EL AND THE GUARDIAN ARE--
--WHY THEY'RE GONE IS A MYSTERY--
--THE QUESTION NOW...

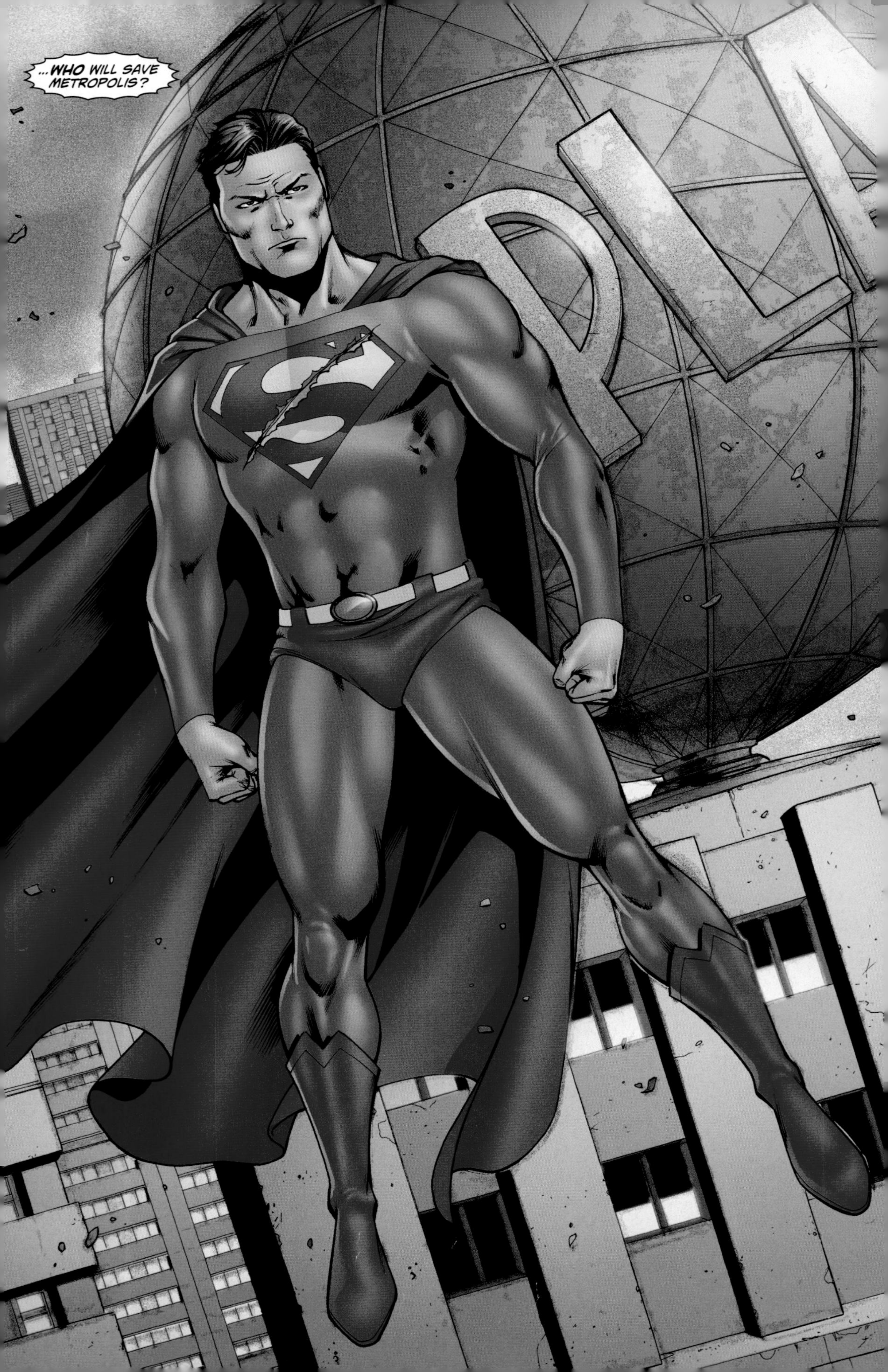
...WHO WILL SAVE METROPOLIS?

PART 4: THE BATTLE FOR SURVIVAL Cover by EDDY BARROWS, J.P. MAYER & ROD REIS

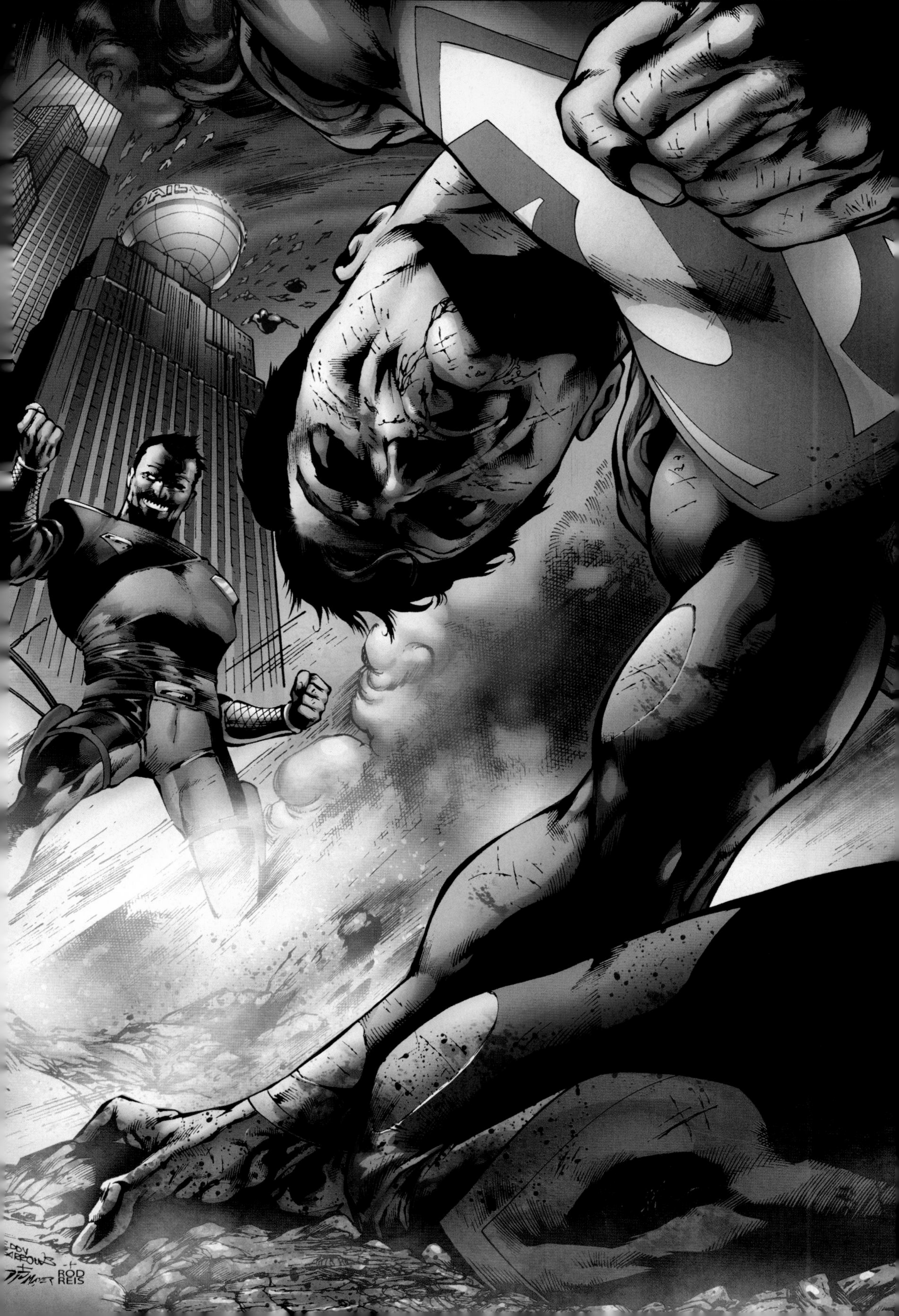

ROD REIS

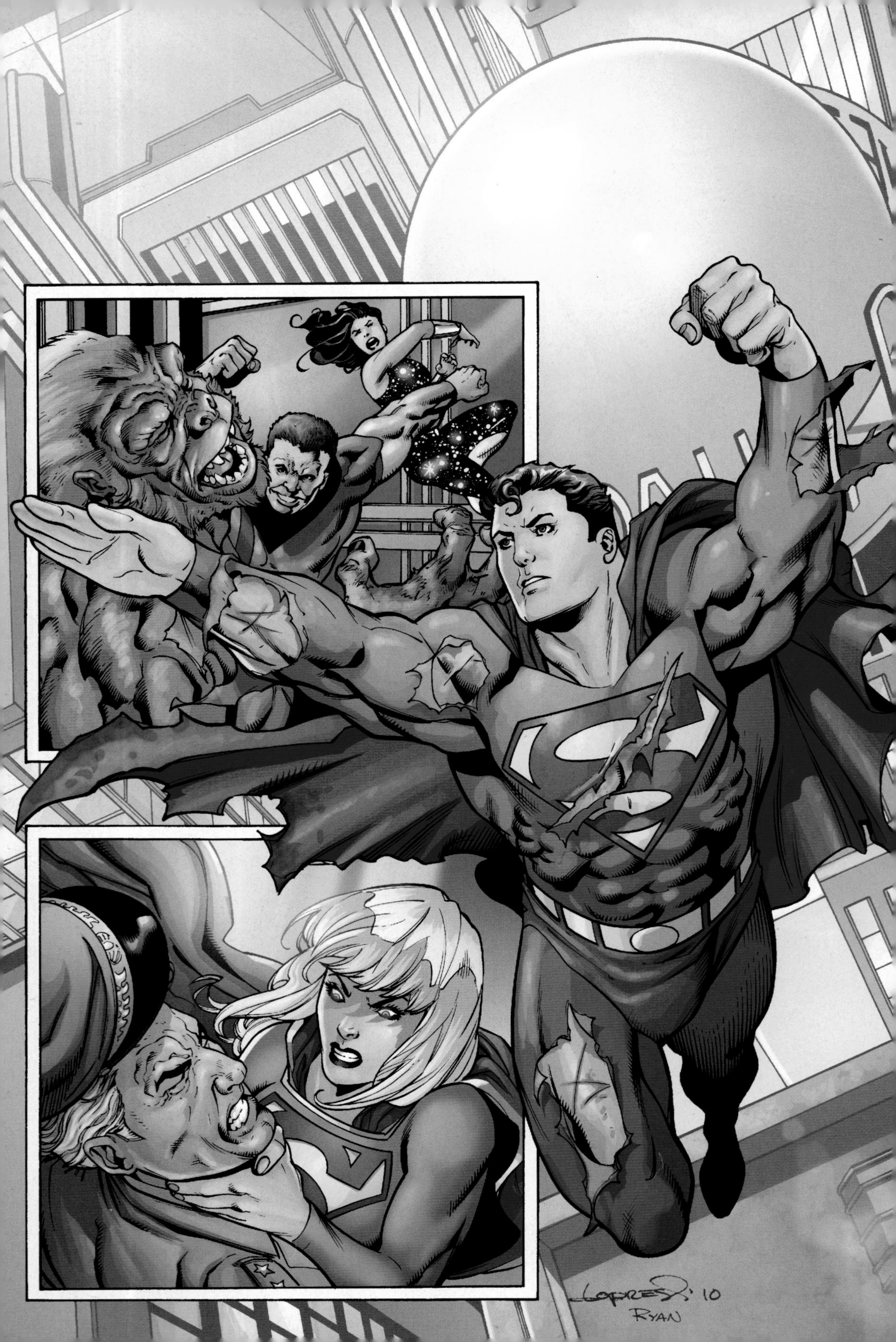

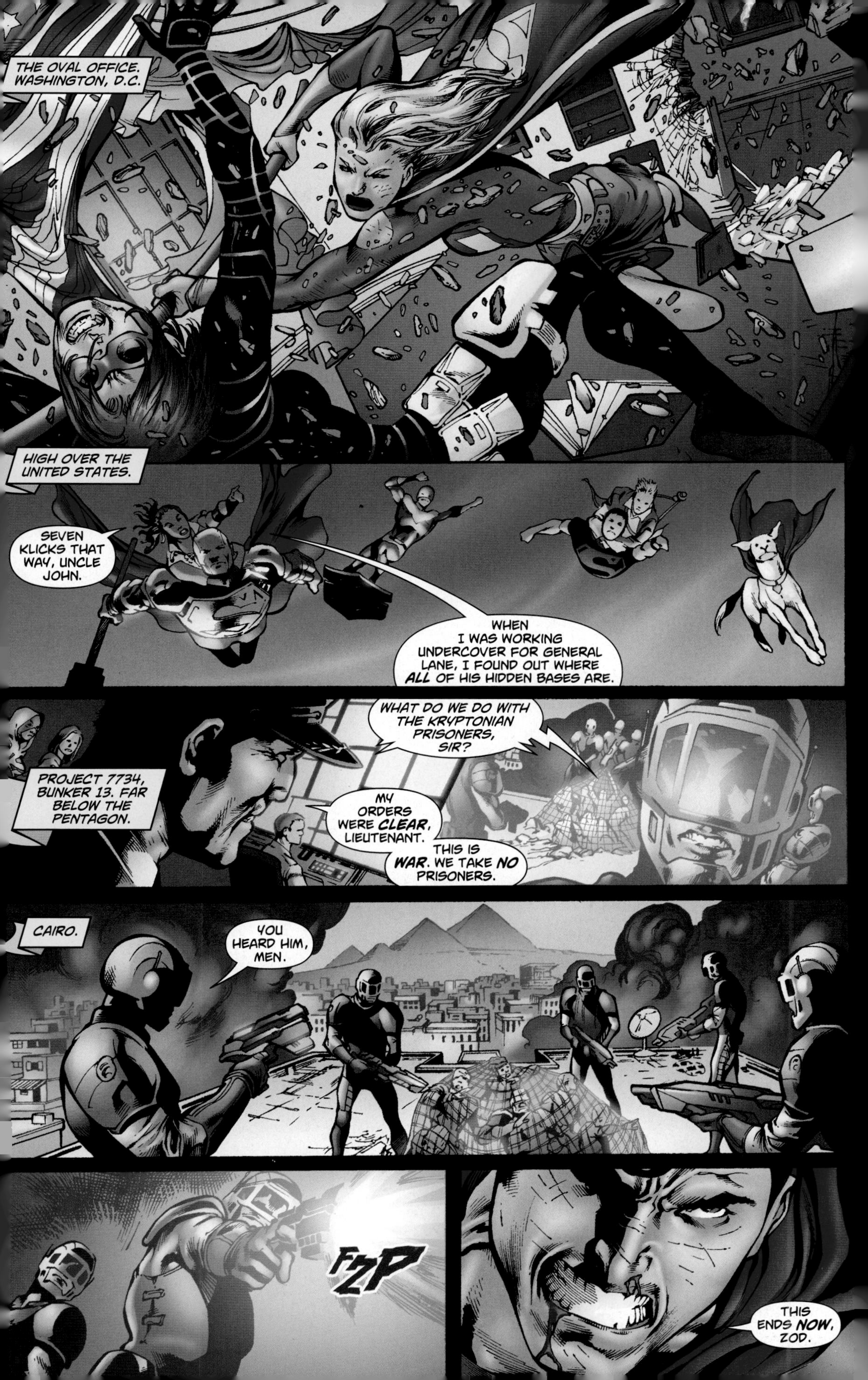
THE OVAL OFFICE. WASHINGTON, D.C.
HIGH OVER THE UNITED STATES.
SEVEN KLICKS THAT WAY, UNCLE JOHN.
WHEN I WAS WORKING UNDERCOVER FOR GENERAL LANE, I FOUND OUT WHERE ALL OF HIS HIDDEN BASES ARE.
PROJECT 7734, BUNKER 13. FAR BELOW THE PENTAGON.
WHAT DO WE DO WITH THE KRYPTONIAN PRISONERS, SIR?
MY ORDERS WERE CLEAR, LIEUTENANT.
THIS IS WAR. WE TAKE NO PRISONERS.
CAIRO.
YOU HEARD HIM, MEN.
FZZP
THIS ENDS NOW, ZOD.

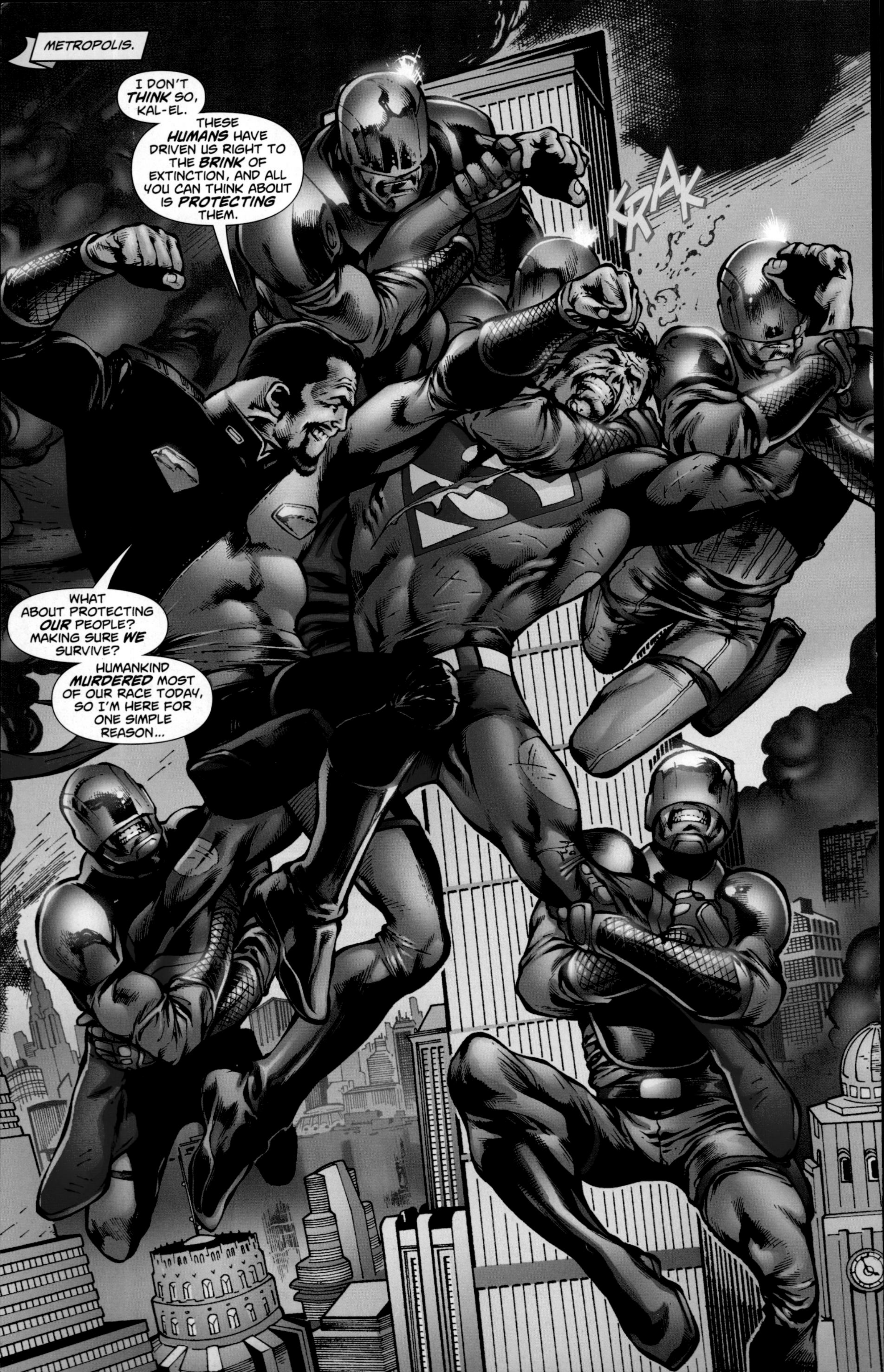
METROPOLIS.
I DON'T THINK SO, KAL-EL.
THESE HUMANS HAVE DRIVEN US RIGHT TO THE BRINK OF EXTINCTION, AND ALL YOU CAN THINK ABOUT IS PROTECTING THEM.
KRAK
WHAT ABOUT PROTECTING OUR PEOPLE? MAKING SURE WE SURVIVE?
HUMANKIND MURDERED MOST OF OUR RACE TODAY, SO I'M HERE FOR ONE SIMPLE REASON...

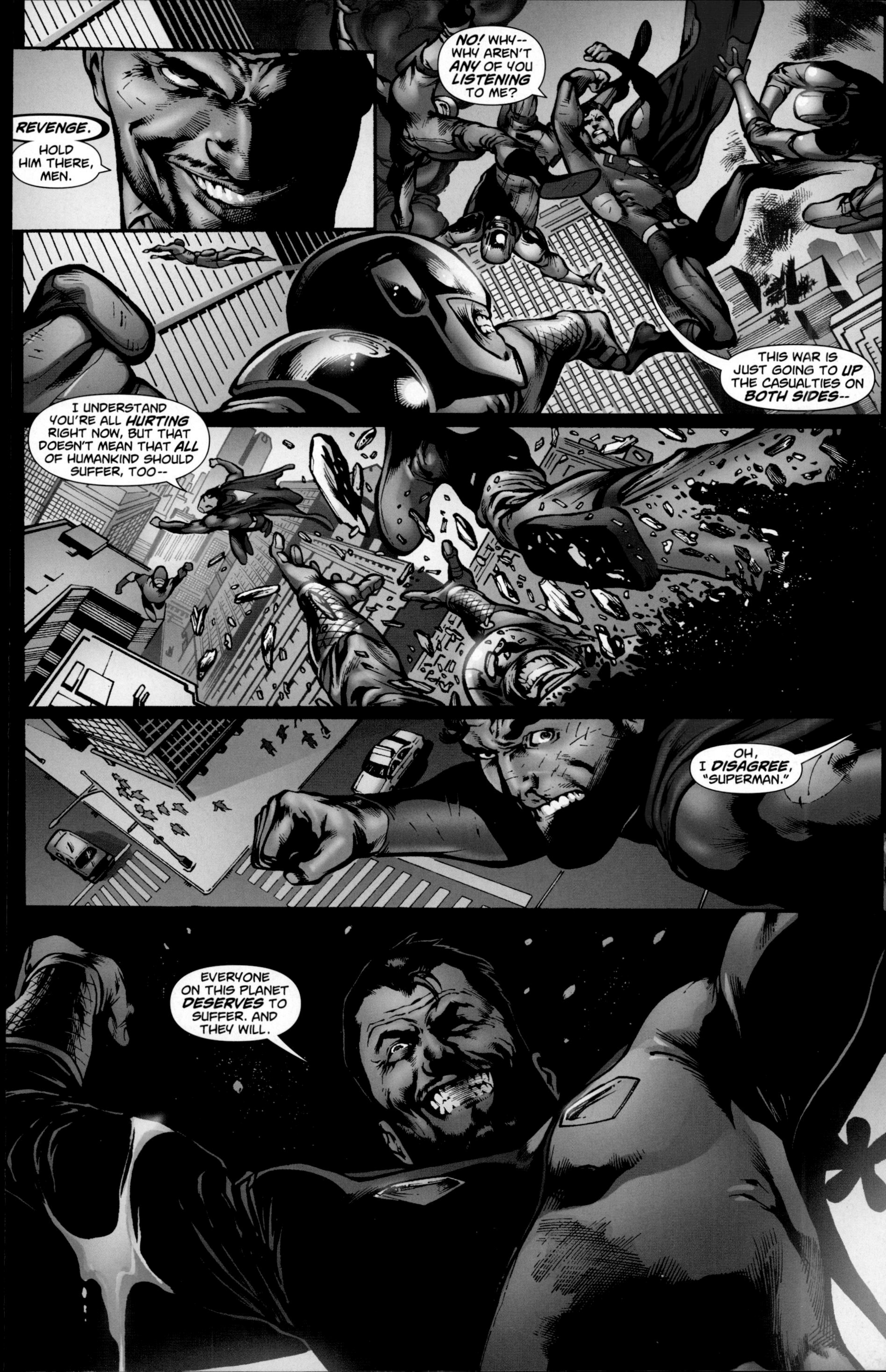

REVENGE.
HOLD HIM THERE, MEN.
NO! WHY-- WHY AREN'T ANY OF YOU LISTENING TO ME?
THIS WAR IS JUST GOING TO UP THE CASUALTIES ON BOTH SIDES--
I UNDERSTAND YOU'RE ALL HURTING RIGHT NOW, BUT THAT DOESN'T MEAN THAT ALL OF HUMANKIND SHOULD SUFFER, TOO--
OH, I DISAGREE, "SUPERMAN."
EVERYONE ON THIS PLANET DESERVES TO SUFFER. AND THEY WILL.

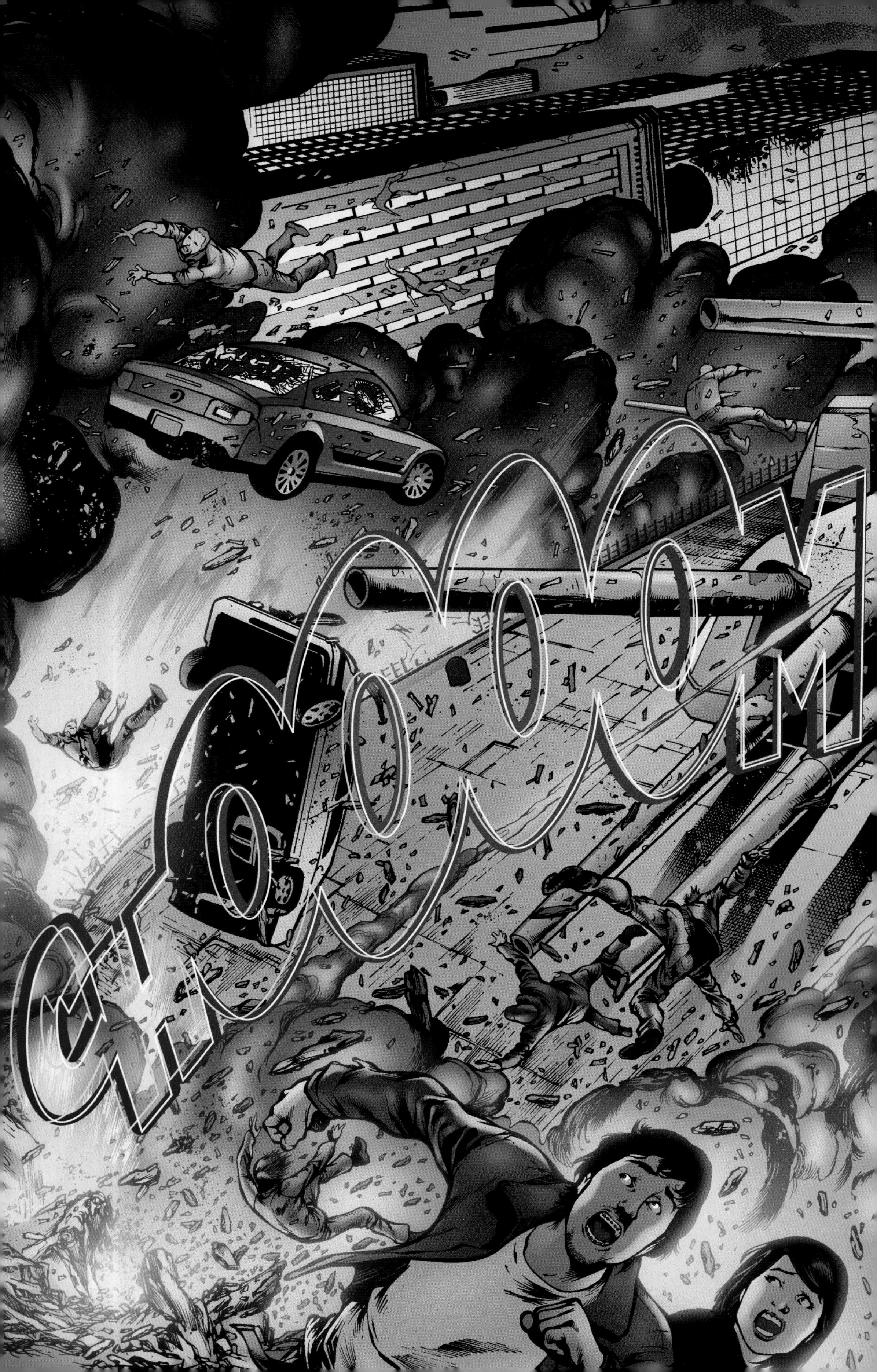
CHOOOOOOOOM

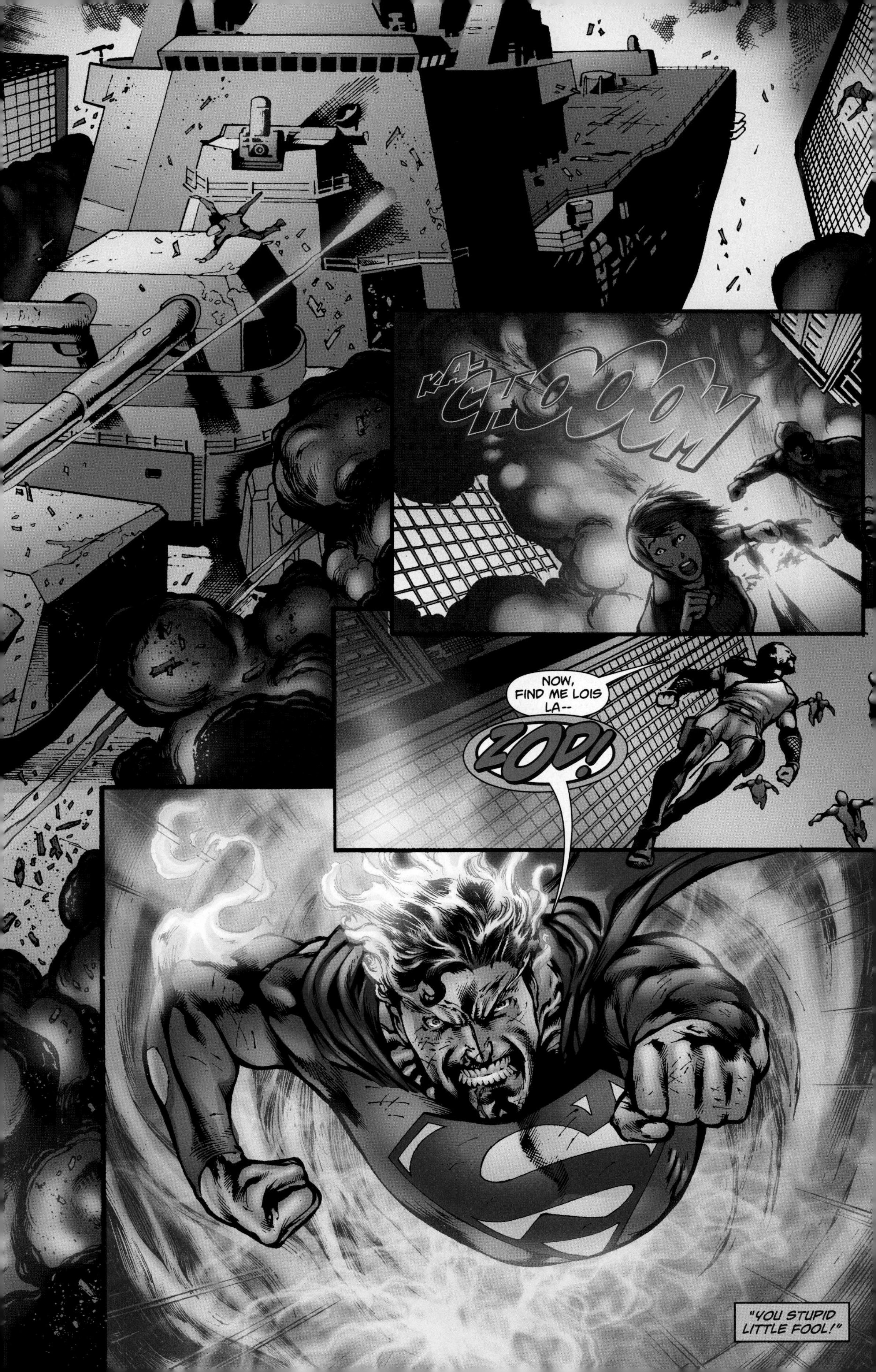
KA-CHOOOOM
NOW, FIND ME LOIS LA--
ZOD!
"YOU STUPID LITTLE FOOL!"

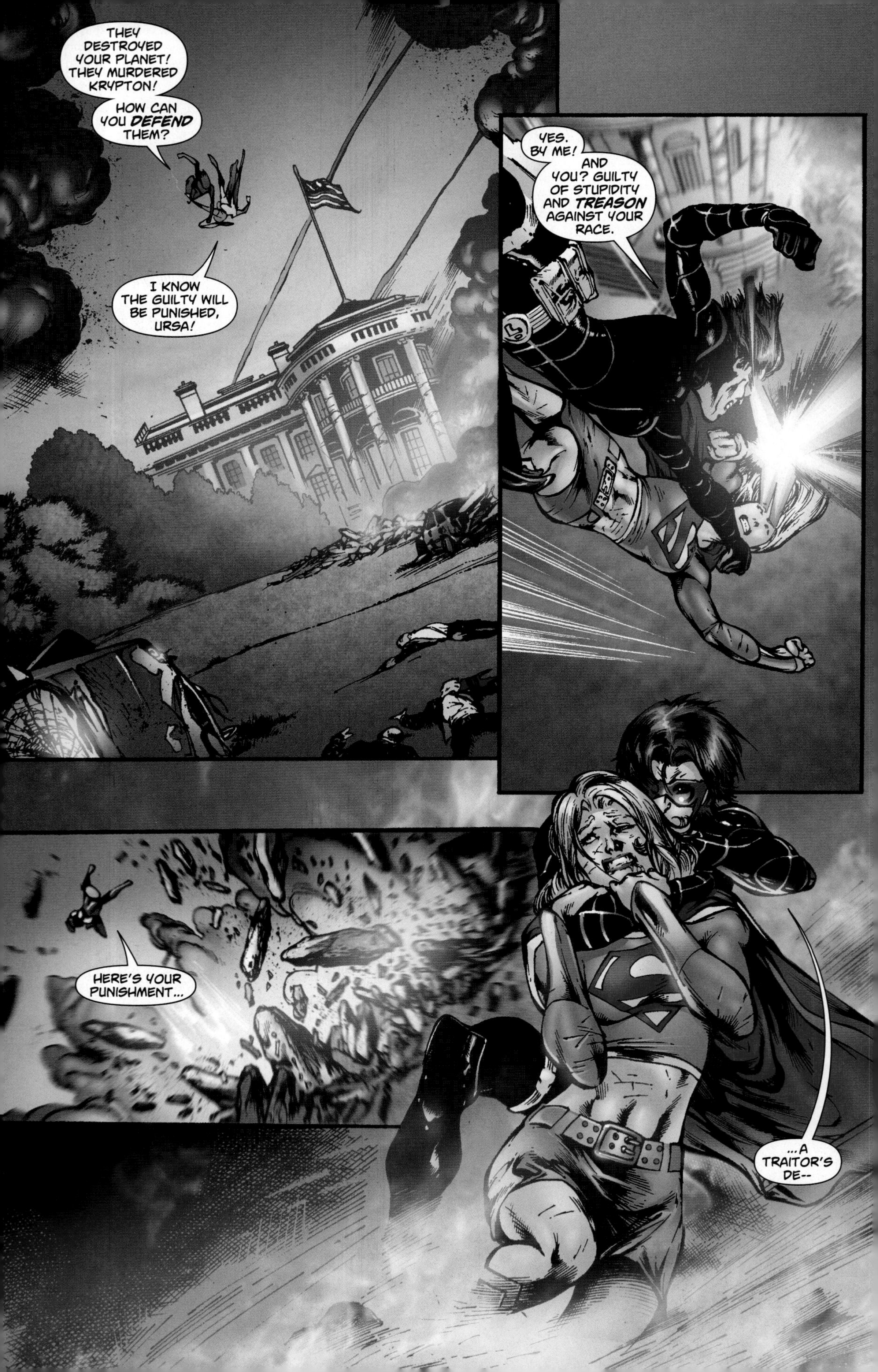
THEY DESTROYED YOUR PLANET! THEY MURDERED KRYPTON!
HOW CAN YOU DEFEND THEM?
I KNOW THE GUILTY WILL BE PUNISHED, URSA!
YES. BY ME!
AND YOU? GUILTY OF STUPIDITY AND TREASON AGAINST YOUR RACE.
HERE'S YOUR PUNISHMENT...
...A TRAITOR'S DE--

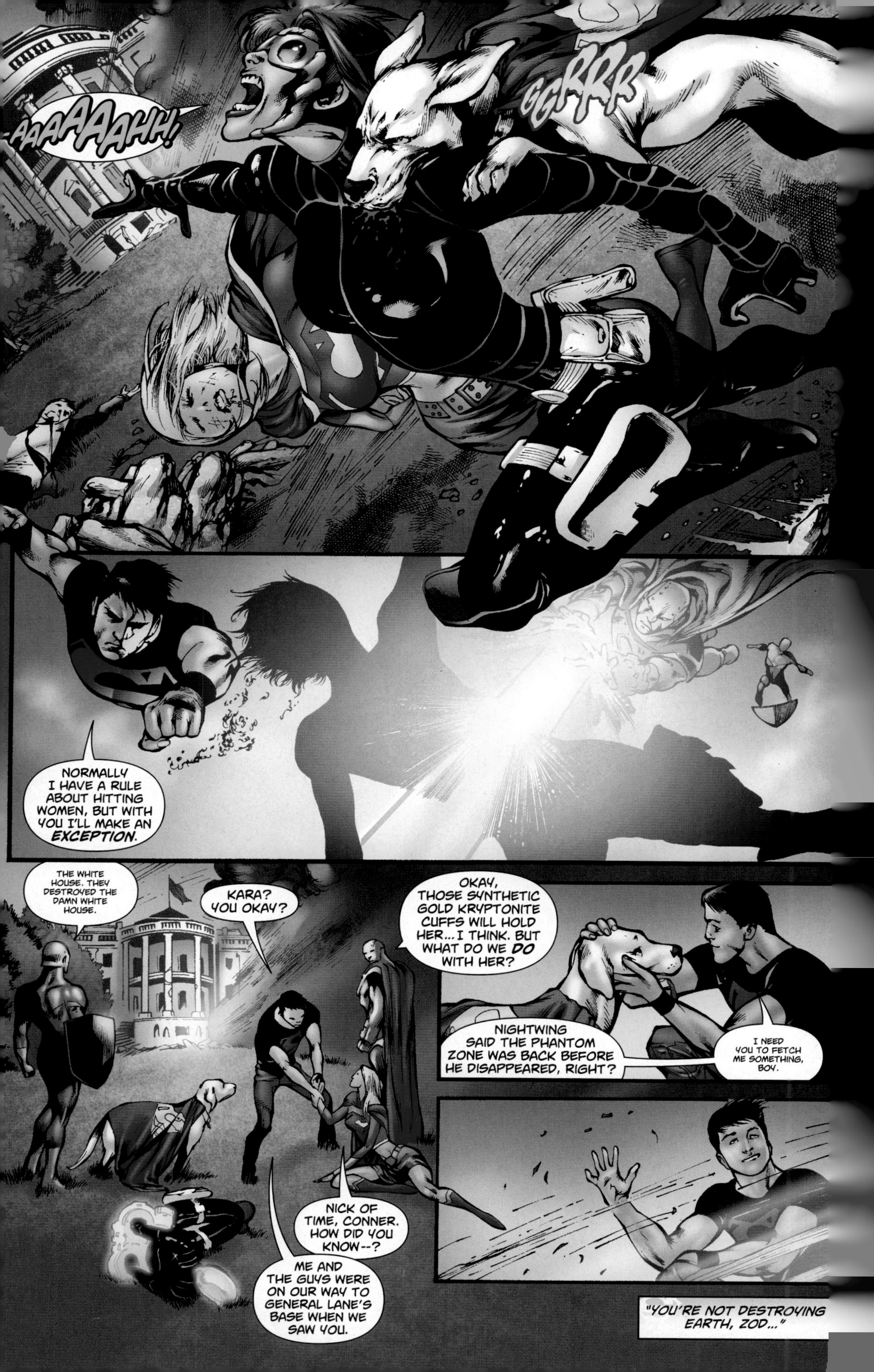
AAAAAAAHH!
GGRRRR
NORMALLY I HAVE A RULE ABOUT HITTING WOMEN, BUT WITH YOU I'LL MAKE AN *EXCEPTION*.
THE WHITE HOUSE. THEY DESTROYED THE DAMN WHITE HOUSE.
KARA? YOU OKAY?
NICK OF TIME, CONNER. HOW DID YOU KNOW--?
ME AND THE GUYS WERE ON OUR WAY TO GENERAL LANE'S BASE WHEN WE SAW YOU.
OKAY, THOSE SYNTHETIC GOLD KRYPTONITE CUFFS WILL HOLD HER... I THINK. BUT WHAT DO WE *DO* WITH HER?
NIGHTWING SAID THE PHANTOM ZONE WAS BACK BEFORE HE DISAPPEARED, RIGHT?
I NEED YOU TO FETCH ME SOMETHING, BOY.
"YOU'RE NOT DESTROYING EARTH, ZOD..."

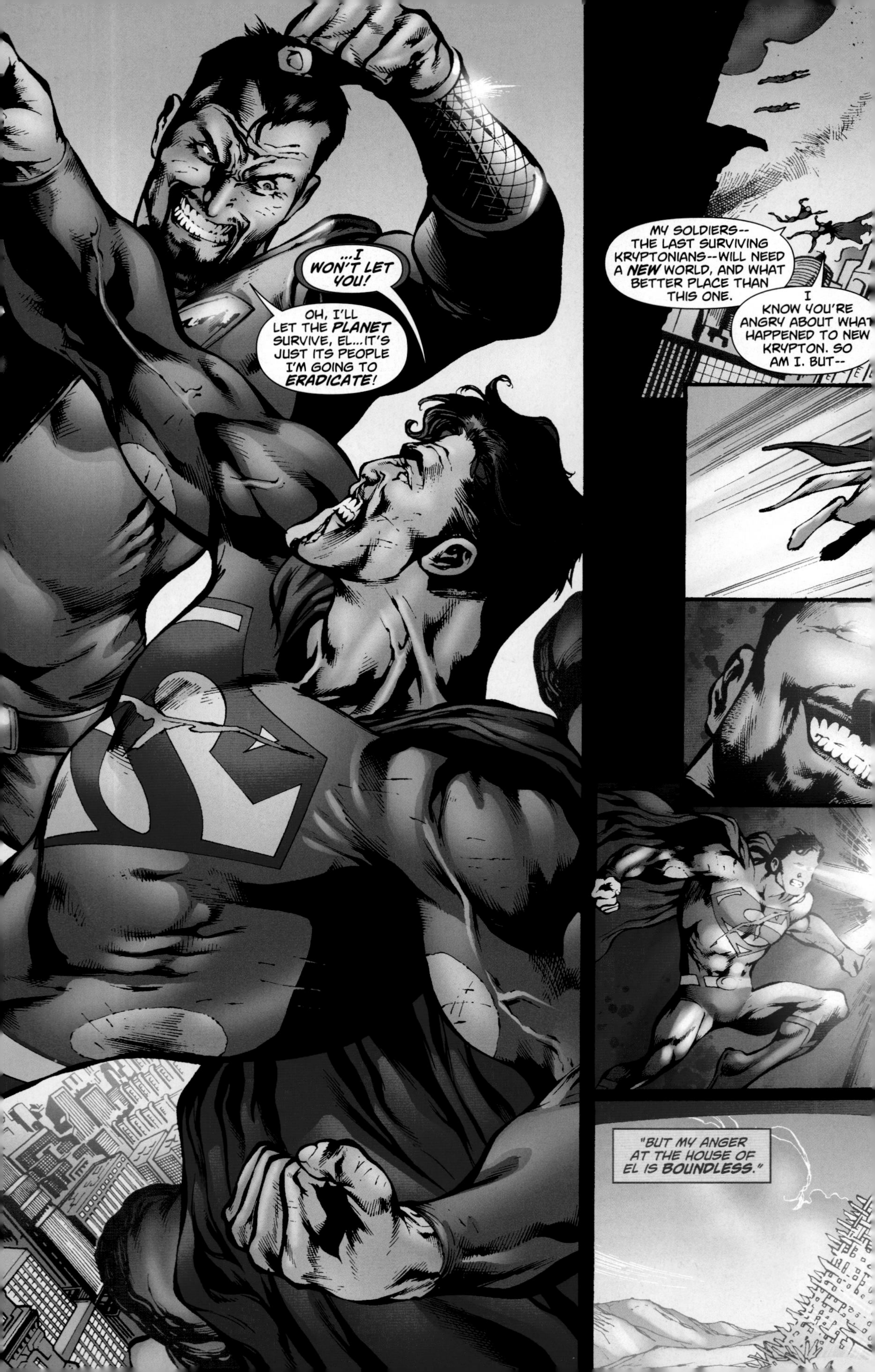

...I WON'T LET YOU!
OH, I'LL LET THE PLANET SURVIVE, EL...IT'S JUST ITS PEOPLE I'M GOING TO ERADICATE!
MY SOLDIERS-- THE LAST SURVIVING KRYPTONIANS--WILL NEED A NEW WORLD, AND WHAT BETTER PLACE THAN THIS ONE.
I KNOW YOU'RE ANGRY ABOUT WHAT HAPPENED TO NEW KRYPTON. SO AM I. BUT--
"BUT MY ANGER AT THE HOUSE OF EL IS BOUNDLESS."

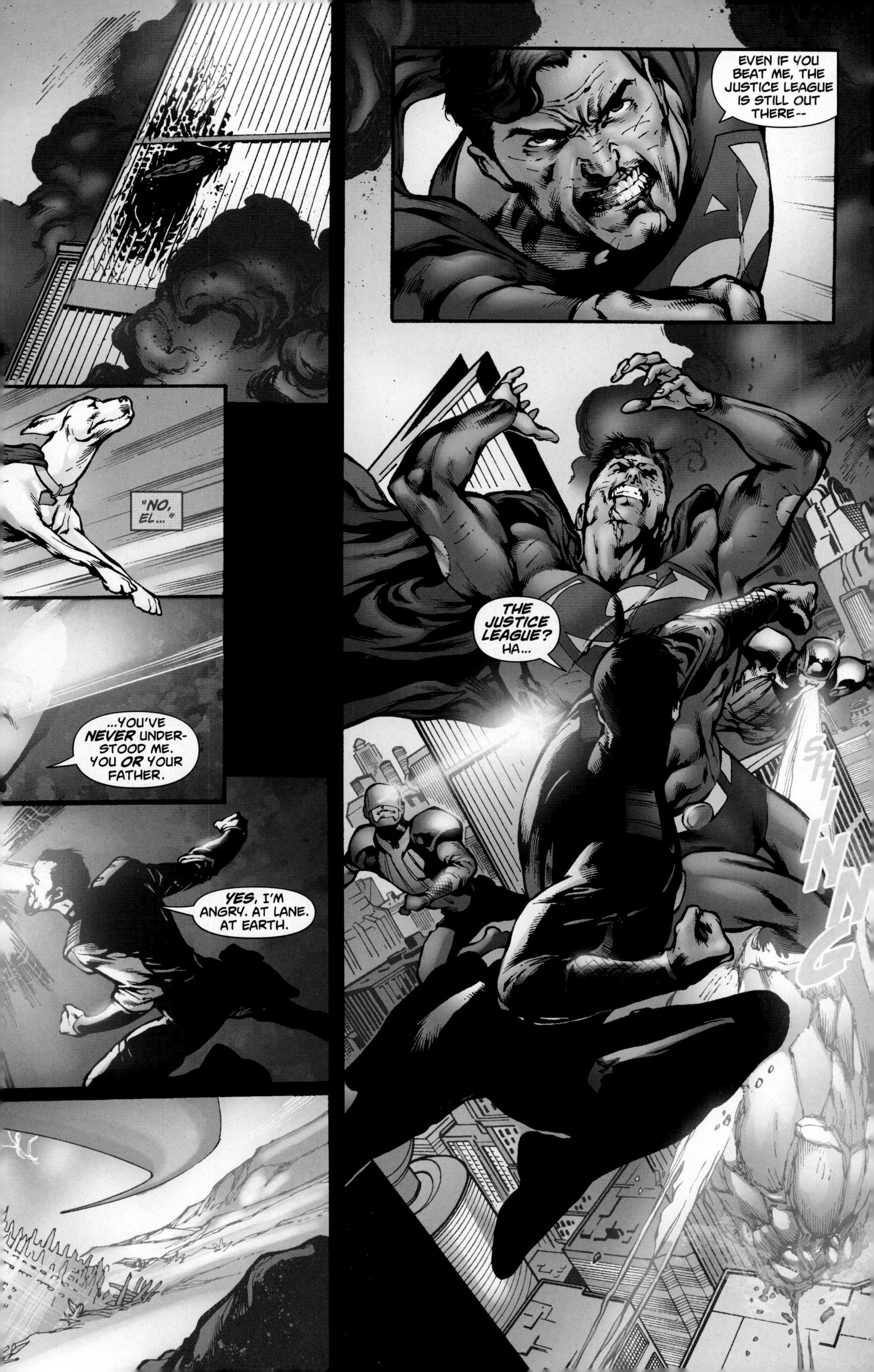
"NO, EL..."
...YOU'VE NEVER UNDERSTOOD ME. YOU OR YOUR FATHER.
YES, I'M ANGRY. AT LANE. AT EARTH.
EVEN IF YOU BEAT ME, THE JUSTICE LEAGUE IS STILL OUT THERE--
THE JUSTICE LEAGUE? HA...
SHIIINNG

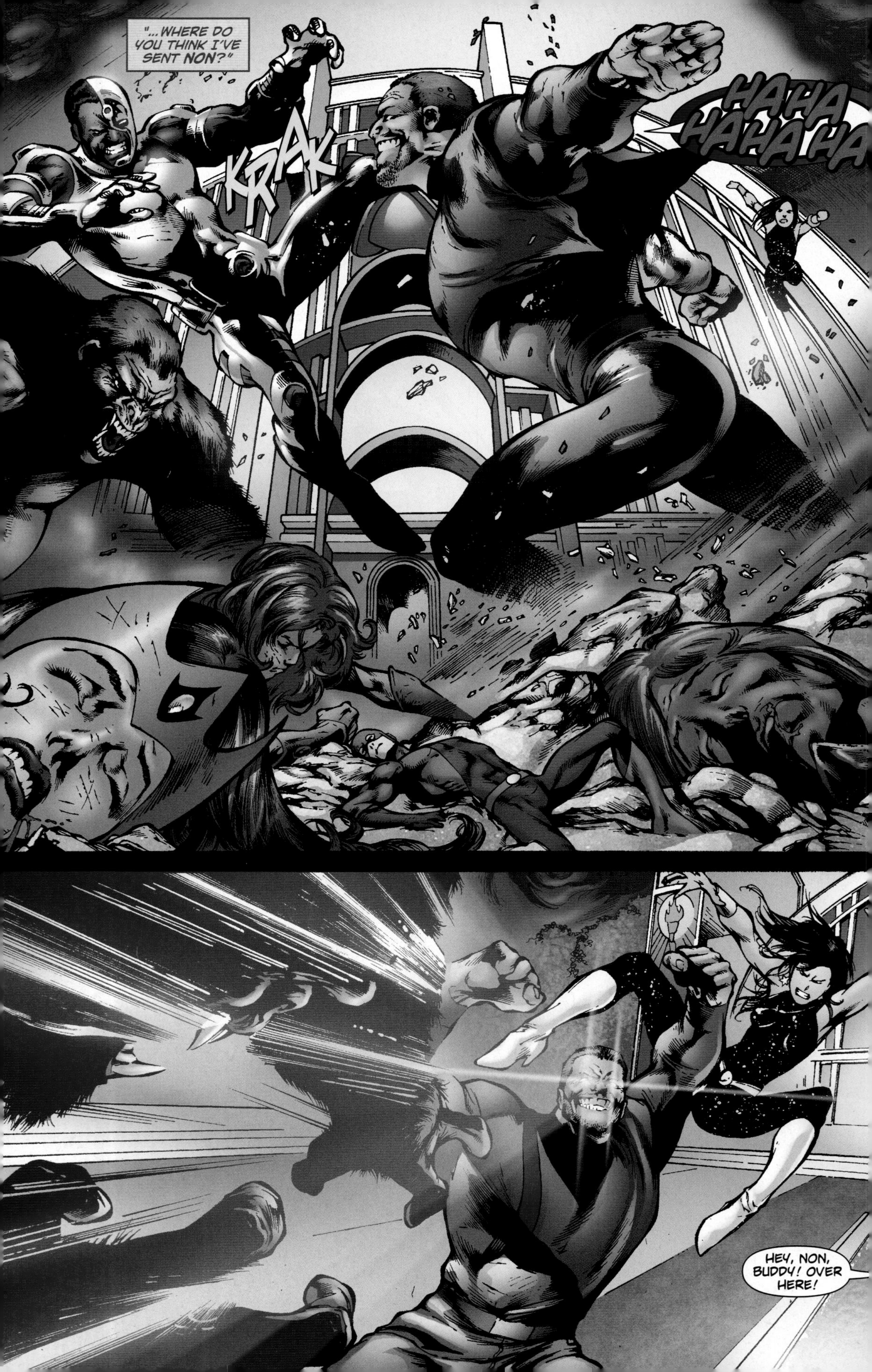
"...WHERE DO YOU THINK I'VE SENT NON?"
KRAK
HAHA HAHA HA HA
HEY, NON, BUDDY! OVER HERE!

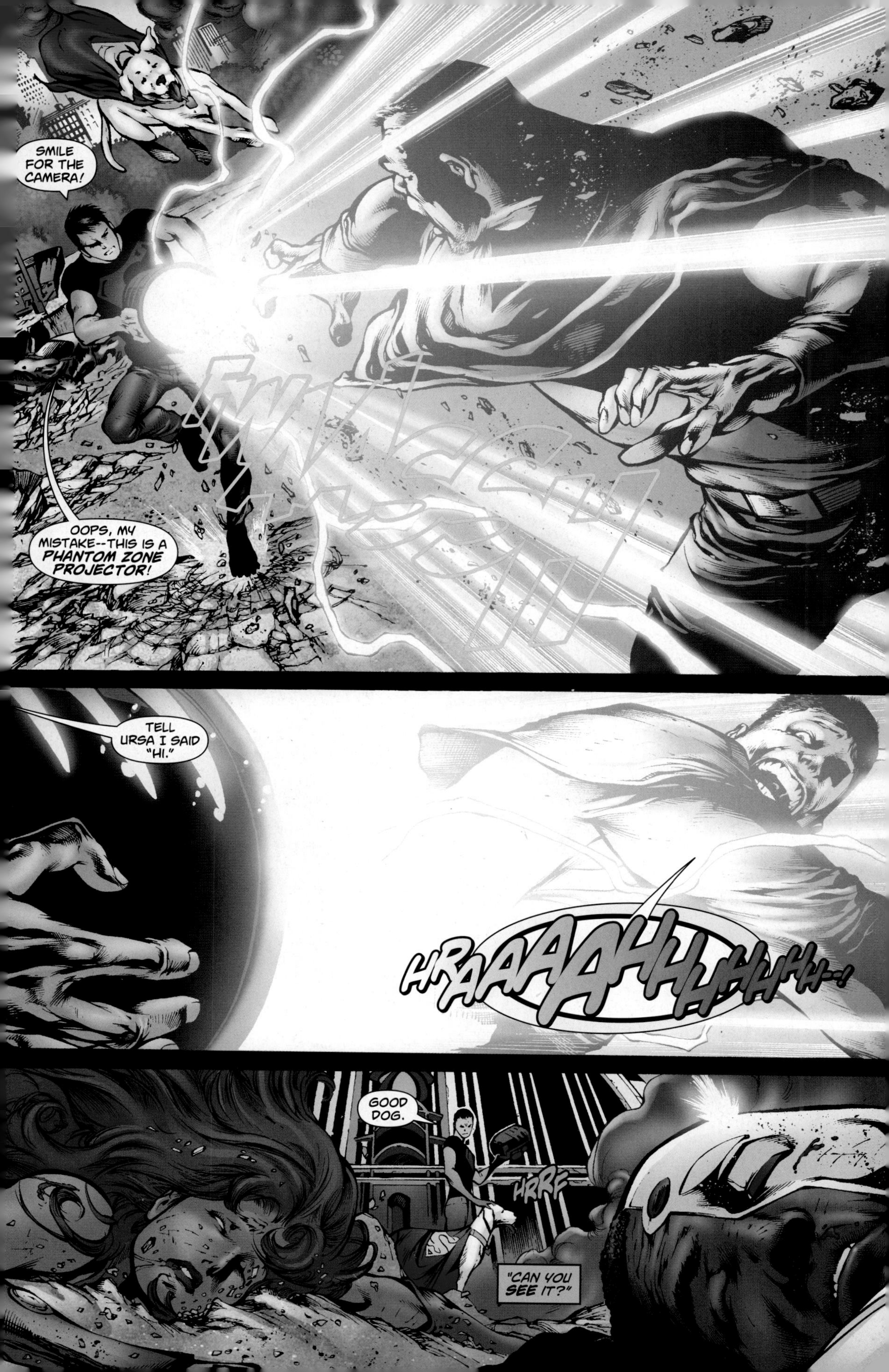

SMILE FOR THE CAMERA!
FWAAAAAAAAAAAAAAAA
OOPS, MY MISTAKE--THIS IS A PHANTOM ZONE PROJECTOR!
TELL URSA I SAID "HI."
HRAAAAAHHHHHH--!
GOOD DOG.
HRRF
"CAN YOU SEE IT?"

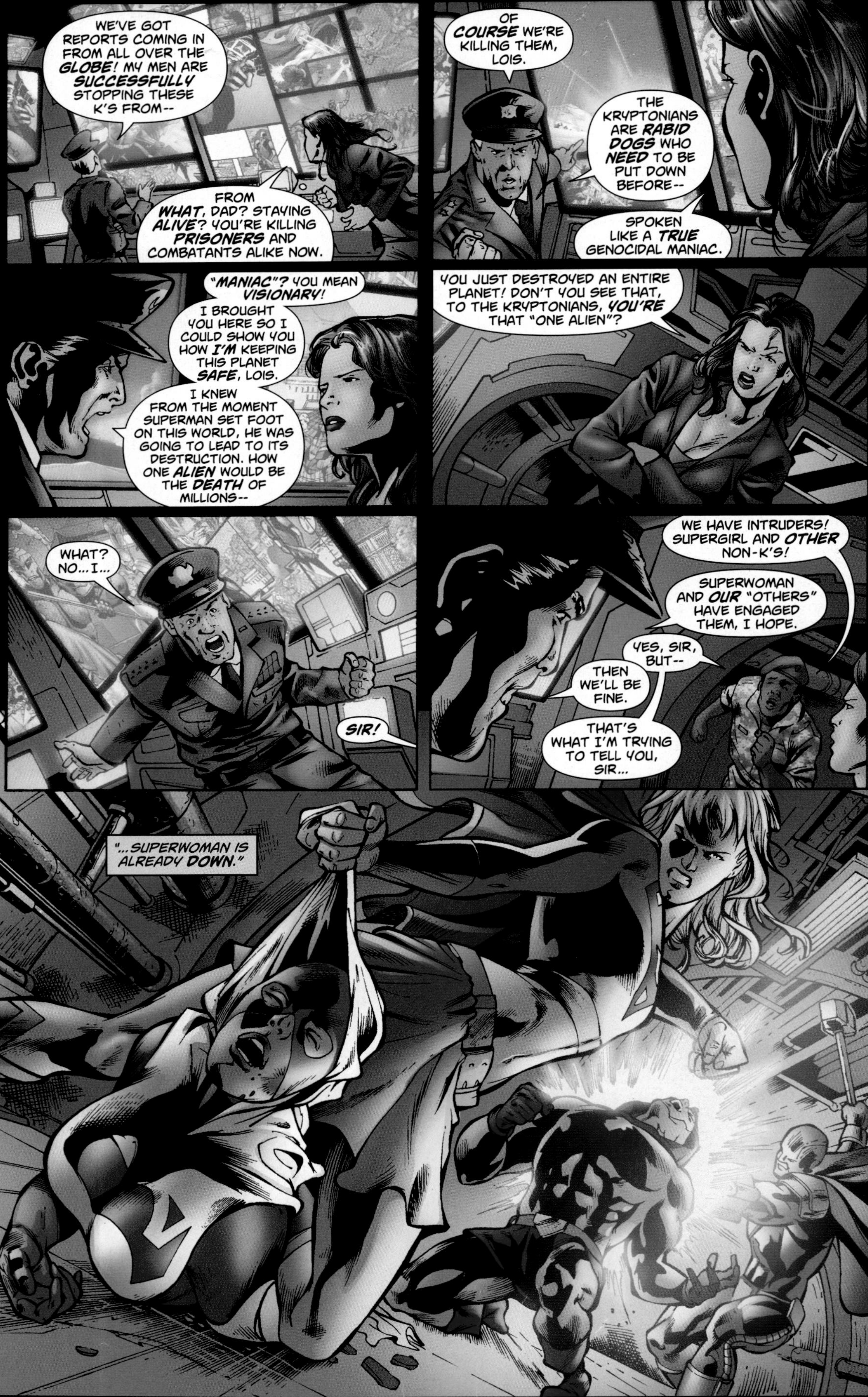
WE'VE GOT REPORTS COMING IN FROM ALL OVER THE GLOBE! MY MEN ARE SUCCESSFULLY STOPPING THESE K'S FROM--
FROM WHAT, DAD? STAYING ALIVE? YOU'RE KILLING PRISONERS AND COMBATANTS ALIKE NOW.
OF COURSE WE'RE KILLING THEM, LOIS.
THE KRYPTONIANS ARE RABID DOGS WHO NEED TO BE PUT DOWN BEFORE--
SPOKEN LIKE A TRUE GENOCIDAL MANIAC.
"MANIAC"? YOU MEAN VISIONARY!
I BROUGHT YOU HERE SO I COULD SHOW YOU HOW I'M KEEPING THIS PLANET SAFE, LOIS.
I KNEW FROM THE MOMENT SUPERMAN SET FOOT ON THIS WORLD, HE WAS GOING TO LEAD TO ITS DESTRUCTION. HOW ONE ALIEN WOULD BE THE DEATH OF MILLIONS--
YOU JUST DESTROYED AN ENTIRE PLANET! DON'T YOU SEE THAT, TO THE KRYPTONIANS, YOU'RE THAT "ONE ALIEN"?
WHAT? NO... I...
SIR!
WE HAVE INTRUDERS! SUPERGIRL AND OTHER NON-K'S!
SUPERWOMAN AND OUR "OTHERS" HAVE ENGAGED THEM, I HOPE.
YES, SIR, BUT--
THEN WE'LL BE FINE.
THAT'S WHAT I'M TRYING TO TELL YOU, SIR...
"...SUPERWOMAN IS ALREADY DOWN."

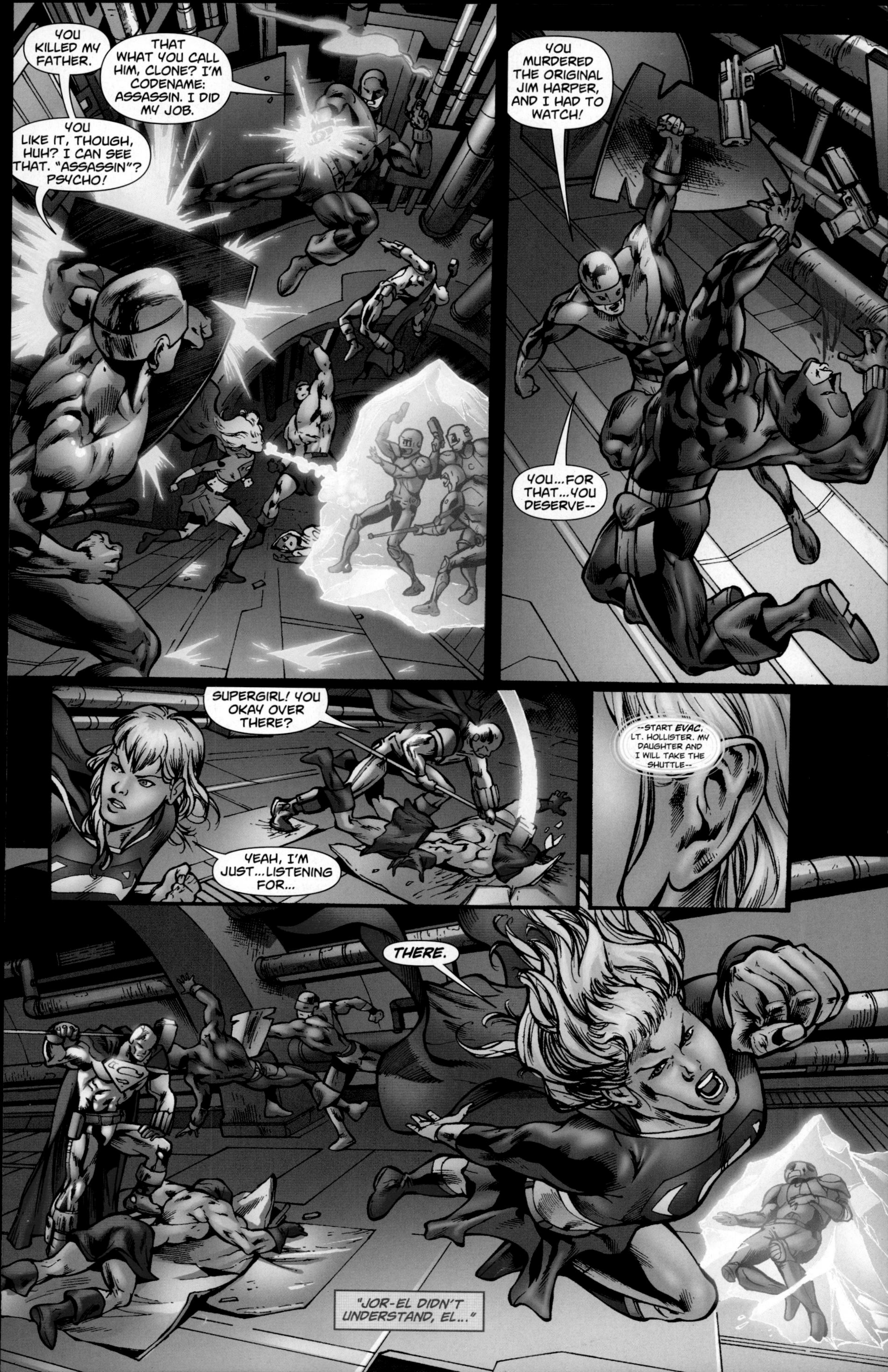
YOU KILLED MY FATHER.
THAT WHAT YOU CALL HIM, CLONE? I'M CODENAME: ASSASSIN. I DID MY JOB.
YOU LIKE IT, THOUGH, HUH? I CAN SEE THAT. "ASSASSIN"? PSYCHO!
YOU MURDERED THE ORIGINAL JIM HARPER, AND I HAD TO WATCH!
YOU...FOR THAT...YOU DESERVE--
SUPERGIRL! YOU OKAY OVER THERE?
YEAH, I'M JUST...LISTENING FOR...
--START EVAC, LT. HOLLISTER. MY DAUGHTER AND I WILL TAKE THE SHUTTLE--
THERE.
"JOR-EL DIDN'T UNDERSTAND, EL..."

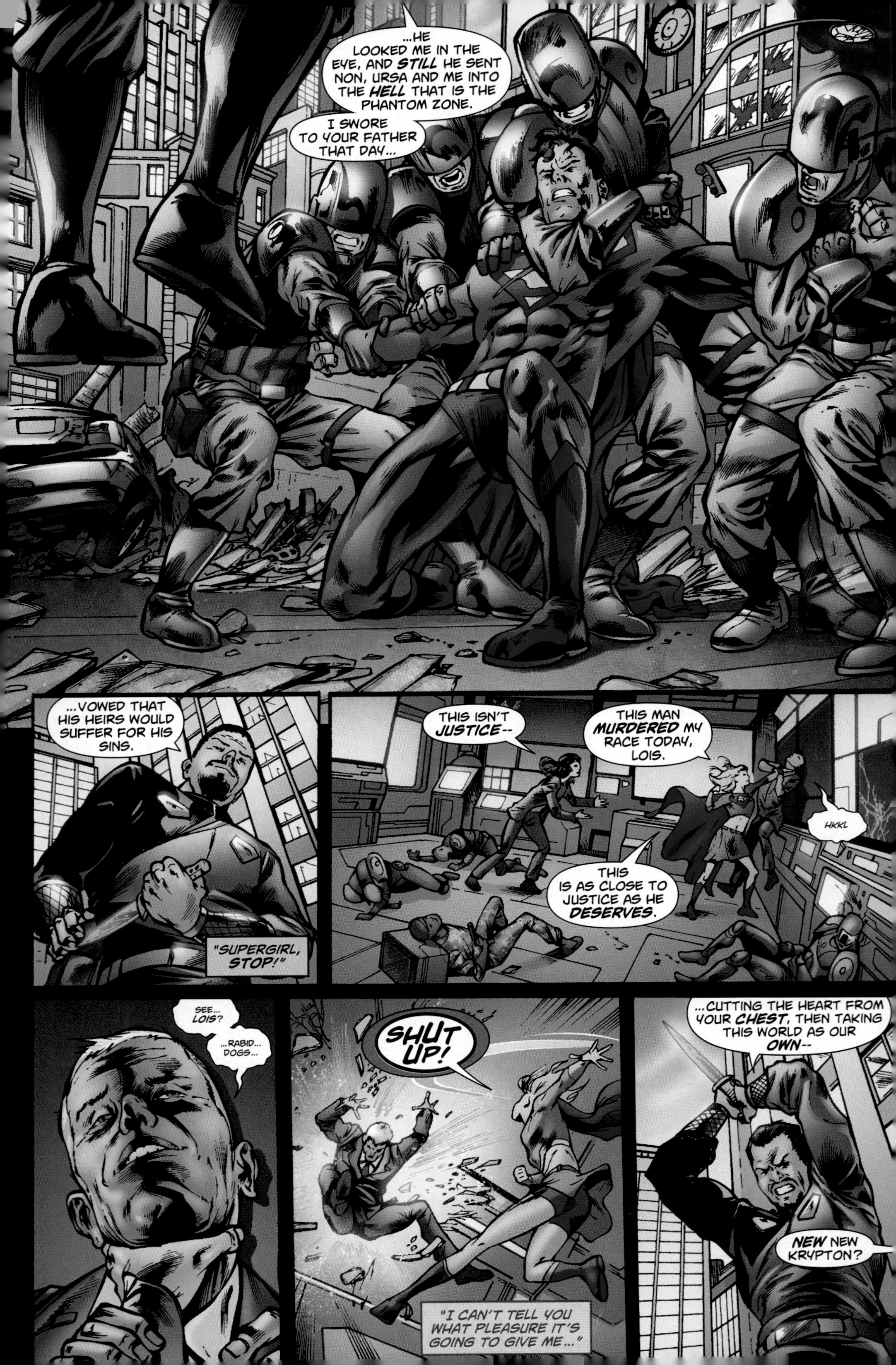
...HE LOOKED ME IN THE EYE, AND **STILL** HE SENT NON, URSA AND ME INTO THE **HELL** THAT IS THE PHANTOM ZONE.
I SWORE TO YOUR FATHER THAT DAY...
...VOWED THAT HIS HEIRS WOULD SUFFER FOR HIS SINS.
"SUPERGIRL, STOP!"
THIS ISN'T **JUSTICE**--
THIS MAN **MURDERED** MY RACE TODAY, LOIS.
HKKL
THIS IS AS CLOSE TO JUSTICE AS HE **DESERVES**.
SEE... LOIS?
...RABID... DOGS...
SHUT UP!
"I CAN'T TELL YOU WHAT PLEASURE IT'S GOING TO GIVE ME..."
...CUTTING THE HEART FROM YOUR **CHEST**, THEN TAKING THIS WORLD AS OUR **OWN**--
NEW NEW KRYPTON?

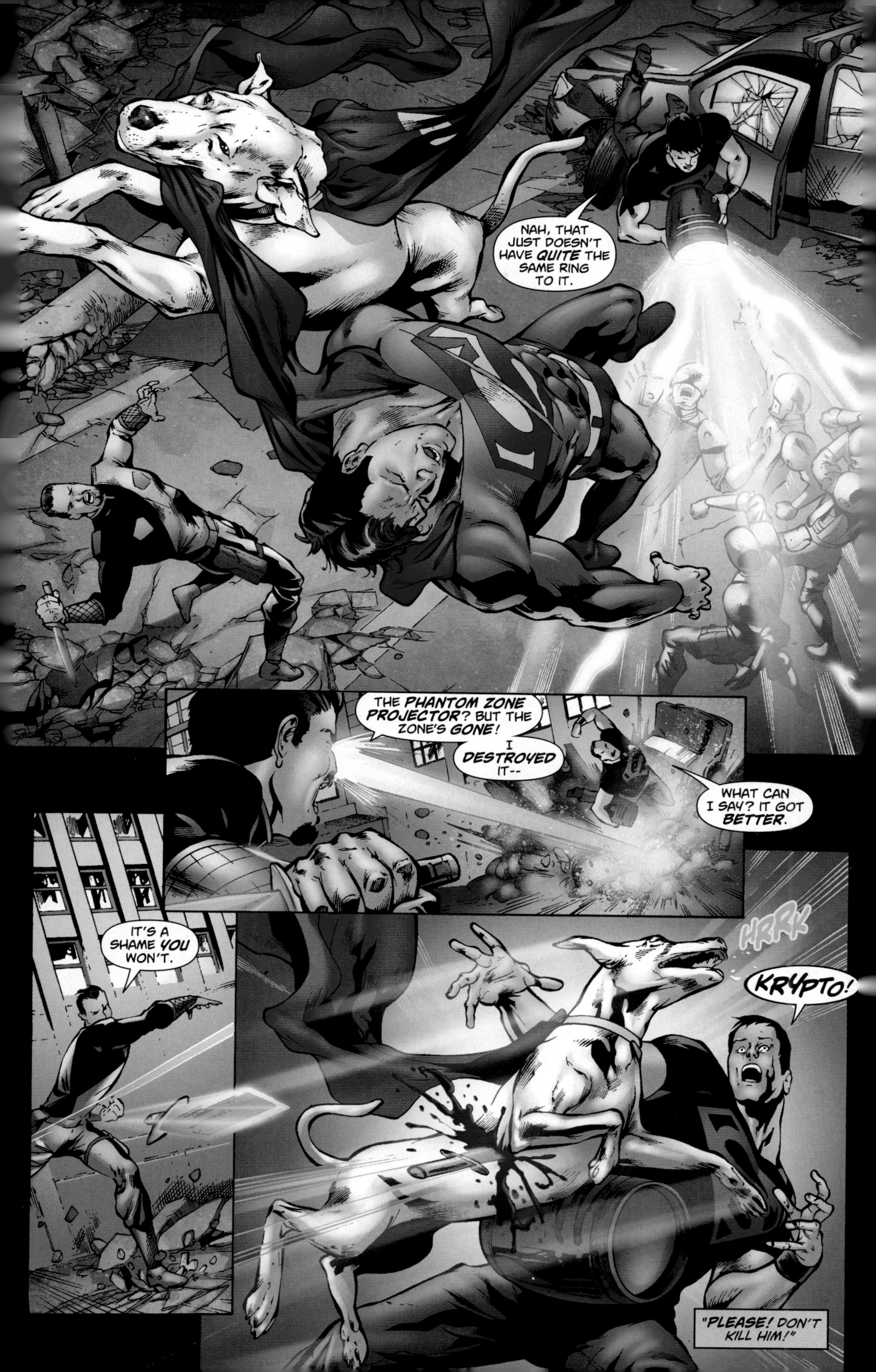
NAH, THAT JUST DOESN'T HAVE QUITE THE SAME RING TO IT.
THE PHANTOM ZONE PROJECTOR? BUT THE ZONE'S GONE!
I DESTROYED IT--
WHAT CAN I SAY? IT GOT BETTER.
IT'S A SHAME YOU WON'T.
HRRK
KRYPTO!
"PLEASE! DON'T KILL HIM!"

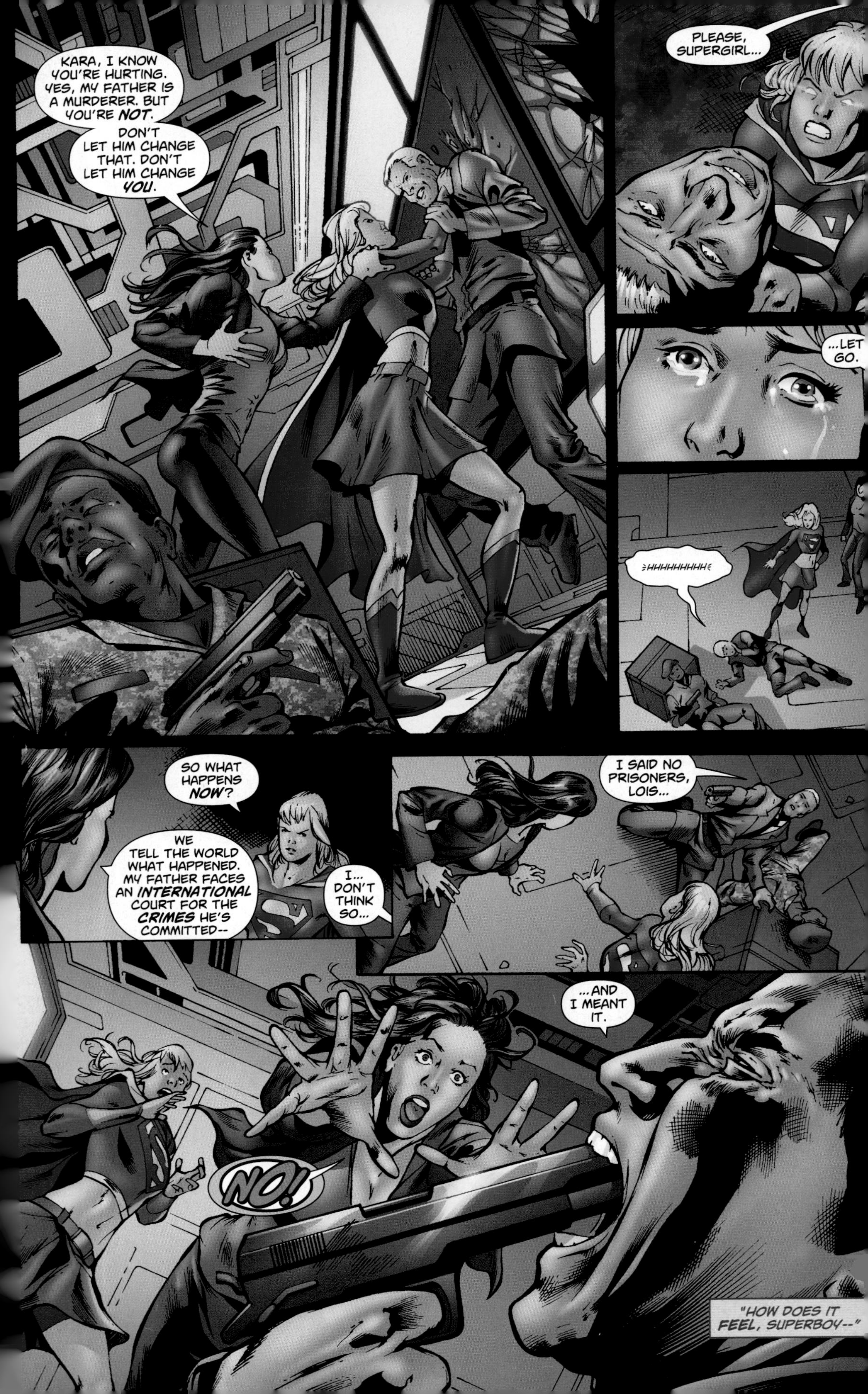
KARA, I KNOW YOU'RE HURTING. YES, MY FATHER IS A MURDERER. BUT YOU'RE NOT.
DON'T LET HIM CHANGE THAT. DON'T LET HIM CHANGE YOU.
PLEASE, SUPERGIRL...
...LET GO.
HHHHHHHHHH
SO WHAT HAPPENS NOW?
WE TELL THE WORLD WHAT HAPPENED. MY FATHER FACES AN INTERNATIONAL COURT FOR THE CRIMES HE'S COMMITTED--
I... DON'T THINK SO...
I SAID NO PRISONERS, LOIS...
...AND I MEANT IT.
NO!
"HOW DOES IT FEEL, SUPERBOY--"

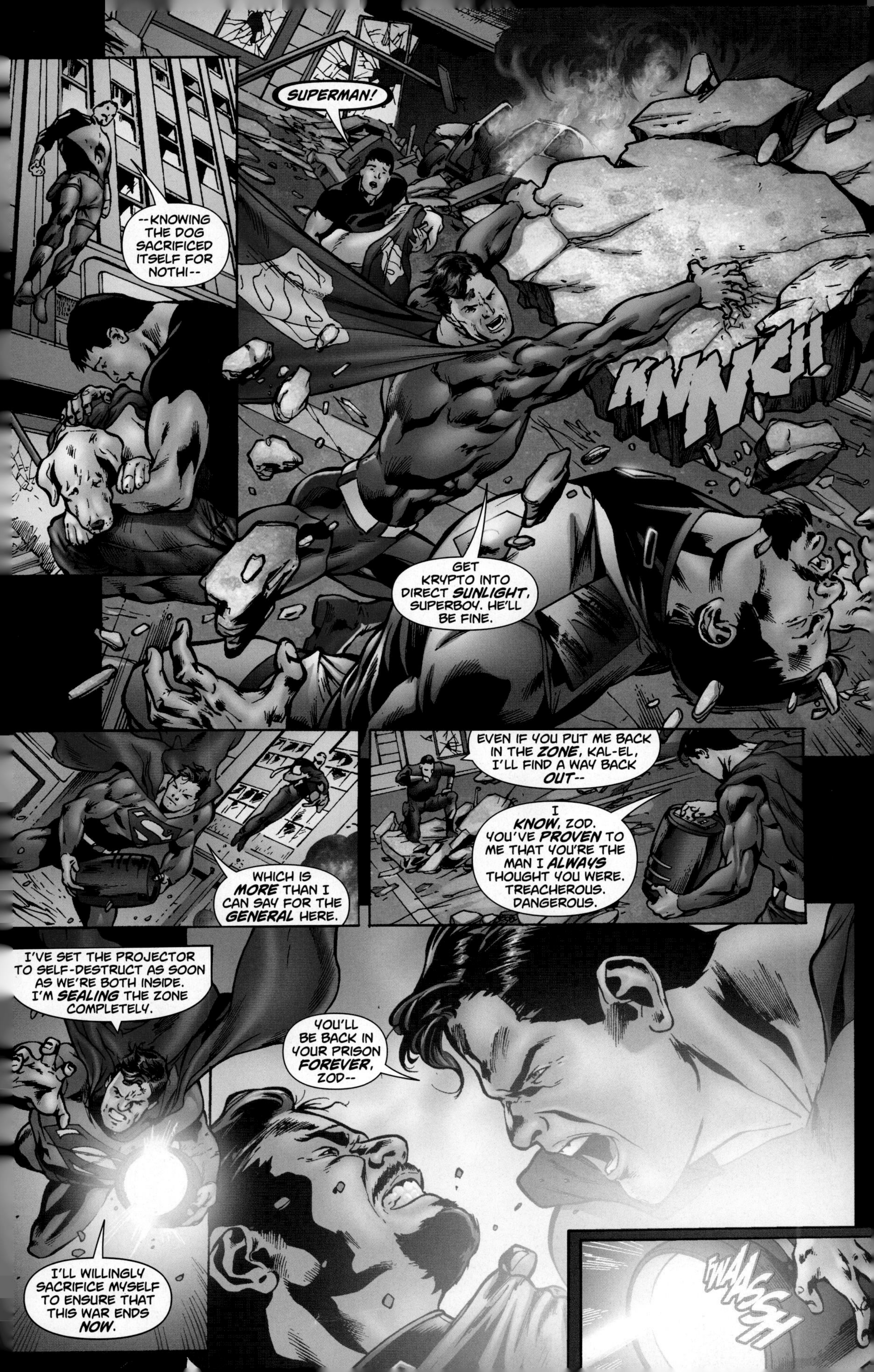
--KNOWING THE DOG SACRIFICED ITSELF FOR NOTHI--
SUPERMAN!
KNNNCH
GET KRYPTO INTO DIRECT SUNLIGHT, SUPERBOY. HE'LL BE FINE.
WHICH IS MORE THAN I CAN SAY FOR THE GENERAL HERE.
EVEN IF YOU PUT ME BACK IN THE ZONE, KAL-EL, I'LL FIND A WAY BACK OUT--
I KNOW, ZOD. YOU'VE PROVEN TO ME THAT YOU'RE THE MAN I ALWAYS THOUGHT YOU WERE. TREACHEROUS. DANGEROUS.
I'VE SET THE PROJECTOR TO SELF-DESTRUCT AS SOON AS WE'RE BOTH INSIDE. I'M SEALING THE ZONE COMPLETELY.
YOU'LL BE BACK IN YOUR PRISON FOREVER, ZOD--
I'LL WILLINGLY SACRIFICE MYSELF TO ENSURE THAT THIS WAR ENDS NOW.
FWAASSH

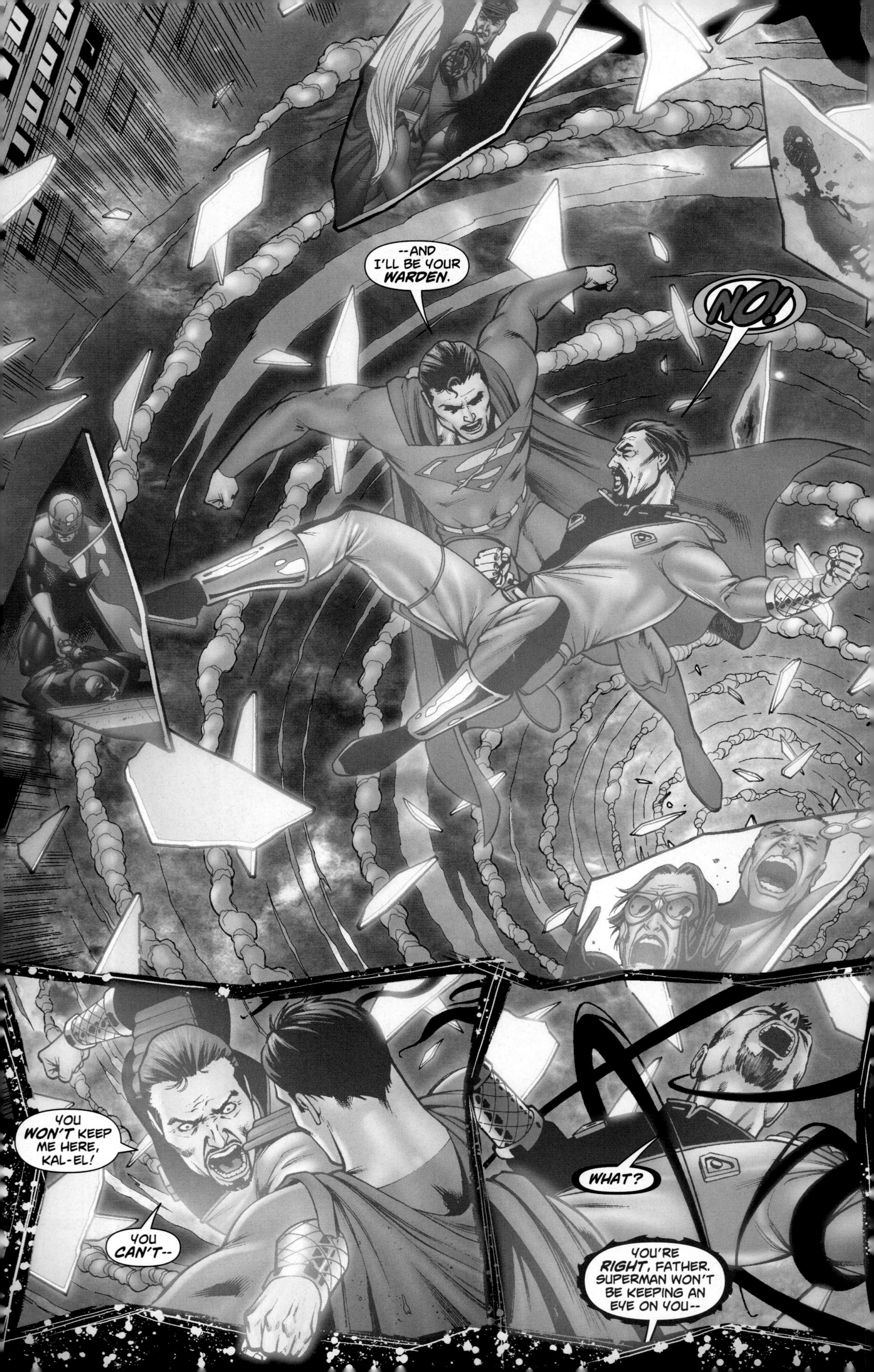
--AND I'LL BE YOUR WARDEN.
NO!
YOU WON'T KEEP ME HERE, KAL-EL!
YOU CAN'T--
WHAT?
YOU'RE RIGHT, FATHER. SUPERMAN WON'T BE KEEPING AN EYE ON YOU--

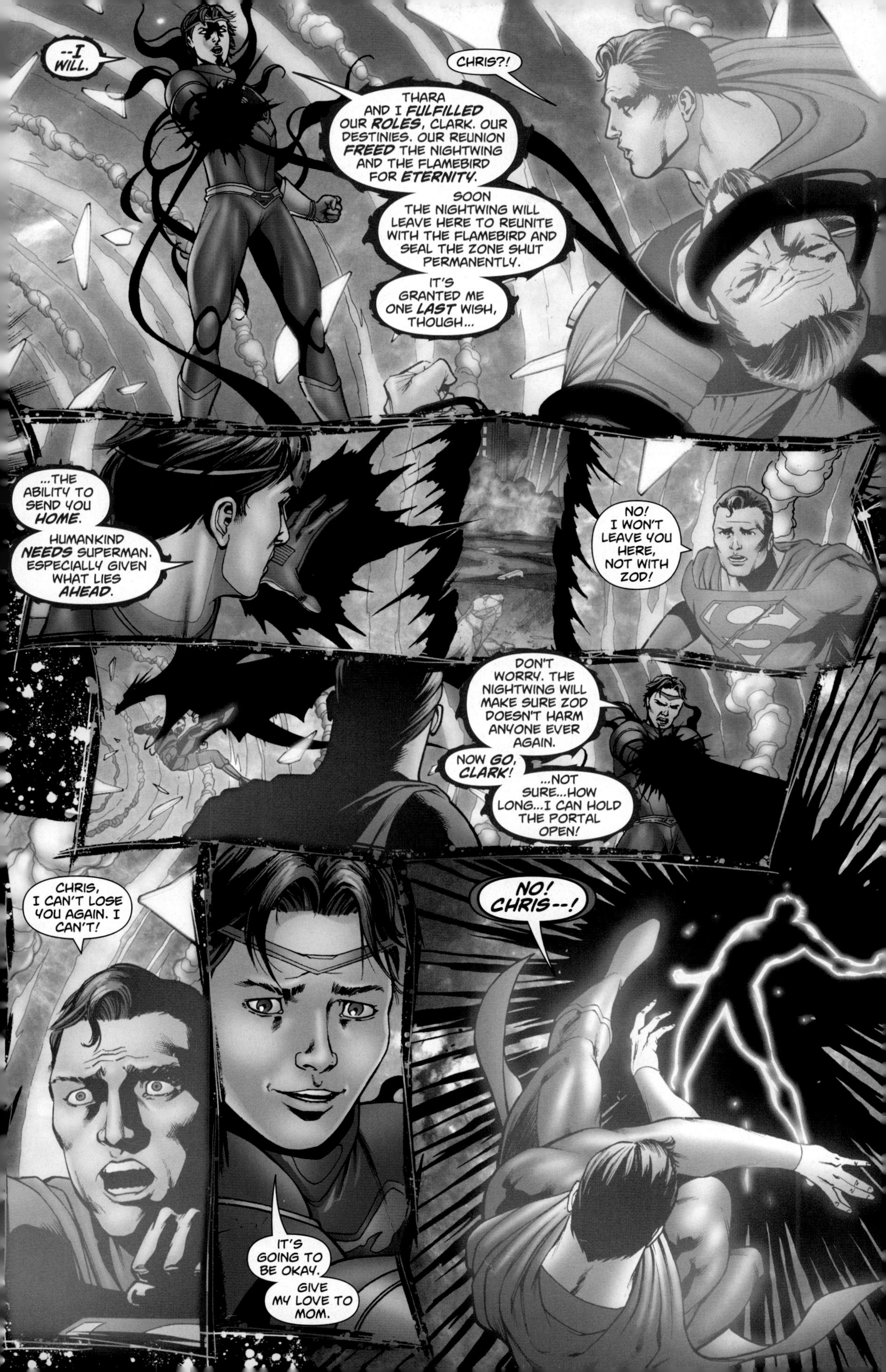
--I WILL.
CHRIS?!
THARA AND I FULFILLED OUR ROLES, CLARK. OUR DESTINIES. OUR REUNION FREED THE NIGHTWING AND THE FLAMEBIRD FOR ETERNITY.
SOON THE NIGHTWING WILL LEAVE HERE TO REUNITE WITH THE FLAMEBIRD AND SEAL THE ZONE SHUT PERMANENTLY.
IT'S GRANTED ME ONE LAST WISH, THOUGH...
...THE ABILITY TO SEND YOU HOME.
HUMANKIND NEEDS SUPERMAN. ESPECIALLY GIVEN WHAT LIES AHEAD.
NO! I WON'T LEAVE YOU HERE, NOT WITH ZOD!
DON'T WORRY. THE NIGHTWING WILL MAKE SURE ZOD DOESN'T HARM ANYONE EVER AGAIN.
NOW GO, CLARK!
...NOT SURE...HOW LONG...I CAN HOLD THE PORTAL OPEN!
CHRIS, I CAN'T LOSE YOU AGAIN. I CAN'T!
IT'S GOING TO BE OKAY.
GIVE MY LOVE TO MOM.
NO! CHRIS--!

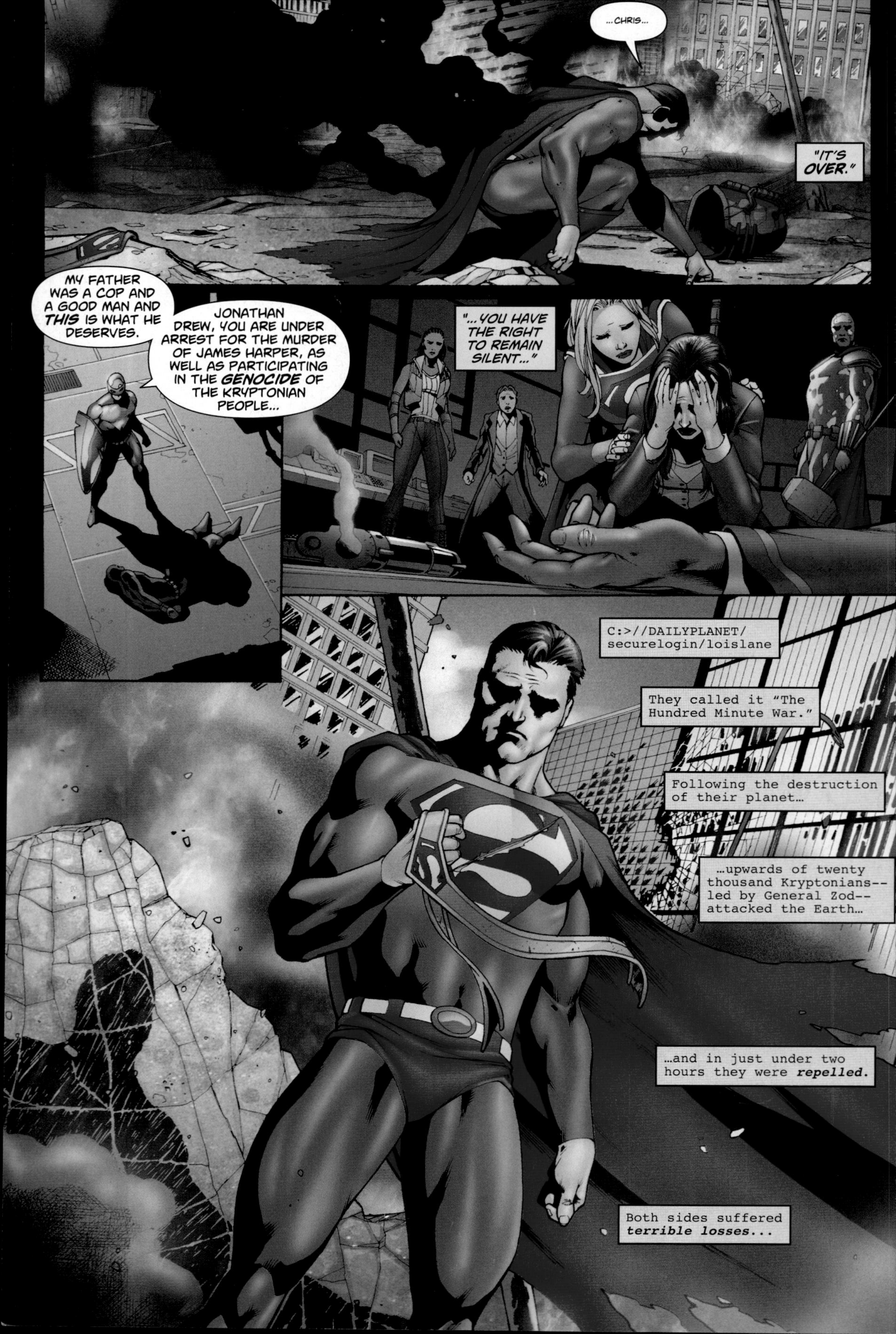

...CHRIS...
"IT'S OVER."
MY FATHER WAS A COP AND A GOOD MAN AND THIS IS WHAT HE DESERVES.
JONATHAN DREW, YOU ARE UNDER ARREST FOR THE MURDER OF JAMES HARPER, AS WELL AS PARTICIPATING IN THE GENOCIDE OF THE KRYPTONIAN PEOPLE...
"...YOU HAVE THE RIGHT TO REMAIN SILENT..."
C:>//DAILYPLANET/ securelogin/loislane
They called it "The Hundred Minute War."
Following the destruction of their planet...
...upwards of twenty thousand Kryptonians--led by General Zod--attacked the Earth...
...and in just under two hours they were repelled.
Both sides suffered terrible losses...

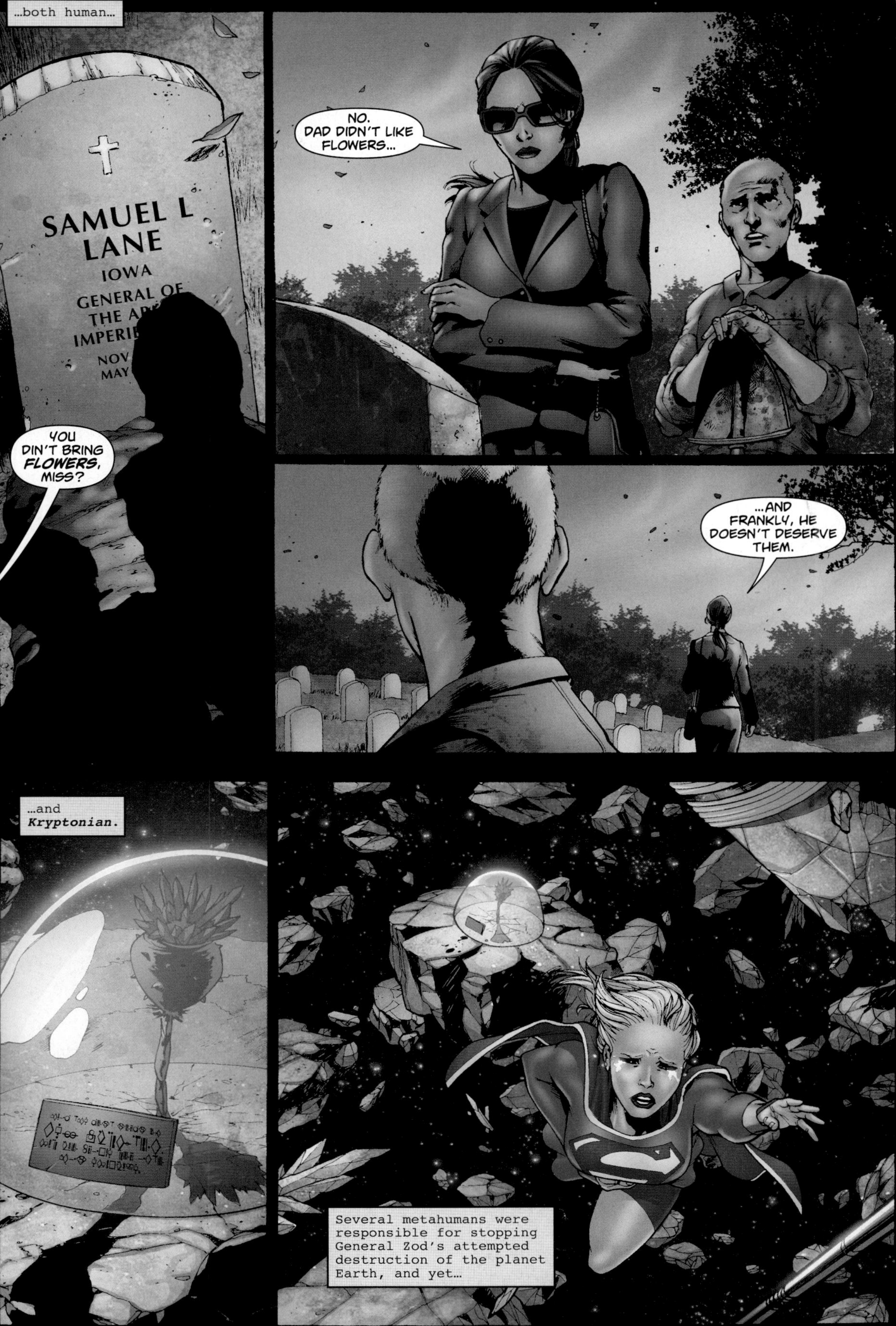
...both human...
SAMUEL L
LANE
IOWA
GENERAL OF
THE AR
IMPERI
NOV
MAY
YOU DIN'T BRING FLOWERS, MISS?
NO. DAD DIDN'T LIKE FLOWERS...
...AND FRANKLY, HE DOESN'T DESERVE THEM.
...and Kryptonian.
Several metahumans were responsible for stopping General Zod's attempted destruction of the planet Earth, and yet...

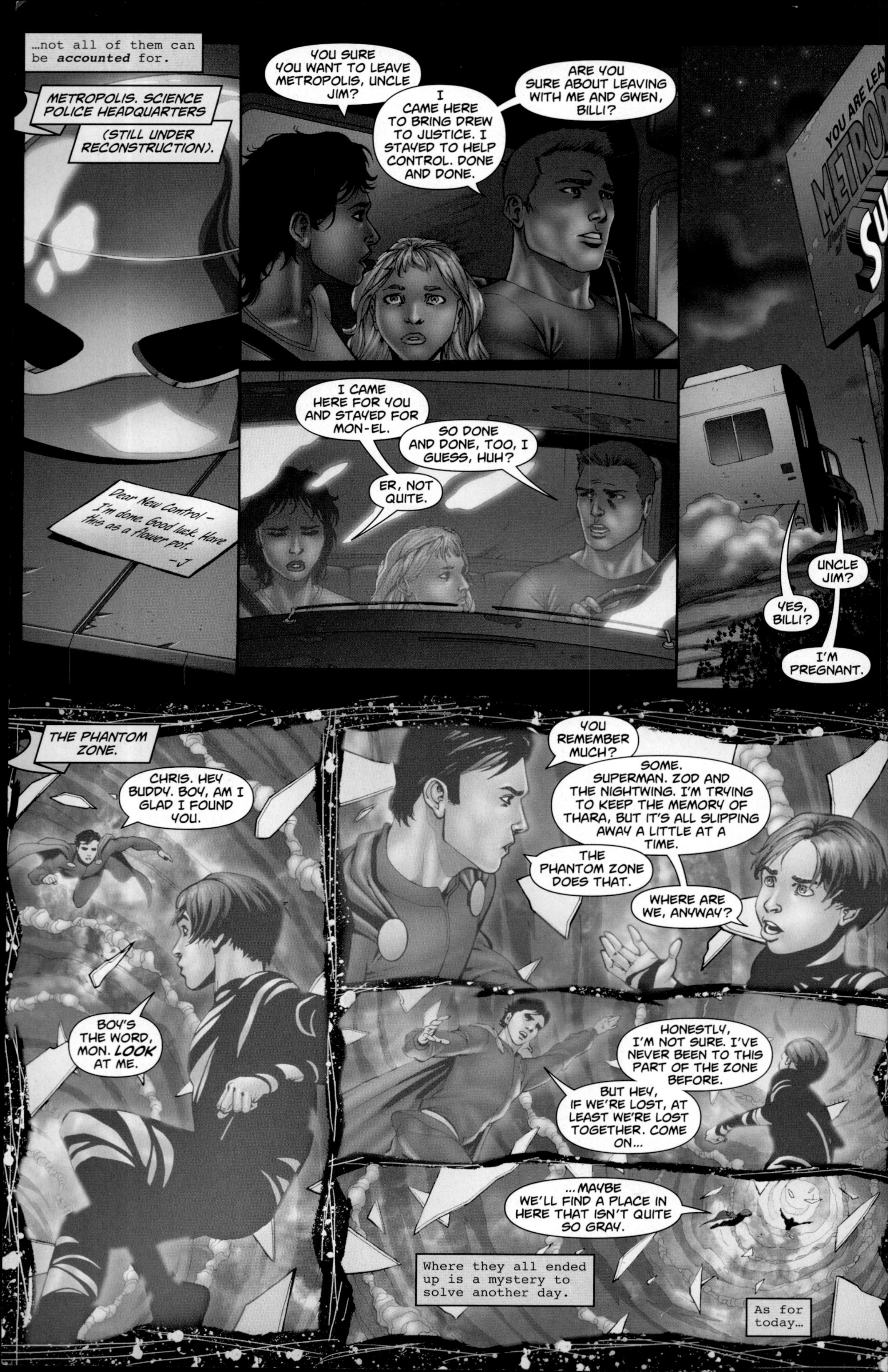
...not all of them can be *accounted* for.
METROPOLIS. SCIENCE POLICE HEADQUARTERS
(STILL UNDER RECONSTRUCTION).
YOU SURE YOU WANT TO LEAVE METROPOLIS, UNCLE JIM?
I CAME HERE TO BRING DREW TO JUSTICE. I STAYED TO HELP CONTROL. DONE AND DONE.
ARE YOU SURE ABOUT LEAVING WITH ME AND GWEN, BILLI?
YOU ARE LEAV
METRO
I CAME HERE FOR YOU AND STAYED FOR MON-EL.
SO DONE AND DONE, TOO, I GUESS, HUH?
ER, NOT QUITE.
Dear New Control — I'm done. Good luck. Have this as a flower pot. —J
UNCLE JIM?
YES, BILLI?
I'M PREGNANT.
THE PHANTOM ZONE.
CHRIS. HEY BUDDY. BOY, AM I GLAD I FOUND YOU.
BOY'S THE WORD, MON. **LOOK** AT ME.
YOU REMEMBER MUCH?
SOME. SUPERMAN. ZOD AND THE NIGHTWING. I'M TRYING TO KEEP THE MEMORY OF THARA, BUT IT'S ALL SLIPPING AWAY A LITTLE AT A TIME.
THE PHANTOM ZONE DOES THAT.
WHERE ARE WE, ANYWAY?
HONESTLY, I'M NOT SURE. I'VE NEVER BEEN TO THIS PART OF THE ZONE BEFORE.
BUT HEY, IF WE'RE LOST, AT LEAST WE'RE LOST TOGETHER. COME ON...
...MAYBE WE'LL FIND A PLACE IN HERE THAT ISN'T QUITE SO GRAY.
Where they all ended up is a mystery to solve another day.
As for today...

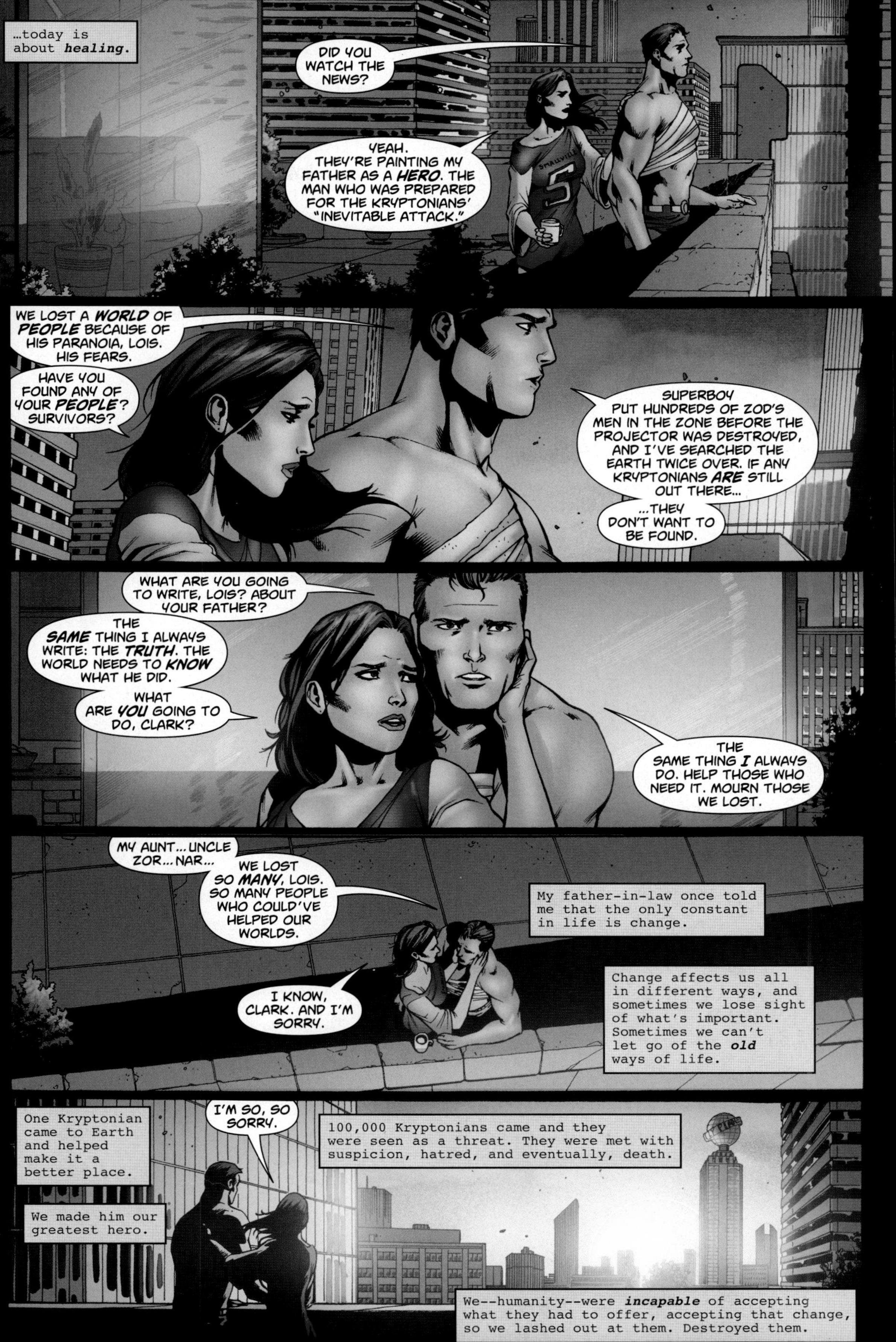

…today is about *healing.*
DID YOU WATCH THE NEWS?
YEAH. THEY'RE PAINTING MY FATHER AS A *HERO*. THE MAN WHO WAS PREPARED FOR THE KRYPTONIANS' "INEVITABLE ATTACK."
SMALLVILLE
WE LOST A *WORLD* OF *PEOPLE* BECAUSE OF HIS PARANOIA, LOIS. HIS FEARS.
HAVE YOU FOUND ANY OF YOUR *PEOPLE*? SURVIVORS?
SUPERBOY PUT HUNDREDS OF ZOD'S MEN IN THE ZONE BEFORE THE PROJECTOR WAS DESTROYED, AND I'VE SEARCHED THE EARTH TWICE OVER. IF ANY KRYPTONIANS *ARE* STILL OUT THERE...
...THEY DON'T WANT TO BE FOUND.
WHAT ARE YOU GOING TO WRITE, LOIS? ABOUT YOUR FATHER?
THE *SAME* THING I ALWAYS WRITE: THE *TRUTH*. THE WORLD NEEDS TO *KNOW* WHAT HE DID.
WHAT ARE *YOU* GOING TO DO, CLARK?
THE SAME THING *I* ALWAYS DO. HELP THOSE WHO NEED IT. MOURN THOSE WE LOST.
MY AUNT... UNCLE ZOR... NAR...
WE LOST SO *MANY*, LOIS. SO MANY PEOPLE WHO COULD'VE HELPED OUR WORLDS.
My father-in-law once told me that the only constant in life is change.
I KNOW, CLARK. AND I'M SORRY.
Change affects us all in different ways, and sometimes we lose sight of what's important. Sometimes we can't let go of the *old* ways of life.
One Kryptonian came to Earth and helped make it a better place.
I'M SO, SO SORRY.
100,000 Kryptonians came and they were seen as a threat. They were met with suspicion, hatred, and eventually, death.
We made him our greatest hero.
We--humanity--were *incapable* of accepting what they had to offer, accepting that change, so we lashed out at them. Destroyed them.

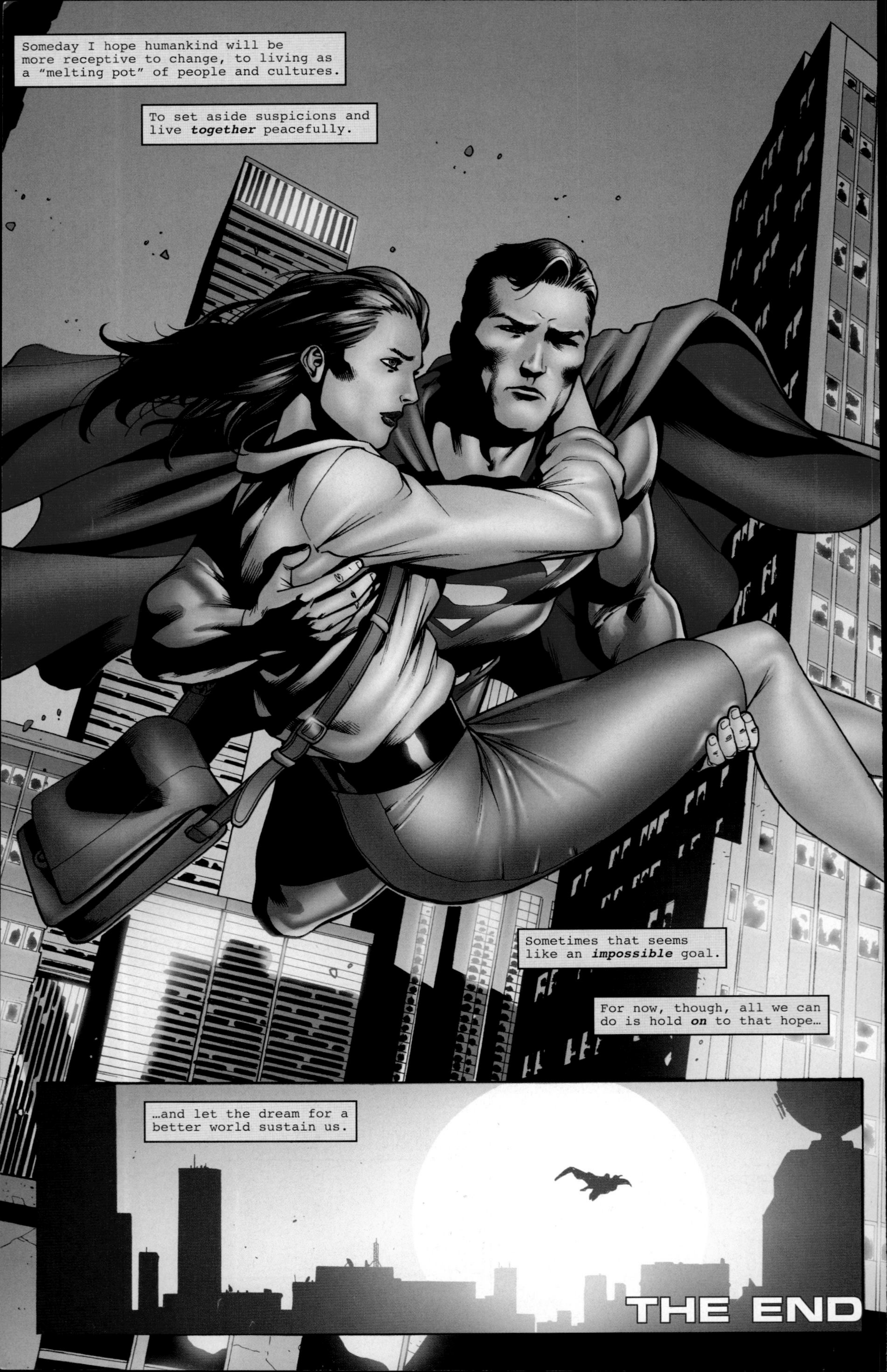
Someday I hope humankind will be more receptive to change, to living as a "melting pot" of people and cultures.
To set aside suspicions and live *together* peacefully.
Sometimes that seems like an *impossible* goal.
For now, though, all we can do is hold *on* to that hope…
…and let the dream for a better world sustain us.
THE END

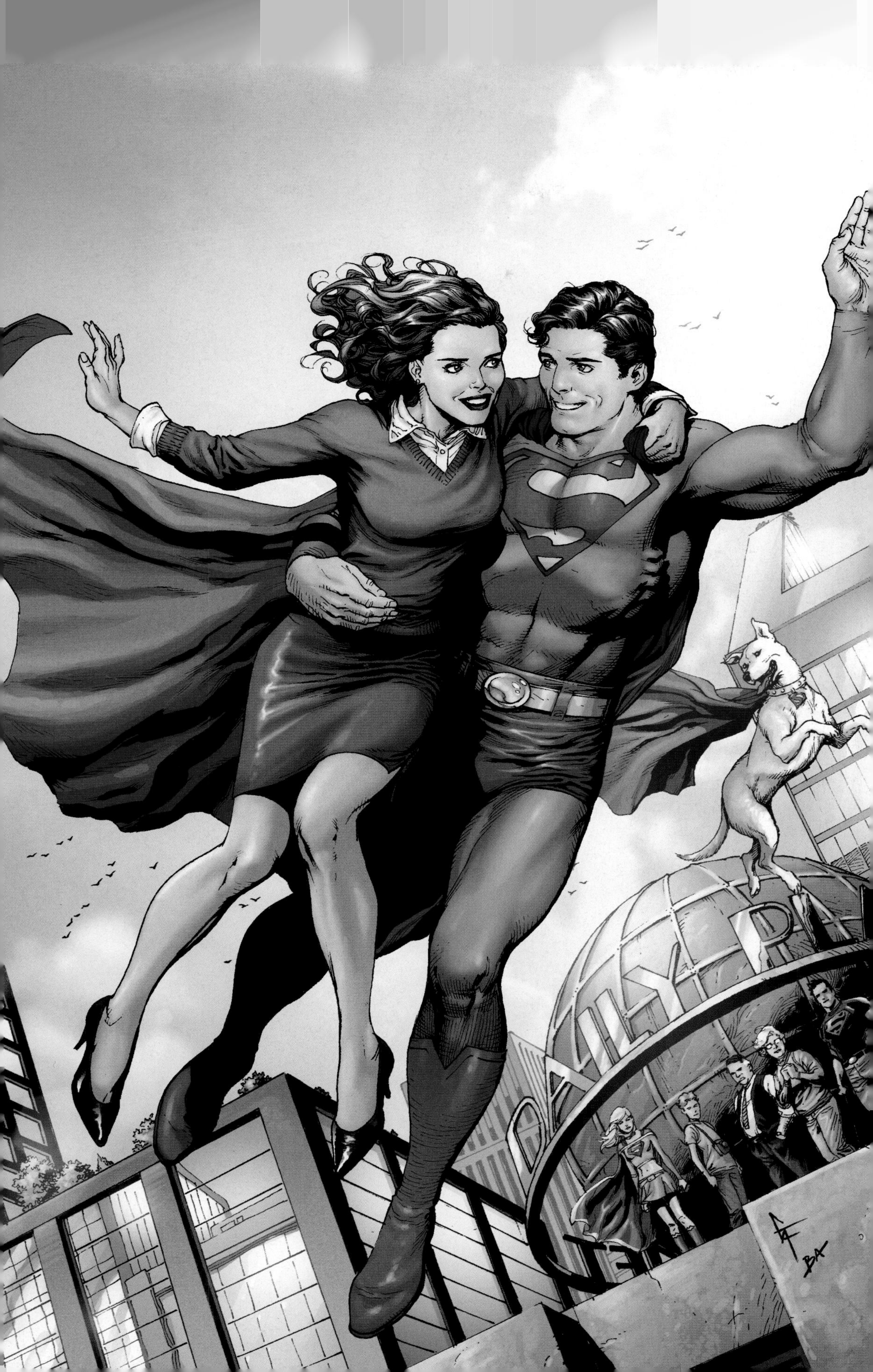

VARIANT by EDUARDO RISSO & MARK CHIARELLO after NEAL ADAMS

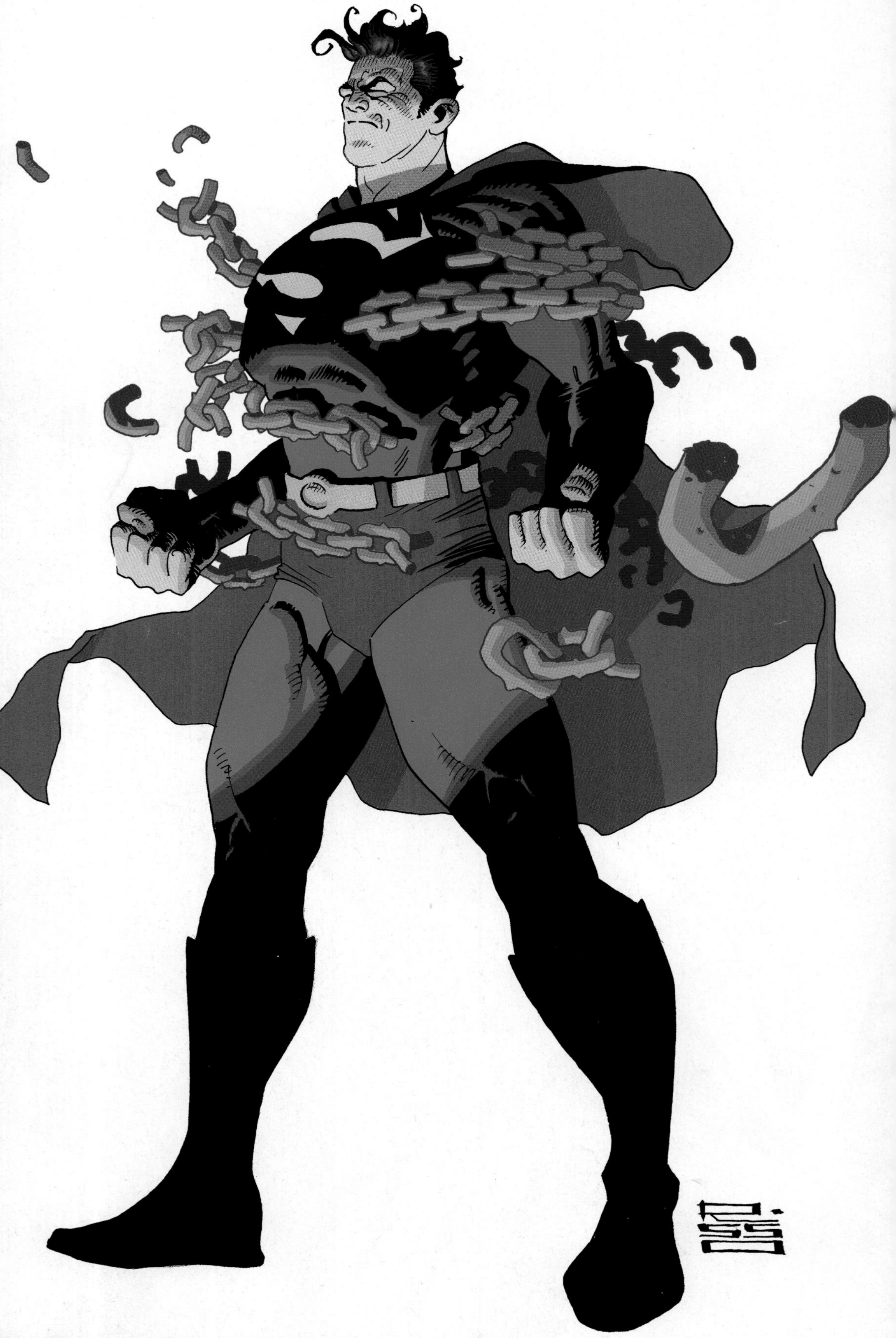

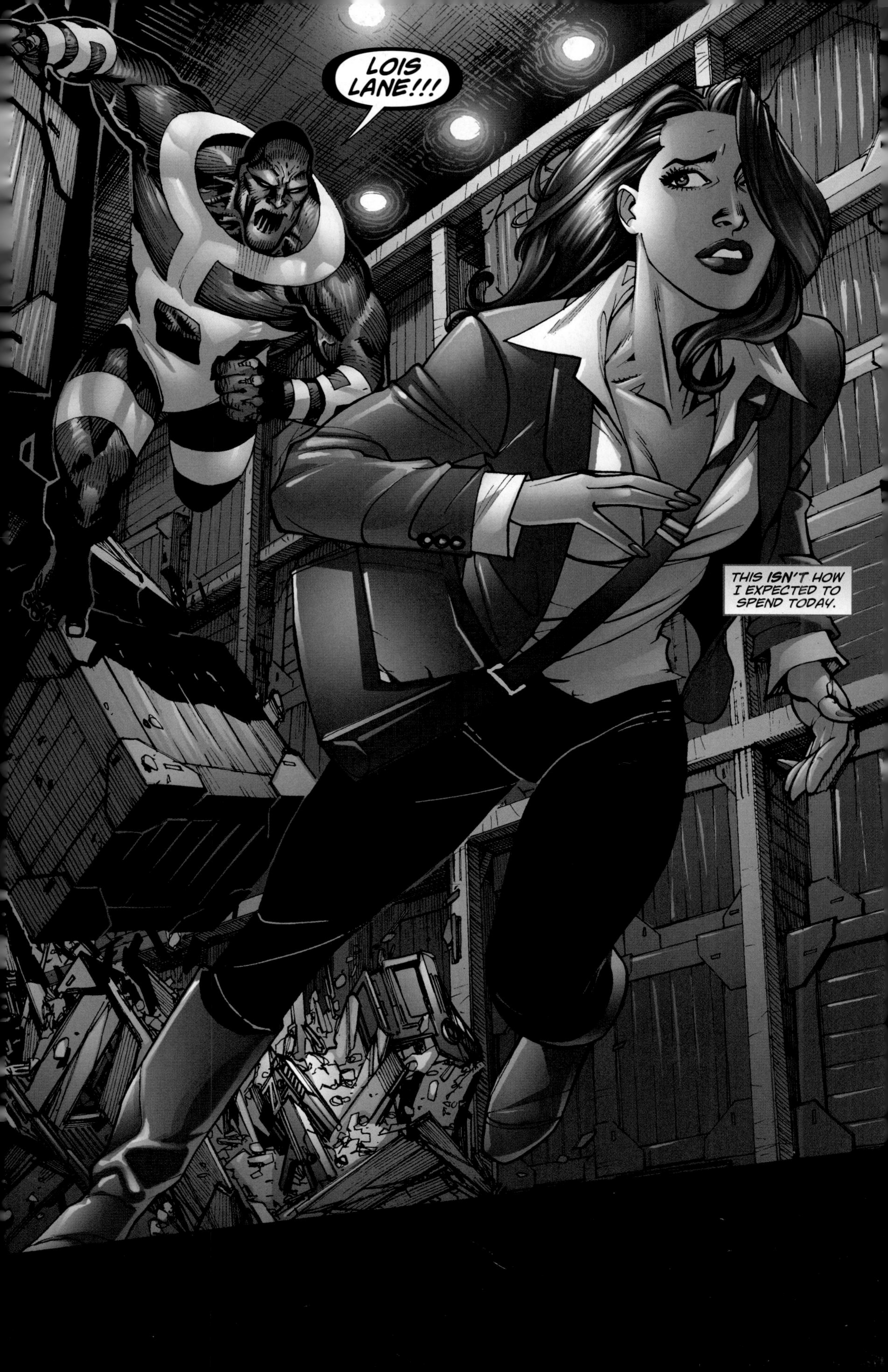
LOIS LANE!!!
THIS ISN'T HOW I EXPECTED TO SPEND TODAY.

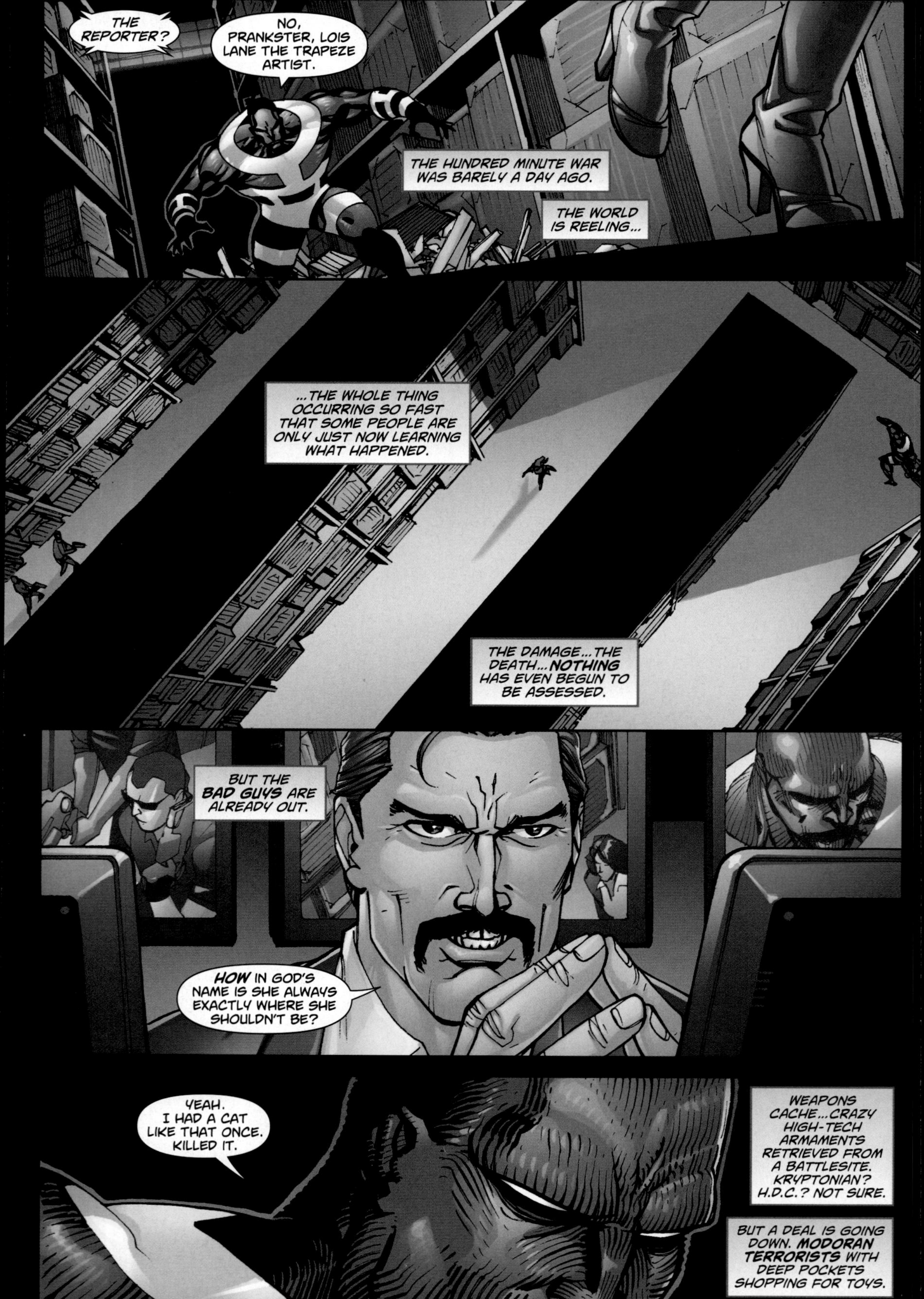
THE REPORTER?
NO, PRANKSTER, LOIS LANE THE TRAPEZE ARTIST.
THE HUNDRED MINUTE WAR WAS BARELY A DAY AGO.
THE WORLD IS REELING...
...THE WHOLE THING OCCURRING SO FAST THAT SOME PEOPLE ARE ONLY JUST NOW LEARNING WHAT HAPPENED.
THE DAMAGE...THE DEATH...NOTHING HAS EVEN BEGUN TO BE ASSESSED.
BUT THE BAD GUYS ARE ALREADY OUT.
HOW IN GOD'S NAME IS SHE ALWAYS EXACTLY WHERE SHE SHOULDN'T BE?
YEAH. I HAD A CAT LIKE THAT ONCE. KILLED IT.
WEAPONS CACHE...CRAZY HIGH-TECH ARMAMENTS RETRIEVED FROM A BATTLESITE. KRYPTONIAN? H.D.C.? NOT SURE.
BUT A DEAL IS GOING DOWN. MODORAN TERRORISTS WITH DEEP POCKETS SHOPPING FOR TOYS.

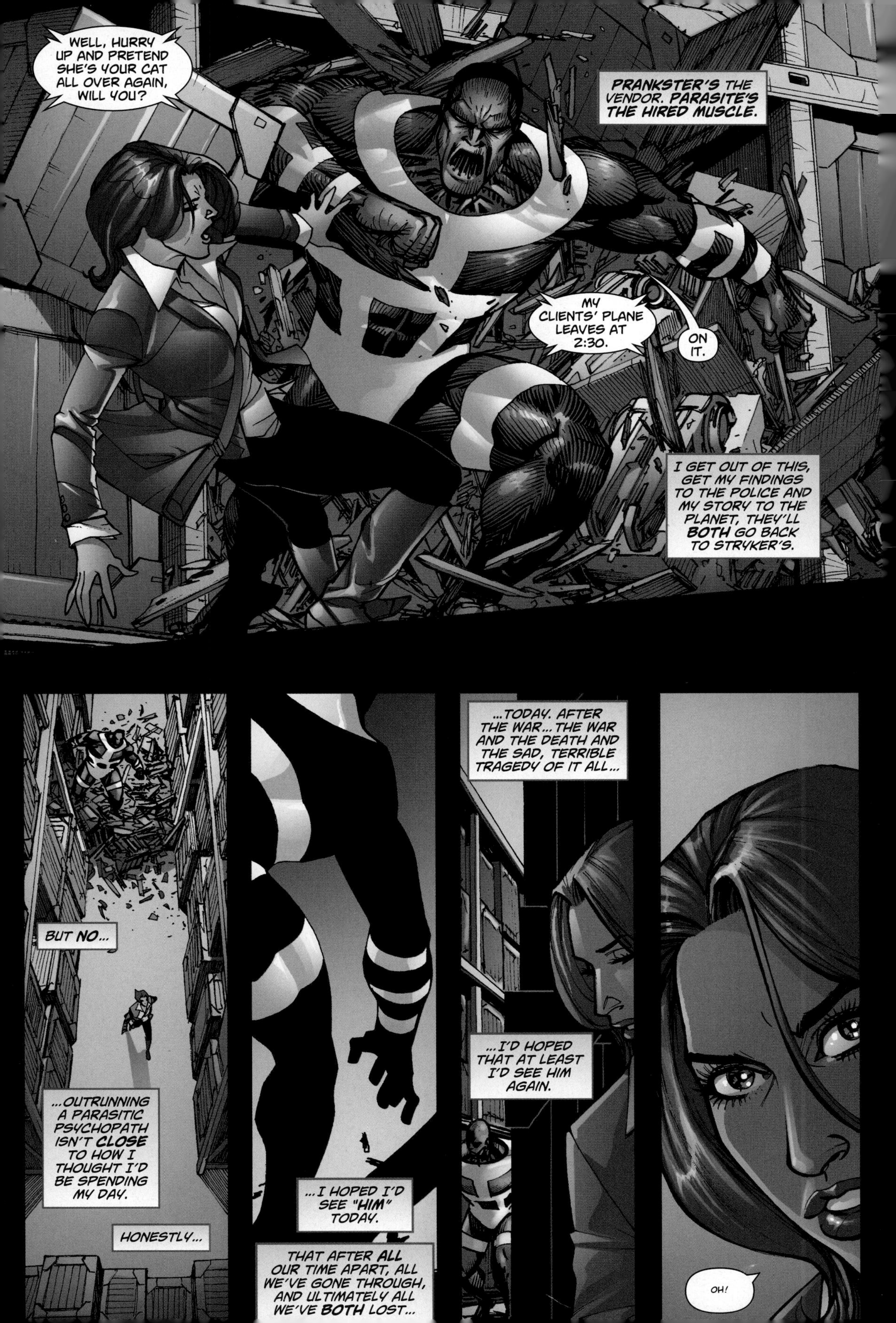

WELL, HURRY UP AND PRETEND SHE'S YOUR CAT ALL OVER AGAIN, WILL YOU?
PRANKSTER'S THE VENDOR. PARASITE'S THE HIRED MUSCLE.
MY CLIENTS' PLANE LEAVES AT 2:30.
ON IT.
I GET OUT OF THIS, GET MY FINDINGS TO THE POLICE AND MY STORY TO THE PLANET, THEY'LL BOTH GO BACK TO STRYKER'S.
BUT NO...
...OUTRUNNING A PARASITIC PSYCHOPATH ISN'T CLOSE TO HOW I THOUGHT I'D BE SPENDING MY DAY.
HONESTLY...
...I HOPED I'D SEE "HIM" TODAY.
THAT AFTER ALL OUR TIME APART, ALL WE'VE GONE THROUGH, AND ULTIMATELY ALL WE'VE BOTH LOST...
...TODAY. AFTER THE WAR... THE WAR AND THE DEATH AND THE SAD, TERRIBLE TRAGEDY OF IT ALL...
...I'D HOPED THAT AT LEAST I'D SEE HIM AGAIN.
OH!

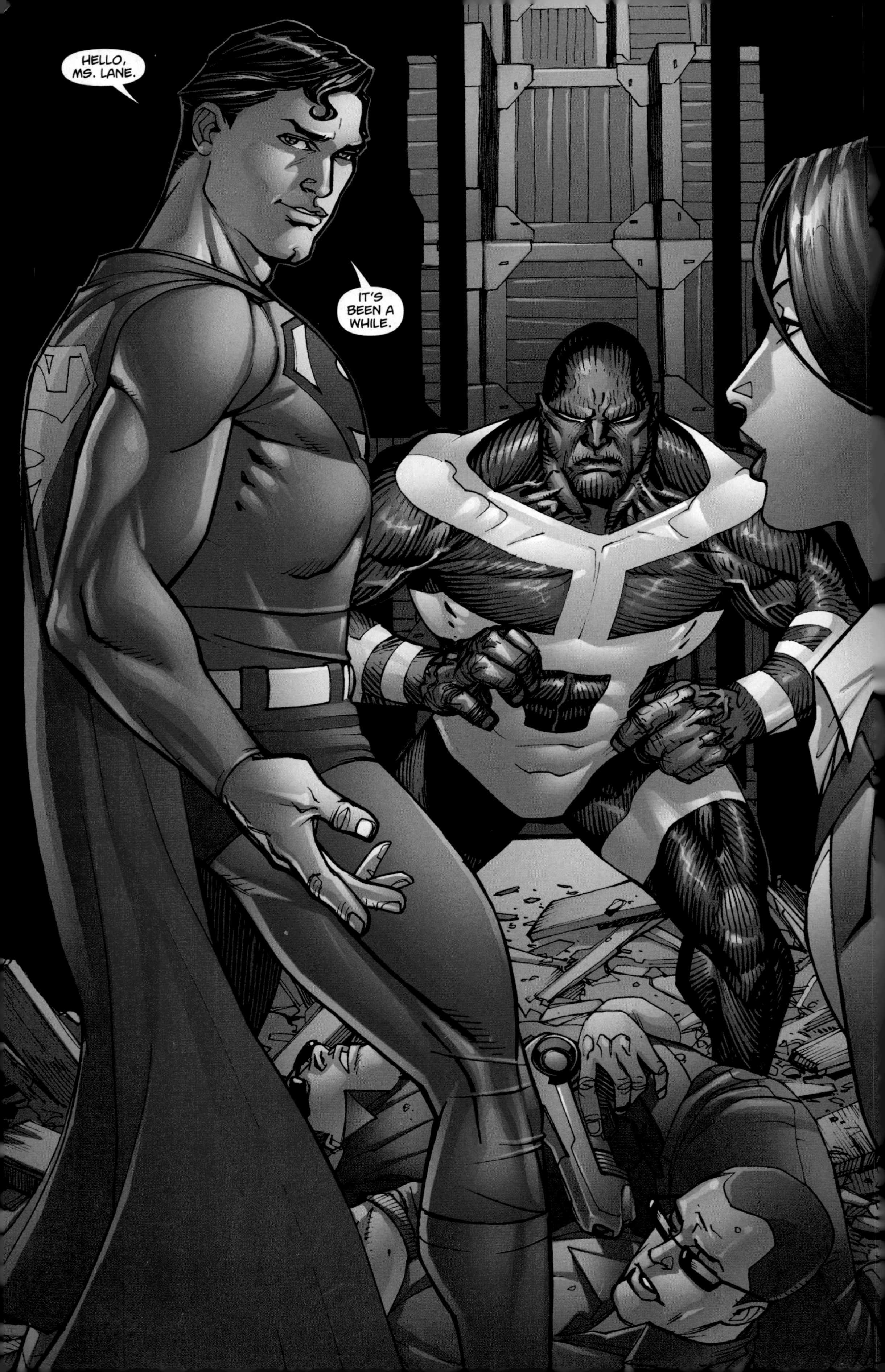
HELLO, MS. LANE.
IT'S BEEN A WHILE.

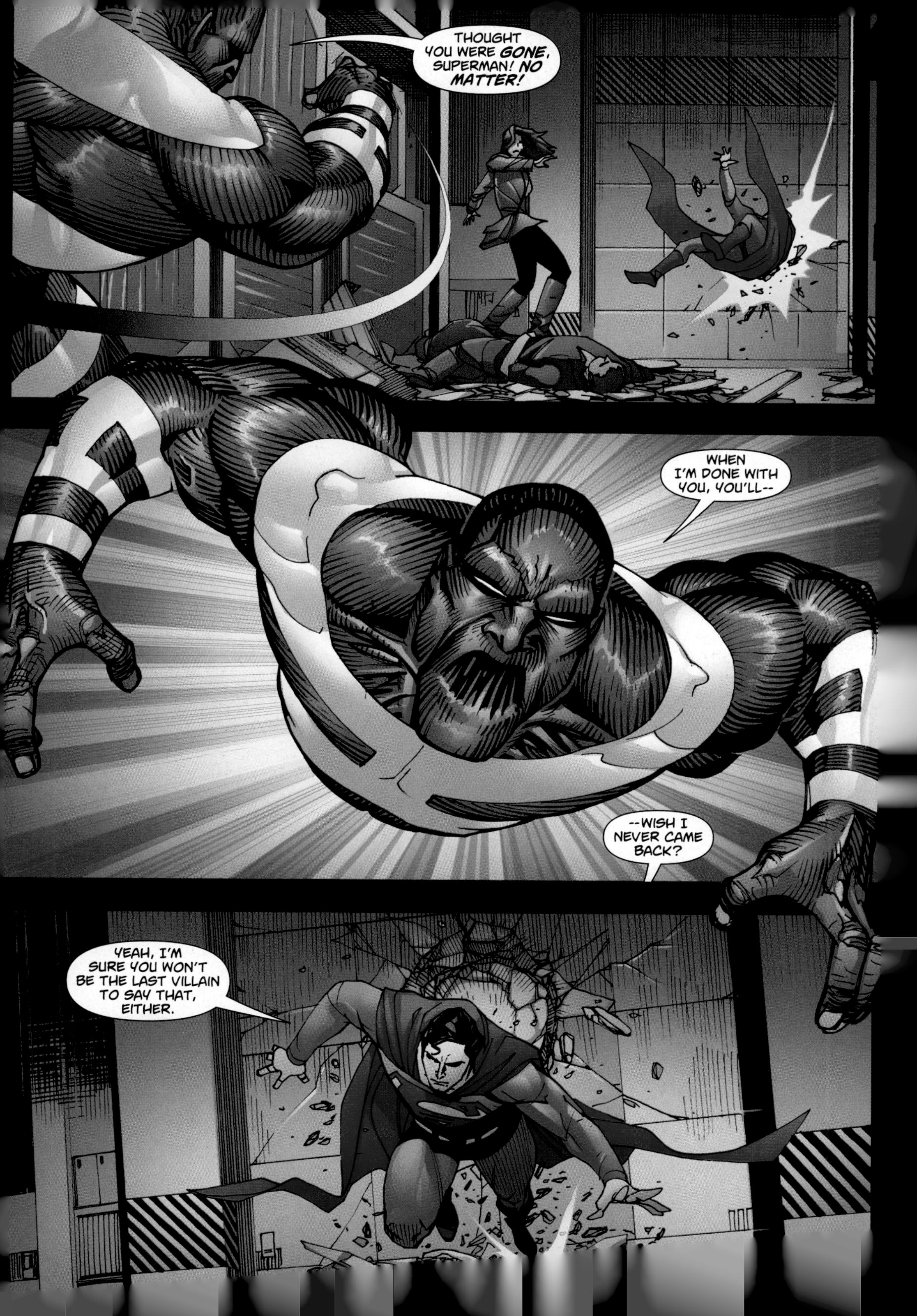
THOUGHT YOU WERE GONE, SUPERMAN! NO MATTER!
WHEN I'M DONE WITH YOU, YOU'LL--
--WISH I NEVER CAME BACK?
YEAH, I'M SURE YOU WON'T BE THE LAST VILLAIN TO SAY THAT, EITHER.

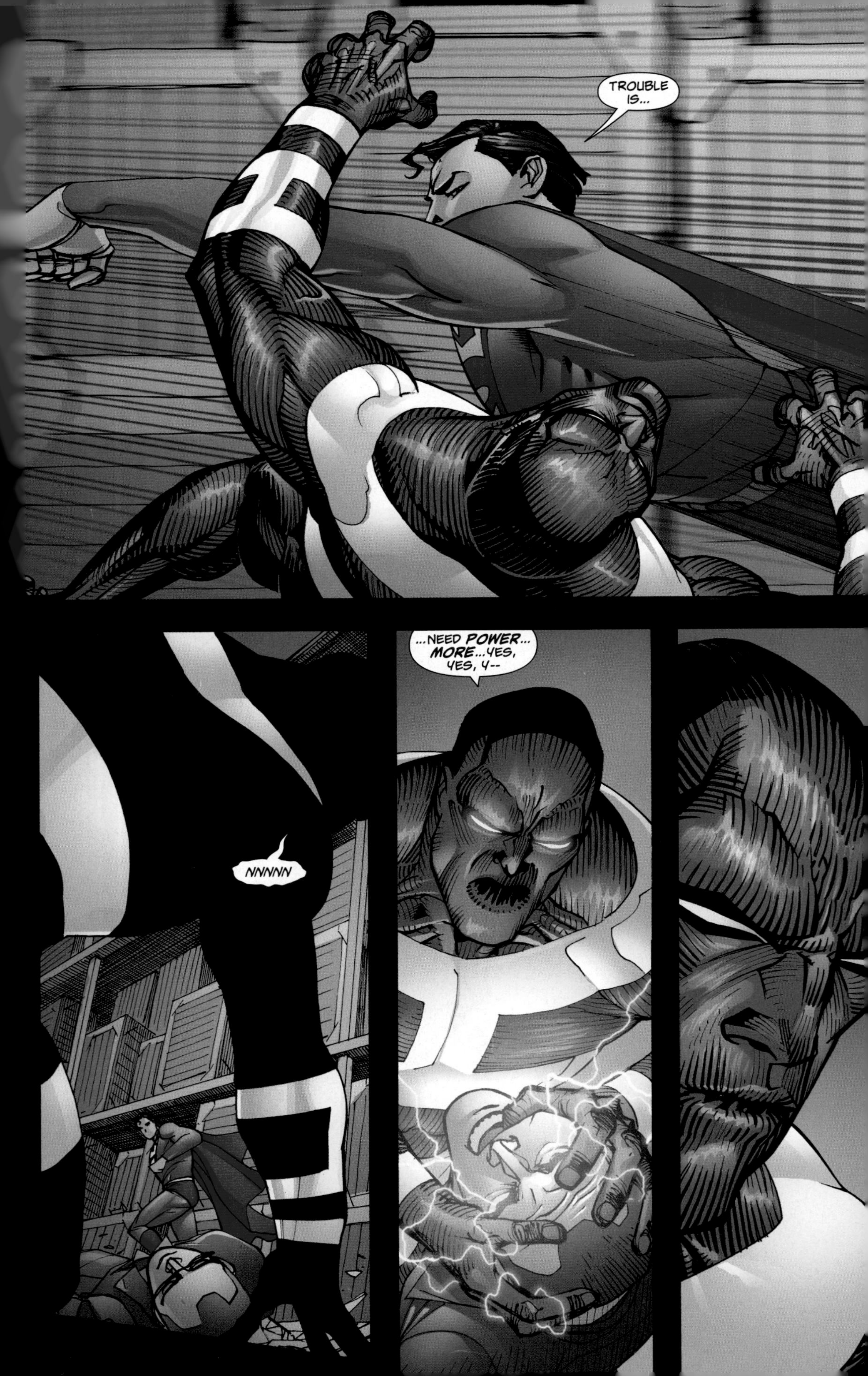
TROUBLE IS...
NNNNN
...NEED **POWER**... **MORE**...YES, YES, Y--

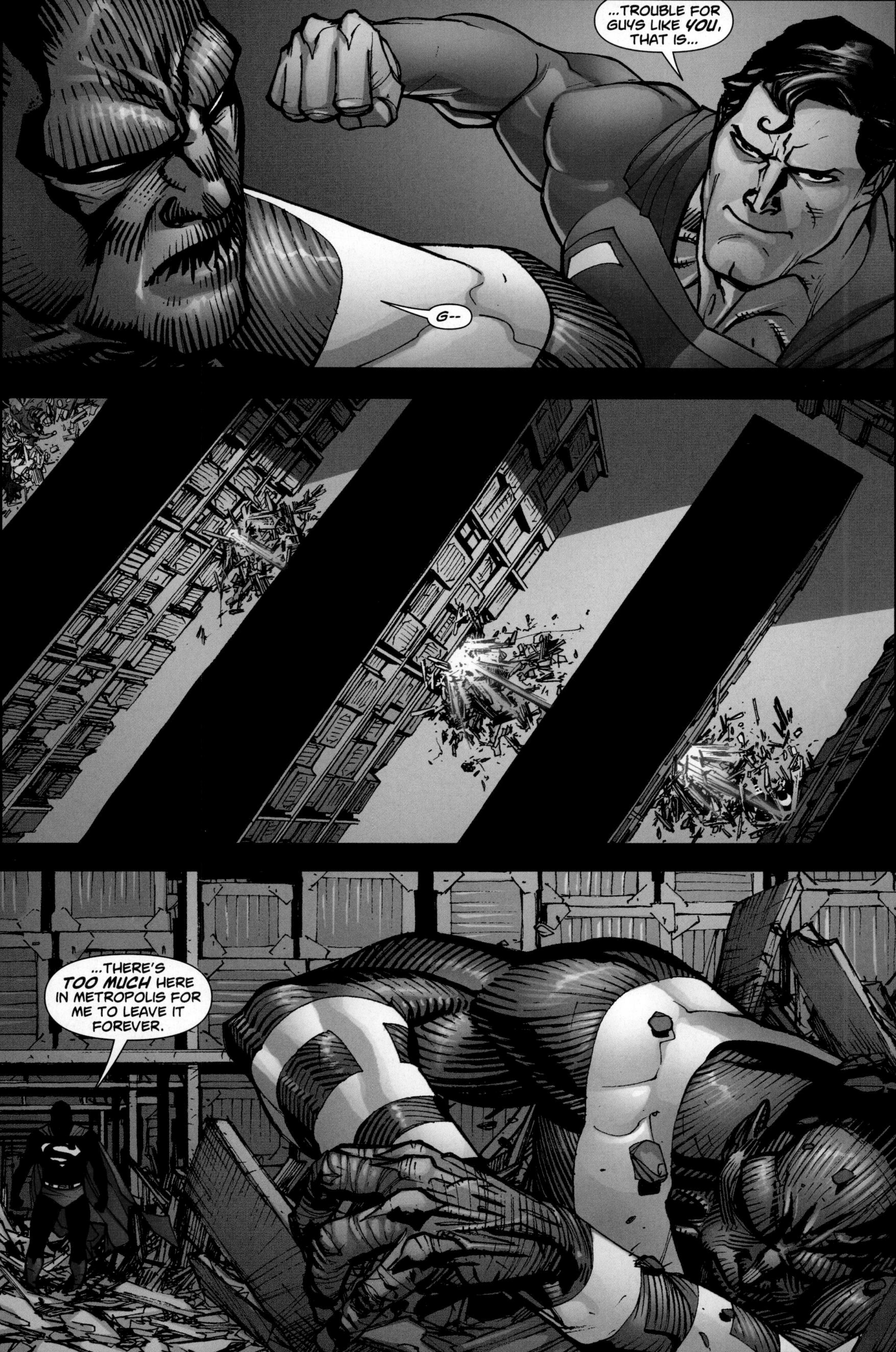
...TROUBLE FOR GUYS LIKE *YOU*, THAT IS...
G--
...THERE'S **TOO MUCH** HERE IN METROPOLIS FOR ME TO LEAVE IT FOREVER.

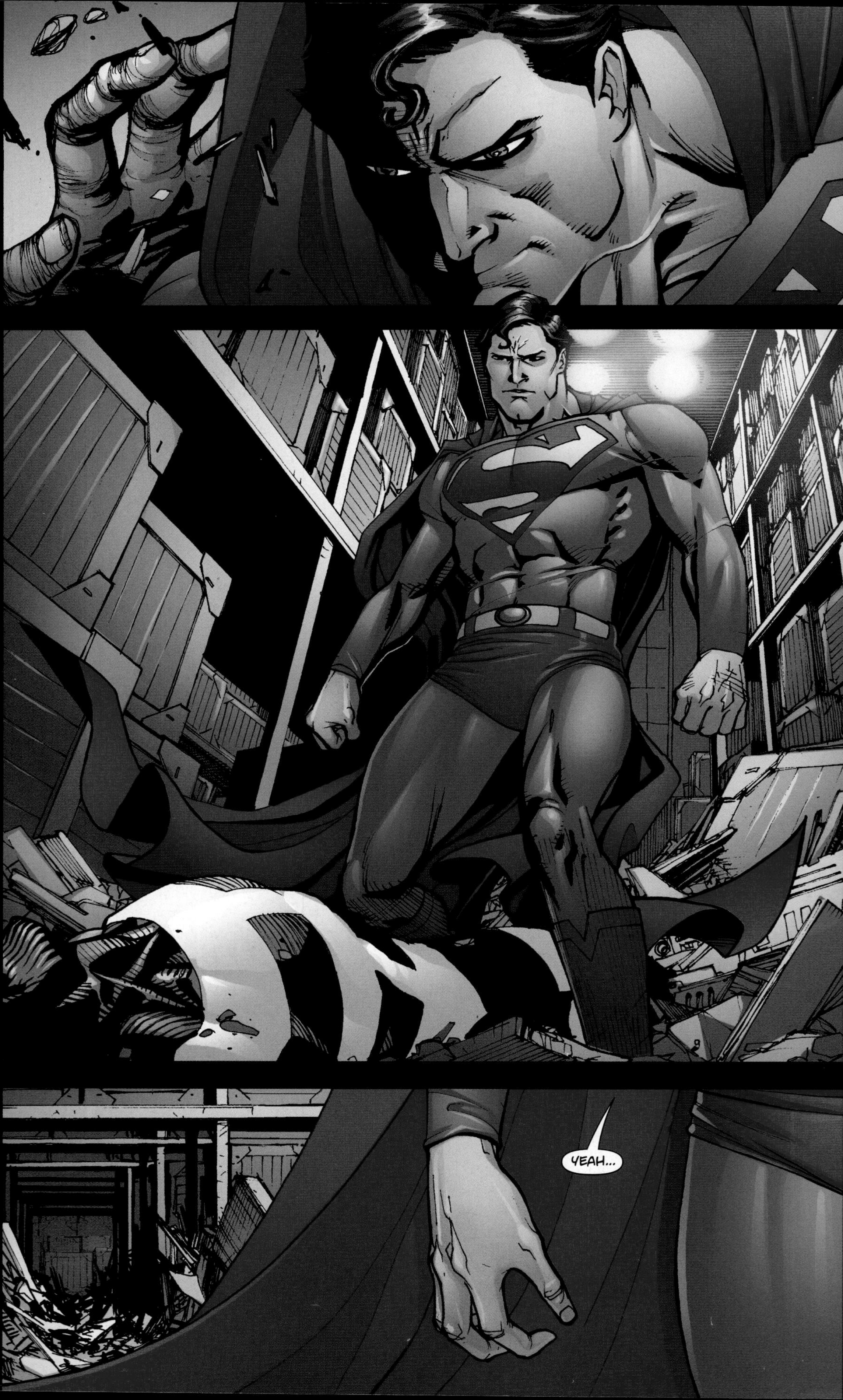
YEAH...

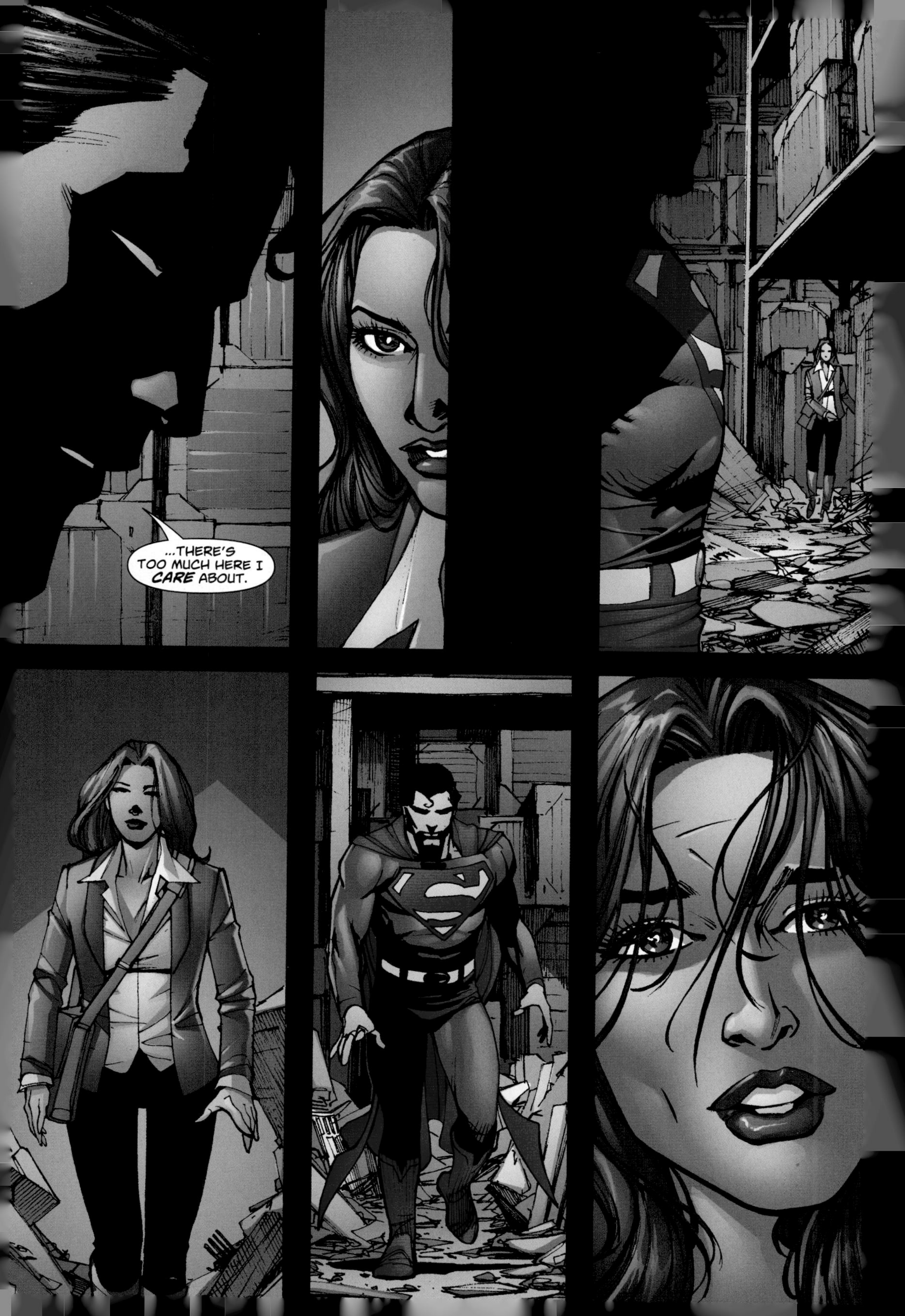
...THERE'S TOO MUCH HERE I CARE ABOUT.

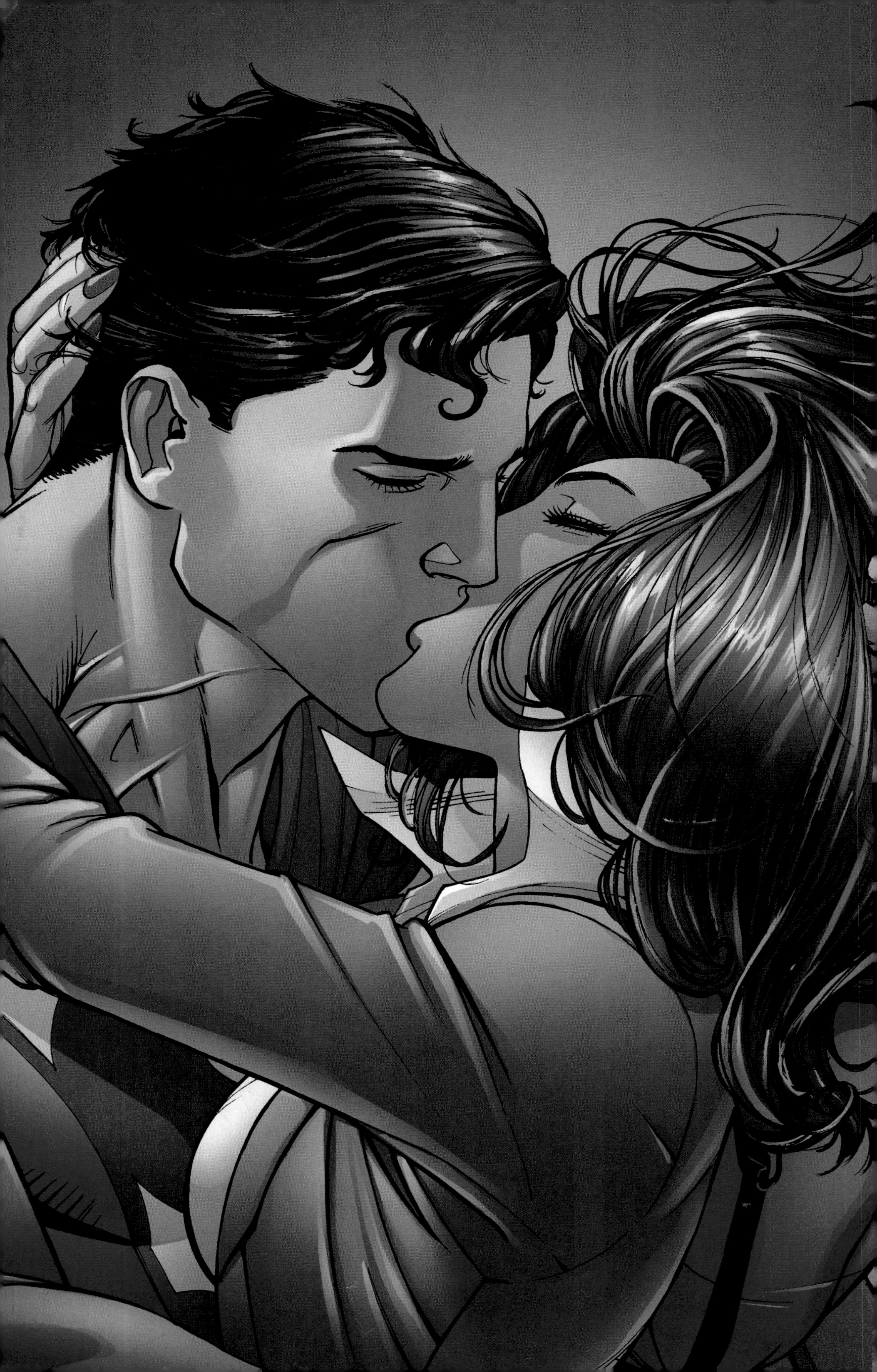

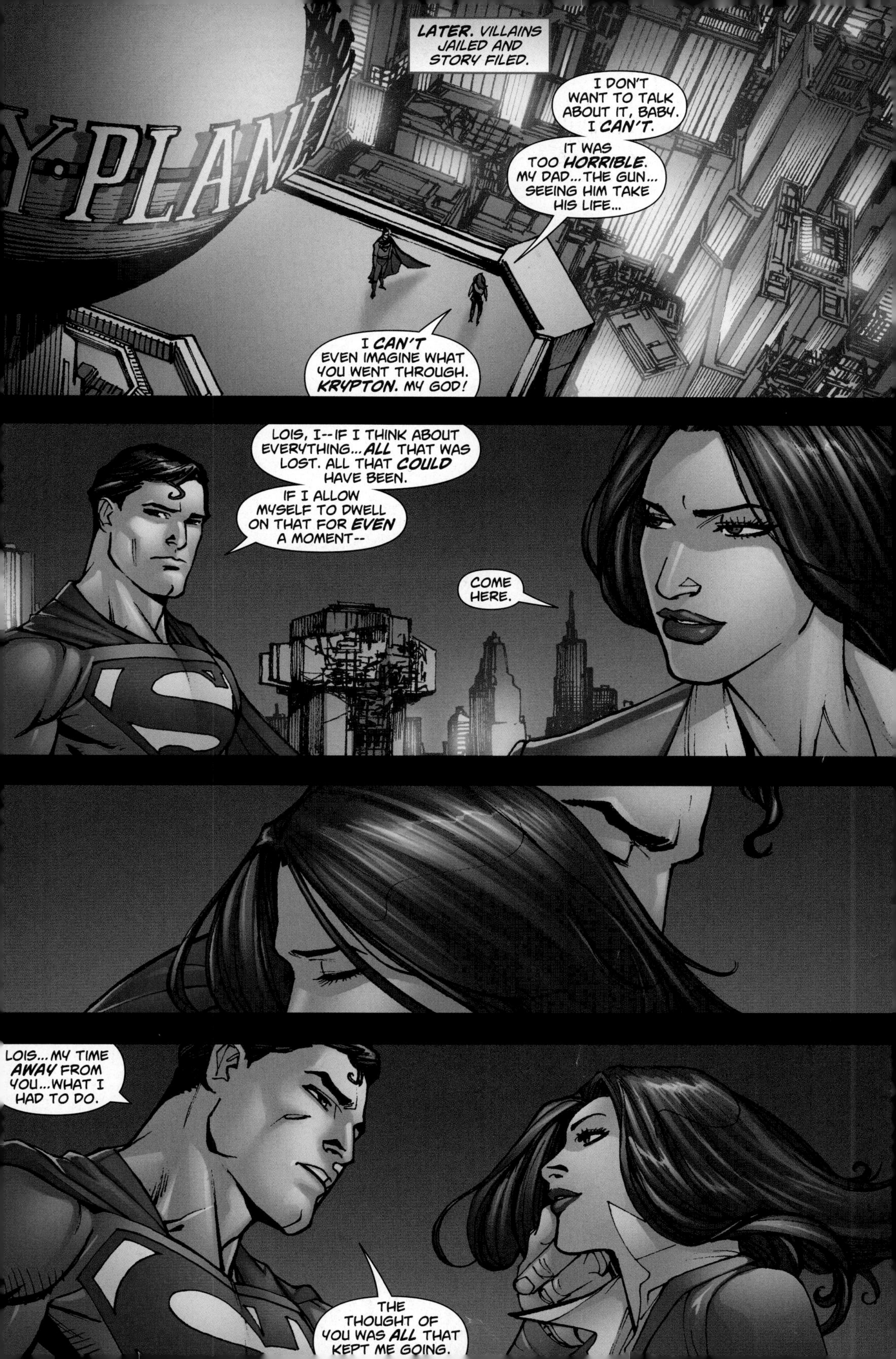

LATER. VILLAINS JAILED AND STORY FILED.
I DON'T WANT TO TALK ABOUT IT, BABY. I CAN'T.
IT WAS TOO HORRIBLE. MY DAD...THE GUN... SEEING HIM TAKE HIS LIFE...
I CAN'T EVEN IMAGINE WHAT YOU WENT THROUGH. KRYPTON. MY GOD!
LOIS, I--IF I THINK ABOUT EVERYTHING...ALL THAT WAS LOST. ALL THAT COULD HAVE BEEN.
IF I ALLOW MYSELF TO DWELL ON THAT FOR EVEN A MOMENT--
COME HERE.
LOIS...MY TIME AWAY FROM YOU...WHAT I HAD TO DO.
THE THOUGHT OF YOU WAS ALL THAT KEPT ME GOING.

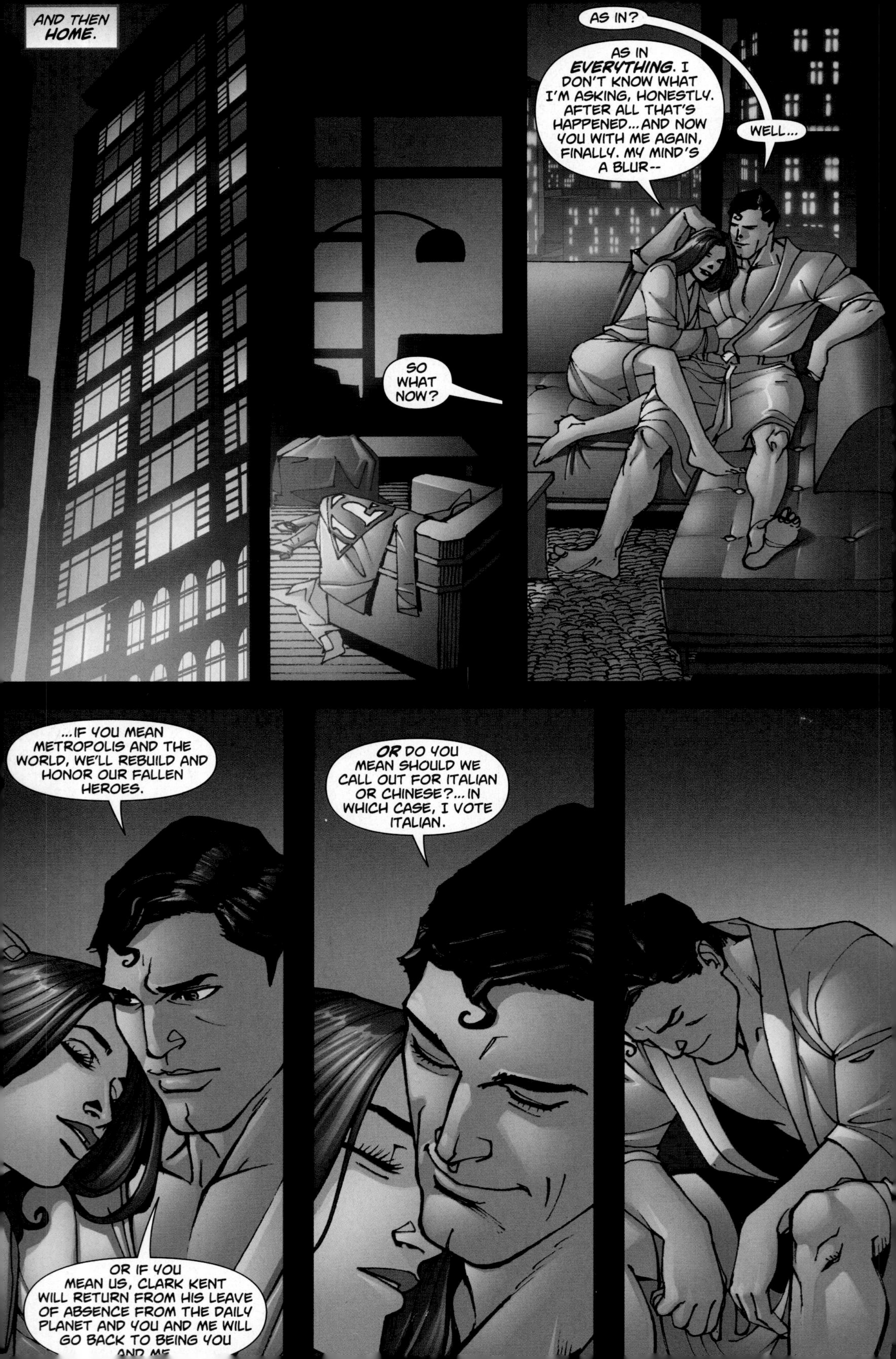
AND THEN HOME.
SO WHAT NOW?
AS IN?
WELL...
AS IN EVERYTHING. I DON'T KNOW WHAT I'M ASKING, HONESTLY. AFTER ALL THAT'S HAPPENED...AND NOW YOU WITH ME AGAIN, FINALLY. MY MIND'S A BLUR--
...IF YOU MEAN METROPOLIS AND THE WORLD, WE'LL REBUILD AND HONOR OUR FALLEN HEROES.
OR IF YOU MEAN US, CLARK KENT WILL RETURN FROM HIS LEAVE OF ABSENCE FROM THE DAILY PLANET AND YOU AND ME WILL GO BACK TO BEING YOU AND ME.
OR DO YOU MEAN SHOULD WE CALL OUT FOR ITALIAN OR CHINESE?...IN WHICH CASE, I VOTE ITALIAN.

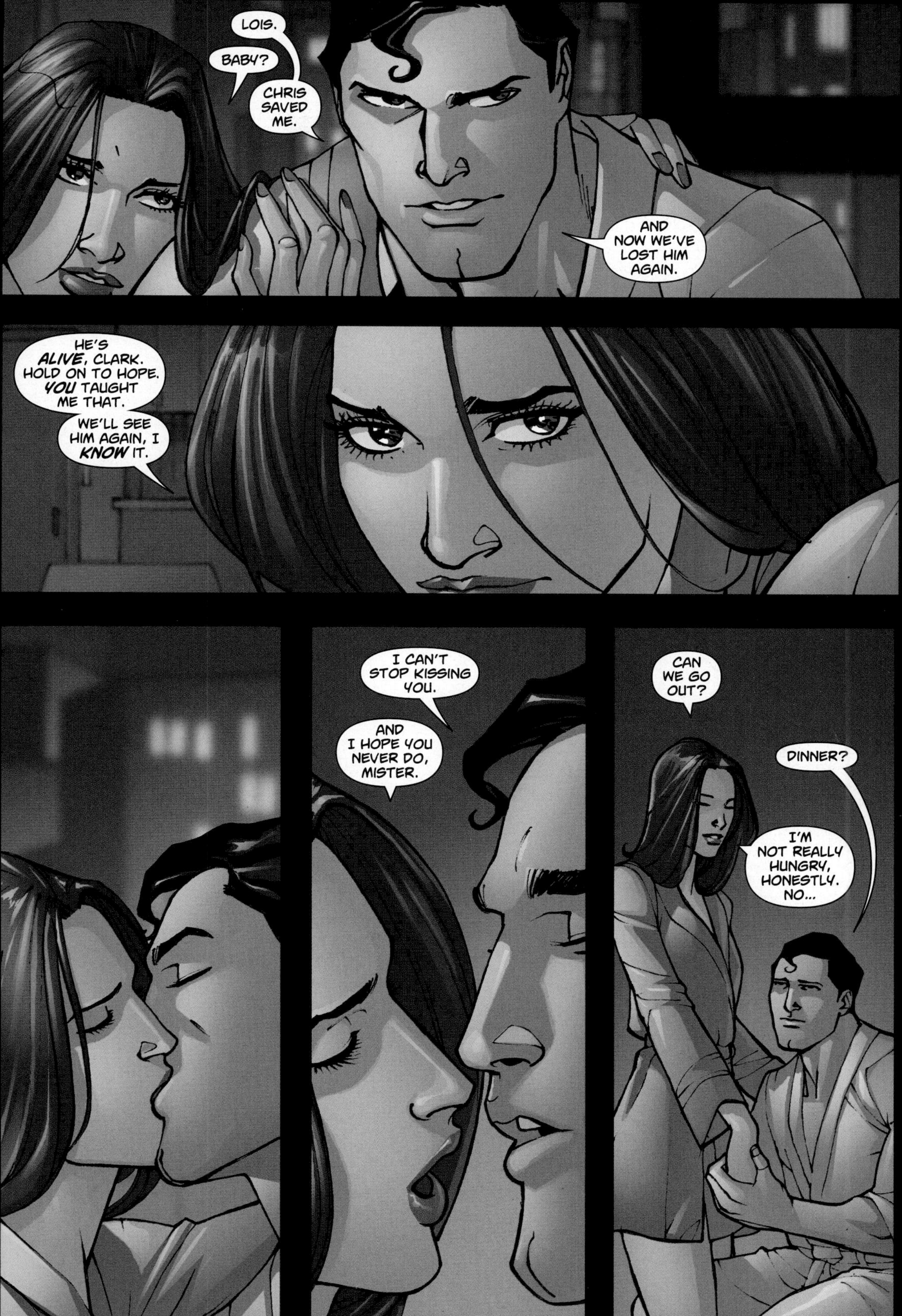
LOIS.
BABY?
CHRIS SAVED ME.
AND NOW WE'VE LOST HIM AGAIN.
HE'S *ALIVE*, CLARK. HOLD ON TO HOPE. *YOU* TAUGHT ME THAT.
WE'LL SEE HIM AGAIN, I *KNOW* IT.
I CAN'T STOP KISSING YOU.
AND I HOPE YOU NEVER DO, MISTER.
CAN WE GO OUT?
DINNER?
I'M NOT REALLY HUNGRY, HONESTLY. NO...

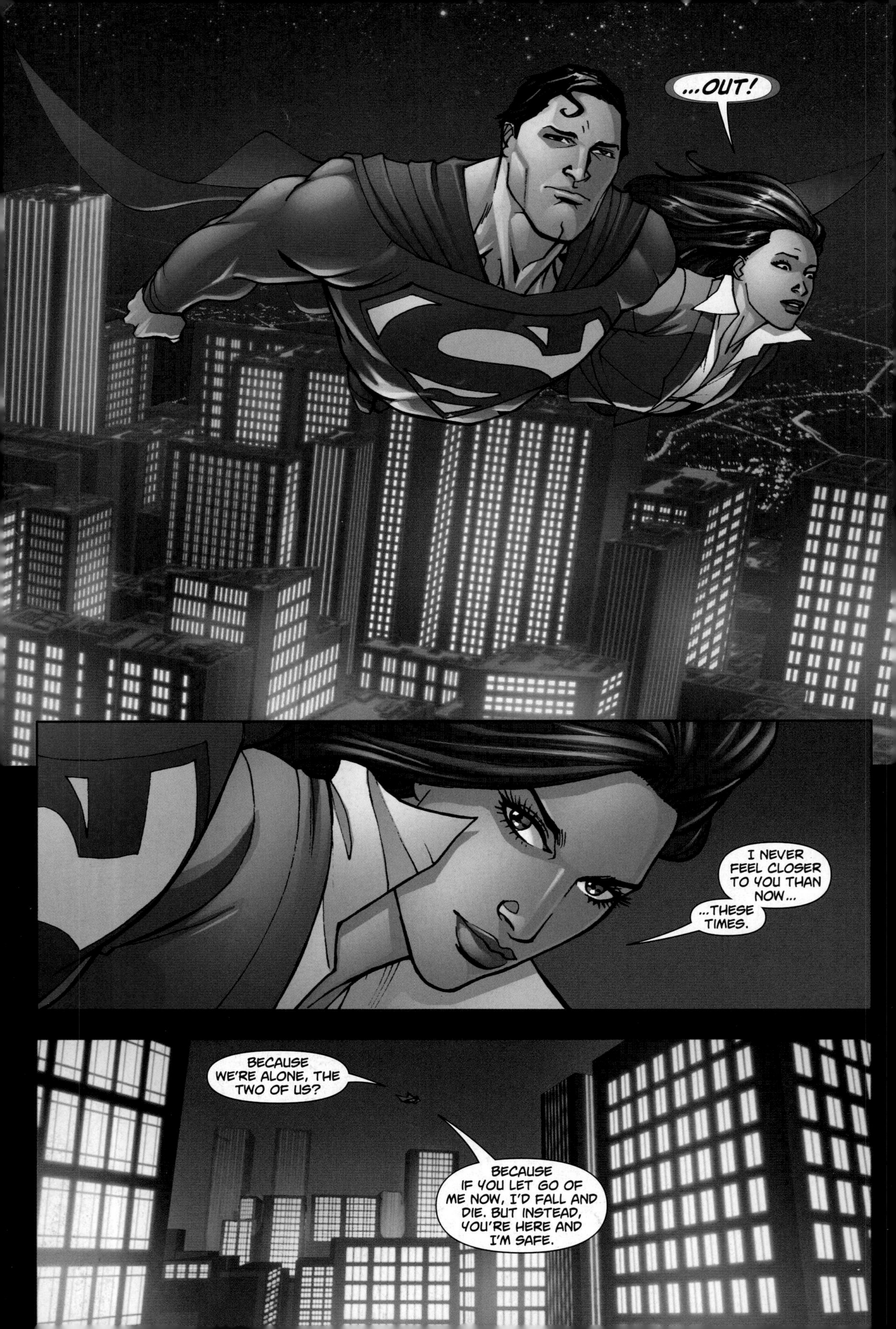
...OUT!
I NEVER FEEL CLOSER TO YOU THAN NOW...
...THESE TIMES.
BECAUSE WE'RE ALONE, THE TWO OF US?
BECAUSE IF YOU LET GO OF ME NOW, I'D FALL AND DIE. BUT INSTEAD, YOU'RE HERE AND I'M SAFE.

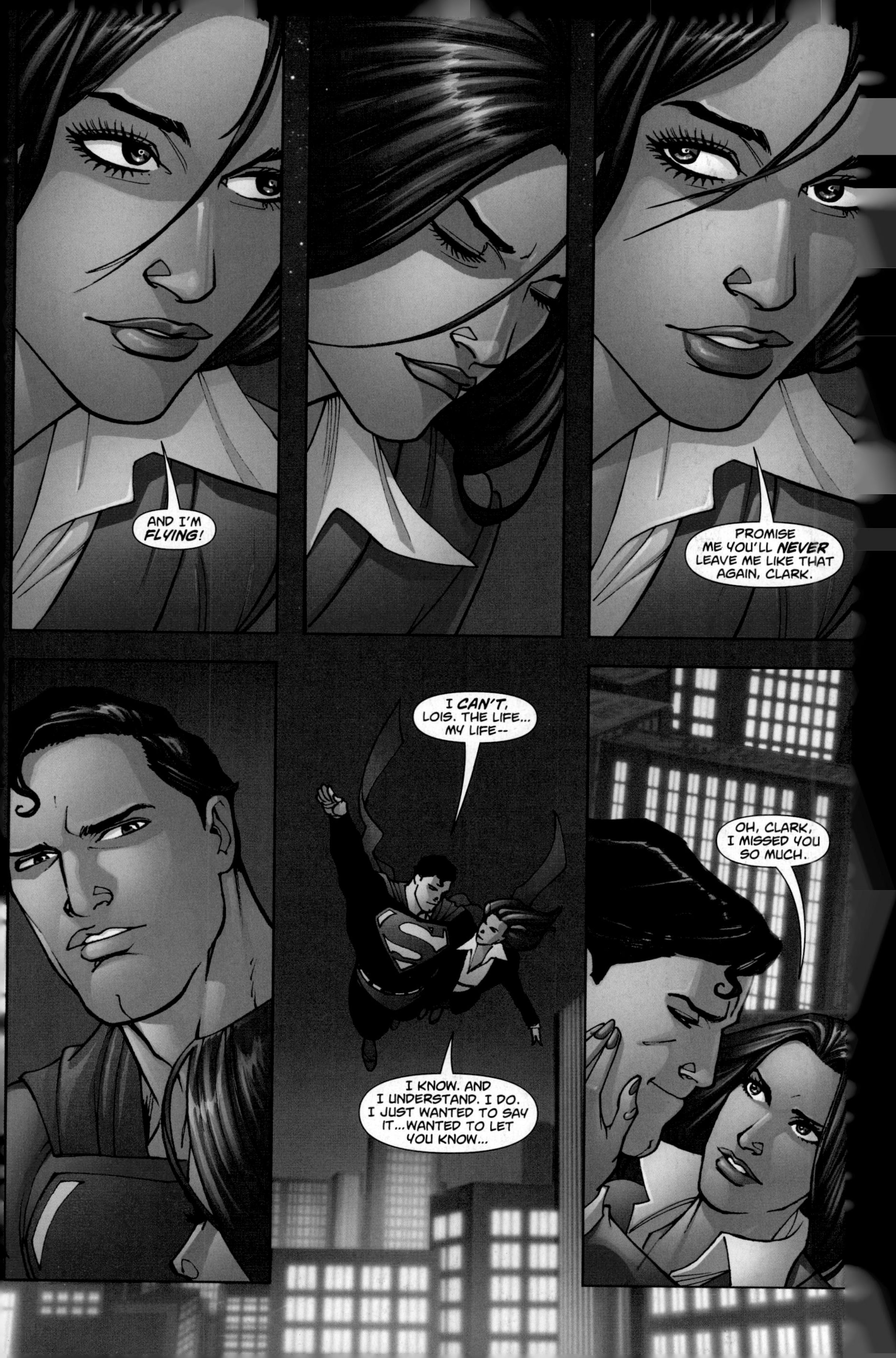
AND I'M FLYING!
PROMISE ME YOU'LL NEVER LEAVE ME LIKE THAT AGAIN, CLARK.
I CAN'T, LOIS. THE LIFE... MY LIFE--
I KNOW. AND I UNDERSTAND. I DO. I JUST WANTED TO SAY IT...WANTED TO LET YOU KNOW...
OH, CLARK, I MISSED YOU SO MUCH.

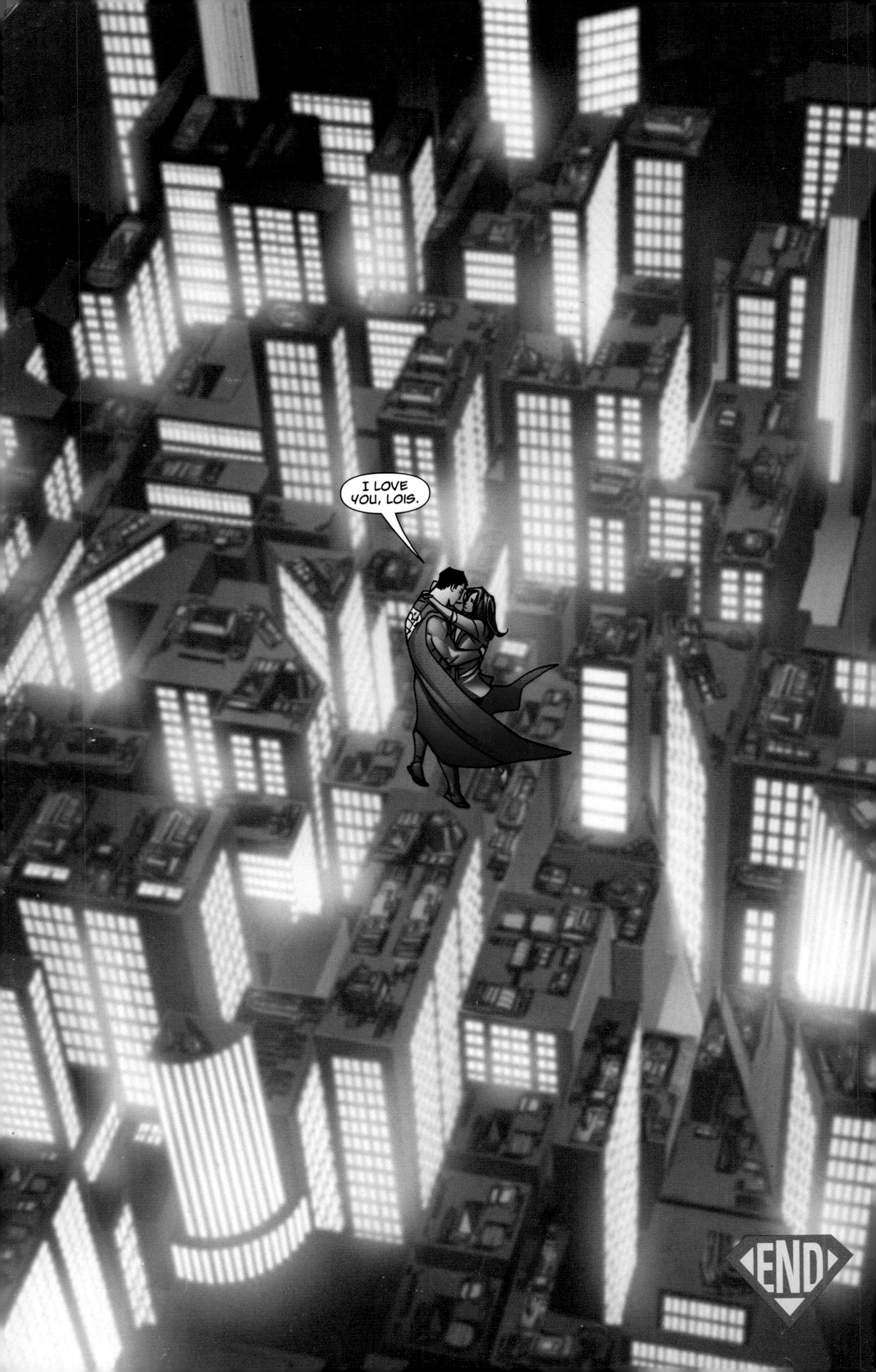
I LOVE YOU, LOIS.
END